Tax Guide for the Intimidated

1995 Edition

By

Joseph F. Markunas, C.P.A., and Lisa Apelt, L.T.C.

CAREER PRESS

180 Fifth Avenue

P.O. Box 34

Hawthorne, NJ 07507

1-800-CAREER-1

201-427-0229 (outside U.S.)

FAX: 201-427-2037

TAX GUIDE FOR THE INTIMIDATED, 1995 EDITION
ISBN 1-56414-144-6, $10.95
Cover design by The Gottry Communications Group, Inc.
Printed in the U.S.A by Book-mart Press

To order this title by mail, please include price as noted above, $2.50 handling per order, and $1.00 for each book ordered. Send to: Career Press, Inc., 180 Fifth Ave., P.O. Box 34, Hawthorne, NJ 07507

Or call toll-free 1-800-CAREER-1 (Canada: 201-427-0229) to order using VISA or MasterCard, or for further information on books from Career Press.

Note: The information in this handbook is based on the tax law as of September 1, 1994. References to IRS forms and tax rates are derived from preliminary proofs or 1993 forms and some adaptation for changes may be necessary. Please consult the Internal Revenue Service or a tax professional for advice regarding problems or situations not covered in this book.

Library of Congress Cataloging-in-Publication Data

Markunas, Joseph F., 1955-
Tax guide for the intimidated / by Joseph F. Markunas and Lisa Apelt. -- 1995 ed.
p. cm.
Includes index.
ISBN 1-56414-144-6 : $10.95
1. Income tax--Law and legislation--United States--Popular works. 2. Tax returns--United States--Popular works. I. Apelt, Lisa, 1945- . II. Title.
KF6369.6.M36 1994
343.7305'2--dc20
(347.30352)

94-22526
CIP

Acknowledgments

We would like to thank:

Delma Garza for her tireless efforts in creating the manuscript.

David Goodwin, whose talent enhances the book and whose good spirit is just as I remembered.

Research Institute of America's RIA Tax Publishing Division for its invaluable assistance in assembling 1994 tax forms and instructions.

To my wife, Maggie, daughter Katie and son Patrick and to the memories of my father Bill Markunas and sister Pamela Markunas.

—Joe Markunas

To John, Mike and Laura for their love and support. And to all my clients for their patience while I did nothing but work on "the book."

—Lisa Apelt

Contents

Chapter One

How to Use This Book

Perhaps you're one of the millions of Americans who are intimidated, even petrified, by the process of preparing your federal income tax returns. The arrival of your tax forms in the mail may cause stomach-churning nausea, the process of gathering your W-2s and other paperwork may leave you dazed and incoherent, the approach of April 15 may bring on insomnia and nightmares...you being led to the torture chamber by an IRS agent, sentenced to an audit that will last 99 years—because your return was off by $2. No matter that it was in the IRS's favor—you were still wrong!

With fears like this, it's no wonder so many Americans shift the burden of tax-preparing responsibility to professionals every year. Hiring a tax preparer can certainly eliminate the hassles that you have to go through each April. But it doesn't diminish that final responsibility for the accuracy of the figures. And if the IRS were to conduct one of its dreaded audits, you may have a more difficult time explaining the outcome if you've had no involvement in the preparation.

We aren't making you feel better? Sorry. It isn't our intention to increase your anxieties. We realize how tough tax time is for everyone. Believe us...if you think *you* break out in cold sweats as the weeks prior to the tax return filing deadline draw near, just imagine how we tax preparers feel every year at this time!

No, it's our belief, after a cumulative 25 years and more than 5,000 tax preparations under our belts, that virtually 99 percent of the tax-paying public is honest in preparing their taxes, and genuine in wanting to pay their fair share. They're just so overwhelmed by all the rules, the fine print, the regulations, the changes in tax code, that they've convinced themselves they're not capable of doing their own taxes.

Nothing could be further from the truth. And while taxes may be as inevitable as death, we are here to show you that preparing your own tax return is not a fate worse than death. Yes, you *can* do it—and you don't need to fear the IRS as you would the Spanish Inquisition.

We Americans have a self-assessing tax system. We report our income and deductions and tell the government what we believe our tax bill should be. This type of honor system would never work without some agency to verify that we are reporting accurately. The IRS is responsible for this task and conducts audits in order to carry out that responsibility. On average, less than 1 percent of all tax returns filed will even be audited, although your chances of an audit increase as income exceeds $100,000 and for taxpayers filing *Schedule C* or *F*. Tax returns are typically audited for one of three reasons:

1. **To develop model returns.** Some returns are randomly selected, and the information obtained by the IRS is used to develop a model of what an average tax return should look like. Other returns are then compared to this mathematical model in order to detect variations from the norm. These variations are known as red flags.
2. **To examine returns that vary from the norm.** Returns are scored by IRS computers, and those that appear to wave red flags will then be selected for further review. If the IRS is unable to reconcile the inconsistencies on its own, then the return will likely be selected for audit.
3. **To reconcile matching differences.** Other sources (your employer, for example) report information via *W-2*s and *1099*s to the IRS as well as to the person receiving the income. If you report contradictory information in your tax return, you will likely receive a matching notice. This is technically an audit, or verification, of just one item on your return, and is usually done by mail.

Most of the time, taxpayers can resolve the IRS's questions and no change takes place. If you've filled out your return as accurately and fairly as possible, then you have merely to explain what you did. If you've made a mistake, or can't provide sufficient proof for what you did, then your return will be adjusted and you will pay any additional tax or receive a refund. That's the end of it!

The key to smooth communication with the IRS is to keep accurate records. You should verify the information, and if there are any discrepancies, attempt to resolve the situation. If that's not feasible, just report what you know to be correct to the IRS and attach a statement describing the apparent discrepancy.

Likewise, you should never assume that an IRS matching notice and/or bill is absolutely correct. Unfortunately, the burden of proof is on you, so once again accurate records are imperative. And don't worry: If you prove the IRS wrong, you won't be put on a "hit list." Don't be intimidated! The IRS tries only to insure that each taxpayer pays his or her fair share in compliance with the law.

As a taxpayer, you are after the same result, to pay your fair share, *but no more!* This book is designed to help you honestly report all income and legitimate deductions. It may even help you avoid some of those nasty red flags.

The Internal Revenue Code (the law enacted by Congress that imposes federal income tax) is now more than 10,000 pages in length (the original in 1913 was only 14 pages!). Every revision, adjustment, reform or rewrite requires pages and pages of legislation to cover all possible exceptions. Tax form instructions and most other tax guides on the market are similar to the code in that they also address all possible scenarios.

This guide, however, addresses only common situations, not all the possible exceptions. Intentionally limiting our scope, we do not veer off the path of an average tax return. Our purpose is to provide clear and concise information to those of you unfamiliar with the tax laws and, at the same time, dispel that common fear we all have of the IRS. We think you will find tax preparation a less frustrating task if you, with the help of this book, just stick to the basics and avoid getting lost in the maze of forms and instructions designed to address all the loopholes.

If yours is a reasonably straightforward tax return, this book is for you. And, for our purposes, *straightforward* includes such sticky but typical situations as:

- Buying or selling investments.
- Buying or selling a home.
- Moving or relocating.
- Paying for childcare.
- Reporting profit from a small business.
- Itemizing deductions.
- Reporting income or loss from rental property, S Corporations, partnerships, trusts or estates.
- Claiming earned income credit.
- Reporting pension distributions.

Our book has a simple and clear consistency throughout, which is important for quick reference and easy understanding. The chapters are arranged in the same order as the lines of *Form 1040*, so you can easily find the parts that apply to you and skip over the rest. The material in each chapter is organized to answer five simple questions:

1. **What you'll need.** Each chapter begins with a list of the documents and instructions you'll need to fill in that line of your return. Optional publications are listed if you require more detailed information or instructions.

2. **What it's all about.** This section provides an overview of this part of your tax return. It offers a general idea of just what is to be reported on which forms and why.
3. **What to do with the forms.** Here, either general instructions or line-by-line instructions are provided for filling out the required forms. In some instances, this section will include worksheets or illustrations.
4. **Watch out!** This section identifies a few common pitfalls that frequently befall taxpayers.
5. **What if?** A question-and-answer section appears at the end of each chapter. It elaborates on the instructions by citing common problems.

In addition to the chapters covering the specific lines of *Form 1040*, we have provided Appendix A, which discusses other general concepts of tax law. These topics are commonly encountered by most taxpayers and warrant a simple explanation.

Appendix B touches upon changes in tax law for 1994.

Appendix C contains a listing of IRS publications and telephone assistance available, with instructions on how you can access these services.

Finally, you will surely encounter some special jargon as you read the forms and instructions. Unfortunately, there are some words and phrases, unique to tax law, that cannot be avoided. To help your understanding, we have provided a glossary of terms in Appendix D.

When You're Ready To Give Up

This book is technically accurate but limited in scope. It addresses average tax returns, and is not designed to answer all questions about all situations. If you find yourself stymied by a particular issue, refer to the IRS publications listed under the "What You'll Need" section in each chapter or Appendix C.

When you've exhausted these sources, you still may determine that your situation is complex enough for you to bundle everything up and haul it off to your local tax preparer.

You will no doubt benefit from your enhanced familiarity with our tax system. Remember, even if you use a professional tax preparer, you are responsible for the information on your tax return. This book will serve as an invaluable tool, whether you prepare your own return or pay a professional to do it for you. And if we are able to eliminate some of the intimidation normally associated with taxes, our mission will have been accomplished.

Chapter Two

Lines 1 through 5: Getting Started

What you'll need

- Copy of last year's tax return
- Check register for the year
- All receipts or notices relating to income or expenses
- *Form 1040*
- 1040 booklet

Optional

- *IRS Publication 501, Exemptions, Standard Deduction and Filing Information*

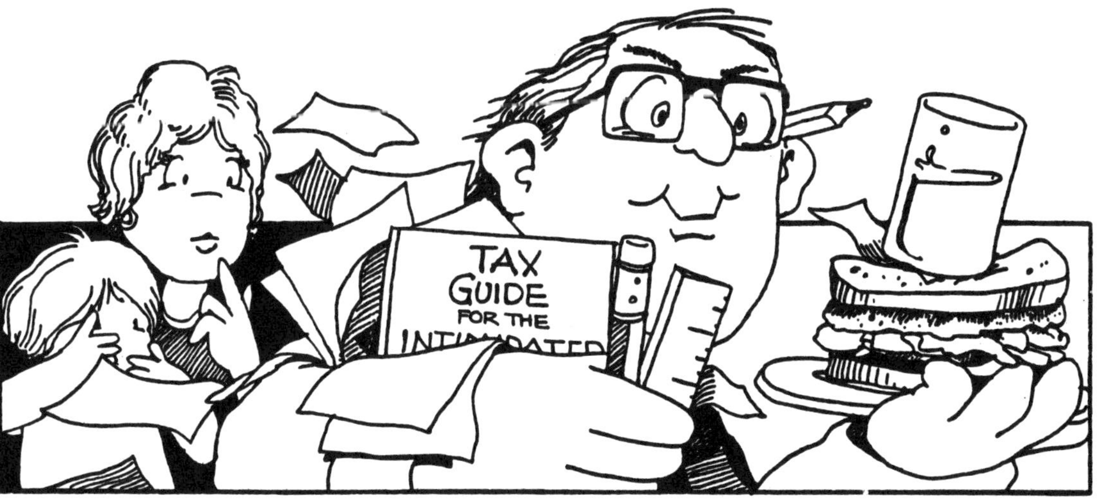

What it's all about

Once again, it's the time of year that accountants fondly call *tax season*. Most taxpayers moan and groan over the complex rules and perplexing forms they are faced with when tax time rolls around. Unless you're anticipating a large refund, chances are you've procrastinated and now find April 17 (since April 15 falls on a

Saturday this year) is just around the corner. Most folks think doing their taxes is about as much fun as going to the dentist. But as the dentist says, "Relax, this won't hurt a bit."

Not everyone is required to file a tax return. The IRS receives more than 1 million unnecessary returns each year, mostly from elderly people who are reluctant to quit filing. Are you required to file a return? It depends on your age, filing status and taxable income. Generally, if your taxable gross income is less than the amount allowed for your standard deduction and personal exemption ($11,250, for example, if you're married filing jointly and both are under age 65), then chances are you don't have to file. If you receive Social Security benefits, read Chapter 18 to help determine if you need to count your benefits as taxable income.

There are, of course, exceptions to every rule and there are instances when you need to file even if you fall below the general income requirement. For instance, you will need to file if you want a refund of withholdings or a payment of earned income credit. You may need to file if you sold your home or other capital assets. And you *definitely* need to file if you are subject to any other taxes, such as the alternative minimum tax or the self-employment tax.

If you filed a return last year, you probably received a booklet of forms and instructions from the IRS for this year. This may not contain everything you'll need for this year, but it's a start. If you didn't receive a booklet you are *not* off the hook for filing an accurate and timely tax return. The IRS will not accept "I didn't get a booklet" as an excuse! You can pick up a copy at most banks or the post office, or contact the IRS at 1-800-TAX-FORM (1-800-829-3676).

Last year's return, your check register, credit card statements and that old shoe box full of receipts and meaningful scraps of paper are the most common sources of information from which you will piece together this year's return. So gather all that up, along with this year's forms, and let's get started.

What to do with the forms

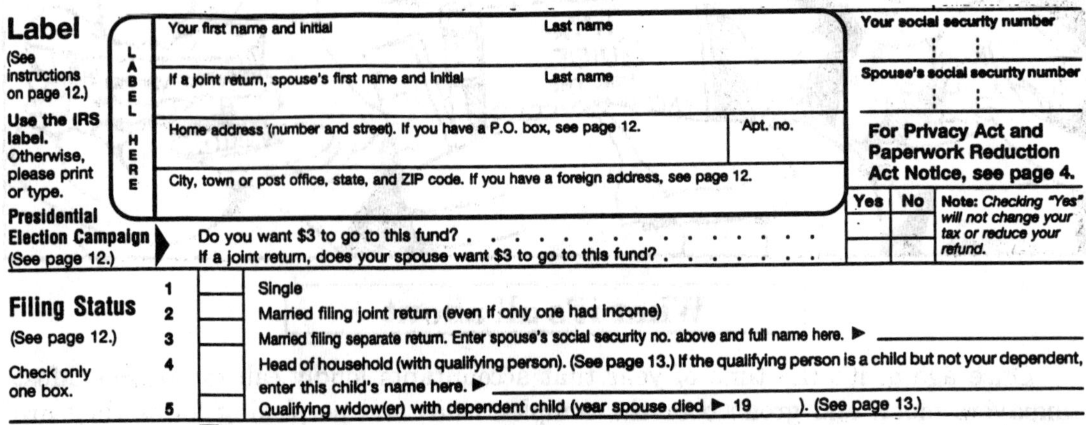

Label (See instructions on page 12.)
Use the IRS label. Otherwise, please print or type.

LABEL HERE

Your first name and initial | Last name | Your social security number

If a joint return, spouse's first name and initial | Last name | Spouse's social security number

Home address (number and street). If you have a P.O. box, see page 12. | Apt. no.

City, town or post office, state, and ZIP code. If you have a foreign address, see page 12.

For Privacy Act and Paperwork Reduction Act Notice, see page 4.

Presidential Election Campaign (See page 12.)
Do you want $3 to go to this fund? . . . .
If a joint return, does your spouse want $3 to go to this fund? . . . .

Yes | No | Note: *Checking "Yes" will not change your tax or reduce your refund.*

Filing Status (See page 12.)
Check only one box.

1 Single
2 Married filing joint return (even if only one had income)
3 Married filing separate return. Enter spouse's social security no. above and full name here. ▶
4 Head of household (with qualifying person). (See page 13.) If the qualifying person is a child but not your dependent, enter this child's name here. ▶
5 Qualifying widow(er) with dependent child (year spouse died ▶ 19). (See page 13.)

Begin by reviewing last year's return. Chances are, you will have many of the same sources of income and deductions from year to year. So a quick review will alert you to possible transactions you need to report this year. Better to include everything on your return than to get a notice from the IRS asking why you reported dividends on ABC stock last year, but this year you reported no dividends and no sale of stock either. What happened to it? Each year's return does not stand completely alone and any tremendous variance from one year to the next can trigger the dreaded audit.

Our book follows the layout of the *Federal Form 1040,* which is the main reporting form for individual income tax returns. Other versions of the *1040* include the *1040EZ,* which can be used by only a select group of taxpayers. If you are single or married filing a joint return, under age 65 Jan. 1, 1995, not blind at the end of 1994, claim no dependents, have only wages, salaries, tips and taxable scholarship or fellowship grants and taxable interest income of $400 or less, did not receive any advanced earned income credit payments and have less than $50,000 taxable income, you may file *Form 1040EZ.* If you or your spouse had wages from two or more employers, those wages, when added together, cannot exceed $60,600. It is a simple form but it covers only limited situations that most people outgrow fairly early in their taxpaying lives.

The next step up is the *1040A,* popularly known as the short form. It's not that short anymore, and while it does address more situations than the *1040EZ,* it does not accommodate certain types of income, taxable income over $50,000 or itemized deductions.

The *Form 1040,* popularly known as the long form, handles any and all situations and can, therefore, be as simple or as complicated as need be. Even if you are eligible to use the *1040EZ,* you can use the *1040* just as well, simply by skipping over the parts that do not apply to you. When in doubt, all taxpayers (except certain nonresident aliens) can use *Form 1040.*

Name, address and Social Security number

Form 1040 is simply a two-page summary of your tax return. As such, it contains a lot of complex information, some of which will take a little work to piece together. But it all begins simply enough—name, address and Social Security number.

This Social Security number is a very important piece of information. The IRS refers to it as your Taxpayer Identification Number. You can change your name, your address, your job, even your sex. But that Social Security number is with you for life. So do make sure you enter the correct number, because a wrong number here will botch up everything. If you are filing a joint return, also enter your spouse's name and Social Security number.

Contributions to presidential candidates?

Next comes the question about whether you want to earmark $3 of your tax for the Presidential Election Campaign Fund. This is a special fund that was set up in 1973 to provide financial support to qualified candidates for president. It's an effort to help keep the candidates for president focused on issues, not fund raising. You can answer yes, no or just ignore the question altogether. In no event will your response have any effect upon the tax you owe or your refund.

Lines 1 through 5: Filing status

Filing status is the last section we will talk about in this chapter. It is based upon your marital status and family situation as of the last day of the year. So if you were single until you married on New Year's Eve, for tax purposes you are considered married for the entire year. Likewise, if your divorce was final in October, you cannot file a joint return for the year. For most of us, filing status is pretty much cut-and-dried. Most married folks file jointly because it provides a more favorable rate than filing separately. If you're not married, you file as *single* unless you have children—in which case you may use *head of household* or *qualifying widow(er)* if you meet certain conditions.

Each status carries with it different standard deduction amounts and different rates. The following is a listing of the five filing statuses and a brief explanation of the general requirements for each:

1. **Single.** This may include those who are divorced or have a decree of separate maintenance. If you have children, you may be able to file as head of household or qualifying widow(er).
2. **Married filing joint.** To file in this status, you must be married at the end of the year for which you are filing. You cannot file in this status if you were divorced at the end of the year for which you are filing. You report the combined total of both spouses' incomes and deductions.
3. **Married filing separate.** In this status, you don't report your income and deductions with your spouse. This is usually the least favorable rate and has limitations on credits you can take. But individuals may prefer to use it in some situations. For example, one spouse may be involved in shaky business practices and the other spouse wants to keep tax issues separate from marriage issues. Or an individual whose spouse is nowhere to be found may be forced to use this filing. If, however, you're providing a home for your child and your spouse was gone for the last six months of the year, you may qualify to file as head of household, which is a better rate.
4. **Head of household.** Unmarried taxpayers paying more than half the cost of keeping a home for themselves and "qualifying person(s)" for more than half the year qualify as heads of household. Sound confusing? It is. As mentioned earlier, even if you are married but your spouse has been gone for the last six months, you may be able to file as head of household. And what is a qualifying person? Generally speaking, an unmarried child or

grandchild who is not necessarily your dependent, a married child or grandchild who *is* your dependent, or any other close relative you can claim as a dependent. If the dependent is your parent, he or she does not necessarily need to live with you. For instance, you could be paying for more than half the cost of keeping your elderly mother in a rest home, which may qualify you to claim her as a dependent.

5. **Qualifying widow(er).** If your spouse is dead and you are paying more than half the cost of keeping a home for you and a child who is your dependent, you may qualify for this status. In the year of the death of your spouse, you can file a joint return, and then, for the next two years, you can use this filing status provided you don't remarry. This allows you to get the same favorable rate as married filing joint for a few years.

On *Form 1040*, check the box opposite the filing status that applies to you. If you are claiming head of household, you need to enter the name of the qualifying person that entitles you to this filing status.

Watch out!

It is not all that unusual today to find oneself in a complex living situation (extended families living under the same roof, for example), and so your tax filing status may not be easy to figure out. It is important that you understand who qualifies as a dependent to help determine the most beneficial filing status for you.

What if?

Q. I got married and moved across the country with my new husband. What should I do about my tax return this year?
A. Send a completed *Form 8822, Change of Address*, to the IRS center where you filed your last return. A change-of-address notice provided by the post office should serve just as well. Also, be sure to notify Social Security so that your name can be changed on its records. Even though your name and address are different, IRS won't skip a beat because it will identify you by your Social Security number, whether on a joint or separate return.

Q. I'm divorced and live with my daughter, but my ex-husband claims her as his dependent. Can I still file as head of household?
A. Yes, if you provide over half the cost of maintaining a home for you and your daughter for over half the year. Do be aware that just as only one of you can claim your daughter as a dependent, so can she qualify only one of you for head of household.

Q. My wife died this year. How do I file my tax return?
A. If you did not remarry before year-end, you can still fill a joint return for the year. Just write "deceased" and include the date of death after your wife's name at the beginning of the return. Then when you sign the return, put "signing as surviving spouse" after your signature and, again, put the date of your wife's death on her signature block. You must also complete and attach *Form 1310* (Statement of Person Claiming Refund Due a Deceased Taxpayer) to your return. This is a very straightforward form which merely requires responses to a series of questions and your signature.

Q. Can I round off the cents when preparing my return?
A. Yes, rounding is allowed. Just be consistent throughout your return. You're not allowed to round all your expenses up and all your income down.

Chapter Three

Line 6: Dependents and Exemptions

What you'll need

- Social Security numbers for all dependents
- *Form 1040*
- 1040 Booklet

Optional

- *IRS Publication 501, Exemptions, Standard Deduction and Filing Information*
- *Form 8332, Release of Claim to Exemption for Child of Divorced / Separated Parents*

What it's all about

Your tax return allows a reduction of income for every exemption claimed. You can claim an exemption for yourself, your spouse (if married filing joint) and your dependents. *Beware!!* The IRS's idea of a dependent is not necessarily the same as yours. In order to claim someone as your dependent (and thereby get the exemption), you must be sure the "dependents" meet *all* of the following five tests:

- **Gross income test.** Dependent must have less than $2,450 gross income. This test does not apply if the dependent is your child under age 19, or under age 24 as of the close of the calendar year and a full-time student. Gross income, in this instance, should almost be termed gross receipts, as many tax-deductible expenses are not taken into account.
- **Member of household test.** A dependent must have lived with you for the entire year unless he or she is your relative. Relatives include your children, grandchildren, parents, brothers, sisters, aunts, uncles, nieces, nephews, in-laws—just about everyone, but *not* cousins.
- **Support test.** You must have provided more than half the cost of supporting the dependent. The tax code does recognize something called a multiple support agreement, which allows for one person to claim the dependency

exemption even though actual support is spread among two or more, with everyone contributing at least 10 percent, but no one contributing more than half. The most common instance of this is when children share in the support of their elderly parents. The person claiming the deduction attaches *Form 2120*, which is a release signed by the persons not claiming the deduction.

- **Citizenship test.** Dependent must be a citizen or resident of the United States or a national or resident of Canada or Mexico.
- **Joint return test.** Dependent may not file a joint return with anyone unless there is no tax liability involved and it is filed only to receive a refund.

Taxpayers seem to have an exaggerated view of the value of dependents. They are not "worth" $2,450—they just reduce your taxable income by that much. So if you are in the 15-percent bracket, each deduction saves only $368 in federal tax. Think about that as you offer to keep supporting that perpetual student.

One person, one exemption—that's the rule. So if someone else can claim you on his or her return, you *cannot* claim yourself on your own return. Say that you're a student who is working, but is still under age 24 and being supported by parents. You must put a *zero* in the exemption box on your return. This does not make for a nonperson in the eyes of the IRS, it just prevents duplication of a tax benefit. And don't think that you can get away with both of you claiming the exemption. Remember that Social Security number? The IRS computers will rapidly spit out a nastygram to filers of both returns, and someone will owe more tax.

What to do with the forms

6a ☐ **Yourself.** If your parent (or someone else) can claim you as a dependent on his or her tax return, **do not** check box 6a. But be sure to check the box on line 33b on page 2 . . . . . **No. of boxes checked on 6a and 6b** ____

b ☐ **Spouse** . . . .

c **Dependents:**

(1) Name (first, initial, and last name)	(2) Check if under age 1	(3) If age 1 or older, dependent's social security number	(4) Dependent's relationship to you	(5) No. of months lived in your home in 1994

No. of your children on 6c who:
- **lived with you** ____
- **didn't live with you due to divorce or separation (see page 14)** ____

Dependents on 6c not entered above ____

d If your child didn't live with you but is claimed as your dependent under a pre-1985 agreement, check here ▶ ☐

e Total number of exemptions claimed . . . . **Add numbers entered on lines above ▶** ☐

Form 1040 Line 6a. Unless someone else can claim you, you will claim your own personal exemption by checking the box marked "yourself."

Form 1040 Line 6b. If married and filing a joint return, you will claim your spouse's personal exemption by checking the box marked "spouse." Indicate on the right-hand side of the form how many boxes you have checked on 6a and 6b (has to be 0, 1 or 2).

Form 1040 Line 6c. List your dependents and check the box if they are under age 1. If they are older, you must provide their Social Security numbers, or you'll be subject to a $50 penalty. If you have applied for a number but don't have it yet, just write "applied for" in the space provided for the number. Do *not* use this tactic next year. The IRS knows that it doesn't take a year to get a Social Security number. Next, you indicate the dependent's relationship to you and the number of months he or she lived in your home. Then summarize on the right-hand side of the form the number and types of dependents you are claiming.

In divorces granted after 1984, the parent with legal custody automatically gets the dependency exemptions for the children. This can be transferred to the other parent if the custodial parent signs *Form 8332, Release of Dependency Exemption*, and gives it to the other parent to return with *Form 1040*.

Form 1040 Line 6d. If your divorce was before 1985, the terms of the divorce will dictate who gets the exemption. If you are claiming a child as a dependent under such a decree, check the box here.

Form 1040 Line 6e. Summarize the total number of exemptions claimed. The total can be no more than you, your spouse and any dependents you have listed by name.

Watch out!

Any complicated living/support situation can give rise to questions of who gets to claim whom as a dependent. The gross income and support tests can be especially tricky. If you have any unusual circumstances, please refer to *IRS Publication 501* or to the 1040 instruction booklet for further information. It might be helpful here to mention those who are *never* your dependents: the maid, the foreign exchange student, the foster child you are paid to keep in your home, the freeloading friend who periodically shows up for extended periods of time, the mother-in-law who pays you rent, the third cousin once removed who has been visiting you for the last 10 months, the grown child who is employed but moves back home to save money, the dog and cat.

* * *

In 1991, Congress voted to phase out the tax benefit of exemptions for high-income taxpayers. This little-publicized maneuver kicks in once your adjusted gross income goes above certain levels, which are based on your filing status. See Chapter 22.

What if?

Q. How can I get a Social Security number for my child?
A. To get a Social Security number, you need to file a *Form SS-5* with the Social Security Administration. You will need to show proof of birth and identity when filing the form. Call or visit your nearest Social Security office, or call 1-800-772-1213 for information. It usually takes about two weeks to get a Social Security card.

Q. Our baby was born this year, but lived for only a few days. Can we claim him as a dependent this year?
Q. My elderly father, who was my dependent, died early this year. Can I claim him for this year?
A. In both cases the answer is yes. You can claim the exemption in the year of death as long as the person was alive for some part of the year and otherwise qualified as your dependent.

Q. My son is 26 years old and had income of only $2,000 this year. Can I claim him as a dependent even though he's over age 19?
A. Yes, if he meets the other tests. You can claim him as a dependent no matter what his age as long as his gross income is less than $2,450.

Chapter Four

Line 7: Wages, Salary, Tips and Compensation

What you'll need

- *Forms W-2*
- *Form 1040*
- 1040 Booklet

Optional

- Payroll records or pay stubs
- *IRS Publication 531, Reporting Tip Income*

What it's all about

Were you employed during the year? If so, this is where to report your earnings. Most likely, you received a *Form W-2* summarizing your earnings and withholdings. The amount to report as income is generally the amount from Box 1 of *Form W-2*.

You should receive a *Form W-2* from your employer by January 31. This is a *very* important form, which reports to both you and the government how much you earned and how much you had withheld for various taxes. If your employer did everything right, he or she sent quarterly reports of these same amounts to the IRS and a copy of the *W-2* to the Social Security Administration. Within a year or two, the IRS and Social Security will get together and match up all three items—the *W-2* sent to Social Security, the quarterly reports sent to the IRS and the *W-2* you attached to your tax return. If something doesn't match up, your employer will be required to make any necessary corrections. Employers are not always right and it is possible the amounts reported on your *W-2* are wrong. It behooves you to keep a record of your pay and use that to verify the accuracy of your *W-2*. Your responsibility is to report actual gross wages—whether or not it agrees with your *W-2*.

You may find that the amount of gross wages reported to you is more than you figured. It's possible that you are receiving some fringe benefits that your employer is correctly including in gross wages. Some such common items are cost of life insurance premiums for coverage above $50,000, awards, bonuses, vacation pay and expense allowance in excess of amounts accounted for to your employer. If you have any question or doubt about what is or is not included in your gross wages, you need to review things with your employer.

In 1982, Congress enacted strict regulations regarding tip income, much of which had historically gone unreported and untaxed. Unfortunately, the regulations are not easy ones, and proper reporting on the part of both employee and employer can be a paperwork nightmare. Basically, employees are supposed to report to their employers the amount of tips received. The employer then takes that additional income into account when calculating withholding taxes. Tips are considered a part of your pay for performing your job and, as such, are subject to all employment taxes and need to be included in calculations for Social Security, Medicare, and federal and state unemployment taxes. Certain larger restaurants are required to allocate tip income to employees who do not report enough in tips. You should keep an accurate log of tips received so you can justify what you are claiming.

What to do with the forms

d	If your child didn't live with you but is claimed as your dependent under a pre-1985 agreement, check here ▶ ☐	Add numbers entered on lines above ▶		☐
e	Total number of exemptions claimed			
7	Wages, salaries, tips, etc. Attach Form(s) W-2	7		
8a	**Taxable** interest income (see page 15). Attach Schedule B if over $400	8a		
b	**Tax-exempt** interest (see page 16). DON'T include on line 8a | 8b |			
9	Dividend income. Attach Schedule B if over $400	9		

Form 1040 Line 7, Wages, salaries, tips, etc. Report on this line the total of gross wages reported to you in Box 1 of all your *W-2s*. Do not pick up the Social Security wages reported in Box 3, as this may very well be a different amount. If you are filing a joint return, be sure to include both spouse's gross wages.

The amount of compensation to be reported on Line 7 is the gross amount, *not* the net amount of paychecks that you received. Although some of the amounts withheld may be tax-deductible, that does not reduce the amount of gross income to be reported here.

Watch out!

If your *W-2* is wrong, you should first see your employer about getting a corrected one and use that to prepare your return. If you are unable to get it corrected, attach it with a statement explaining what the error is. Whatever you do, make sure that you file your return with the correct amount—you are not relieved of that obligation.

* * *

Is the box marked "Statutory Employee" checked on your *W-2*? If so, you report your compensation on *Schedule C*, not on Line 7 of *Form 1040*. Being a statutory employee allows you to deduct business expenses directly from gross income, rather than having to deduct them as employee business expenses under itemized deductions. Statutory employees are a select few that are clearly defined by law. Full-time life insurance salespeople are commonly considered statutory employees.

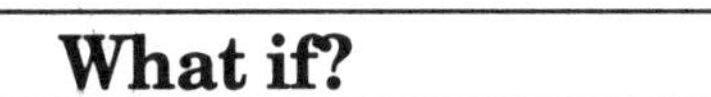

Q. I lost my *W-2*. How can I file my tax return?
A. Try to get a copy from your employer. If you can't, you must still report all earnings. Hopefully, you have kept earnings statements or some type of record of your wages for the year. You can request *Form 4852, Substitute Form W-2*, to attach to your return or just write out a statement of your own. On it, you will report what you think are the correct amounts for wages and withholdings, how you arrived at these amounts and why you don't have a *W-2*.

Q. I worked several jobs last year and received several *W-2s*. Do I need to do anything special?
A. No, just add them all together and report the total figures for gross wages and withholdings on your return. Be sure to attach a copy of *all* the *W-2s* to your return. If the total of your gross wages (Box 1 on the *W-2*) is more than $60,600, you may have had too much Social Security tax withheld. See Chapter 27.

Chapter Five

Line 8: Interest Income

What you'll need

- *Forms 1099-INT*
- *Forms 1099-OID*
- Substitute *Forms 1099*
- *Form 1040*
- 1040 Booklet

Optional

- *Schedule B, Interest and Dividend Income*
- *IRS Publication 550, Investment Income & Expenses*
- *Form 8815, Exclusion of Interest From Series EE US Savings Bonds Issued After 1989*
- *Form 8818, Optional Form to Record Redemption of Series EE Bonds Issued After 1989*

What it's all about

After wages, interest is the most common item of income reported on tax returns. We automatically associate interest with banks, but it can come from many other sources. For example, if you lend money and charge someone for the use of that money you have interest income to report equal to the amount of interest received.

Generally, all interest is taxable, even interest received from the IRS. The only exception is interest on most state and municipal bonds. Many people mistakenly think that savings bond interest is also tax-free, but it is exempt only from state and local taxes. Some savings bonds do, however, allow you to defer payment of the tax until you cash in the bond.

1. Series E and EE bonds

These are issued at a discount and increase in value until maturity. The difference between what you pay for the bond and what you redeem it for is interest income. You may pay tax on the interest as it is earned each year, or you can wait to claim the income until you redeem the bond or until it matures, whichever is later. You should, therefore, keep track of bond maturity dates and plan accordingly, as some bonds may be rolled over and the income deferred. This is a classic example of tax deferral that is both simple and legal. Series EE bonds purchased after 1989 can be "educational bonds," qualifying for tax-exempt status. To qualify, you must be over age 24 at the time of purchase and the proceeds must be used to pay for college tuition for you, your spouse or your dependents. This special exclusion from income is lost to high-income taxpayers, however. At an adjusted gross income (AGI) of $61,850 for married filing joint, you begin to lose the exclusion and it vanishes entirely at $91,850. These amounts are $41,200 to $56,200 for single or head of household payers. If you are married filing separate, you simply don't qualify for it at all.

There are specific rules regarding the Education Savings Bond Program dealing with eligible expenses and educational institutions, excludable amounts and other aspects of this program. You should consult *IRS Publications 17* and *550* as well as *Form 8815* for more information.

2. Series H and HH bonds

These are issued at face value and interest is paid twice a year with the income being taxed in the year received. No deferral here. Series E and EE bonds can be converted into HH Bonds, but not vice versa.

3. Original Issue Discount (OID) bonds

These are corporate or government bonds that you buy at a price less than face value. Just as with Series E and Series EE bonds, the difference between purchase price and maturity value is interest income. Unlike the savings bonds, you cannot defer the interest that is computed each year. A *1099-OID* will show stated interest that you must include in income, even though you didn't receive it.

All banks, stockbrokers and financial institutions are required to prepare a *Form 1099-INT* or *1099-OID* reporting the amount of interest paid to you during the year. If it's less than $10, they are relieved of this responsibility, but you are *not* relieved of the responsibility to report it on your tax return. Just like people, the *Form 1099-INT* comes in all different shapes and sizes. Some look suspiciously like *W-2s*, some like bank statements. Whatever they look like, a duplicate copy has been sent to the IRS. Unlike a *W-2*, the *Forms 1099* do *not* get attached to your return. Do, however, be sure to keep them for your records.

What to do with the forms

7	Wages, salaries, tips, etc. Attach Form(s) W-2		7	
8a	Taxable interest income (see page 15). Attach Schedule B if over $400		8a	
b	Tax-exempt interest (see page 16). DON'T include on line 8a	8b		
9	Dividend income. Attach Schedule B if over $400		9	
10	Taxable refunds, credits, or offsets of state and local income taxes (see page 16) . .		10	

Form 1040 Line 8a. Total up all the interest income you received during the year. If the total is less than $400 (and you are not claiming any Series EE interest exclusion for educational purposes), you need only enter the total amount on Line 8a. If the total is more than $400, then you need to provide the IRS with some additional information. This information is reported on *Schedule B* and it is simply a listing of who paid you and how much.

Form 1040 Line 8b. Report all tax-exempt interest income here. It will not affect your taxable income, but it will satisfy that pesky matching program, and you may be doing calculations later in your return that also require this figure.

Now go to *Schedule B* if necessary.

Schedule B Line 1. Simply list who paid you the interest and the amount paid. If you received interest from financing a mortgage on a piece of property you sold and the buyer used the property as a personal residence, list first any interest paid to you by that buyer. You must show the buyer's name, address and Social Security number and give him your number, or you may be subject to a $50 penalty.

Schedule B Line 2. Total amounts from Line 1.

Schedule B Line 3. If you have interest from Series EE bonds that you are excluding for educational purposes, you subtract that interest here. You must also complete and attach *Form 8815,* which provides details of your qualification for the exclusion.

Schedule B Line 4. Subtract Line 3 from Line 2. This is your total taxable interest income, which is carried forward to Line 8a on *Form 1040*.

Now skip down to the bottom of the page and answer Lines 11 and 12. Everyone who is required to file a *Schedule B* is required to answer yes or no to these questions regarding foreign investments. If you have none, simply check the "no" box. If you do have any foreign bank accounts or trusts, check the "yes" box and read the IRS instructions for further direction.

Watch out!

Do not include interest earned on your IRA accounts. This is not taxable to you until you actually withdraw it. Many taxpayers mistakenly include this in their taxable income.

* * *

Do not include interest paid on accounts you hold as custodian for your children if those accounts are under the child's Social Security number and your child has ownership control of the account. This is income taxable to your child. Be aware that you may want to include it in your income anyway, but that's another chapter. (See Appendix A, Section 6, Kiddie Tax.)

* * *

If you have interest income from financing a mortgage, you may also be required to file a *Form 6252, Installment Sales.* (See Appendix A, Section 5.) If, for instance, your installment sale involved a sale of a residence, or you elected out of installment sale treatment, a *Form 6252* may not be required.

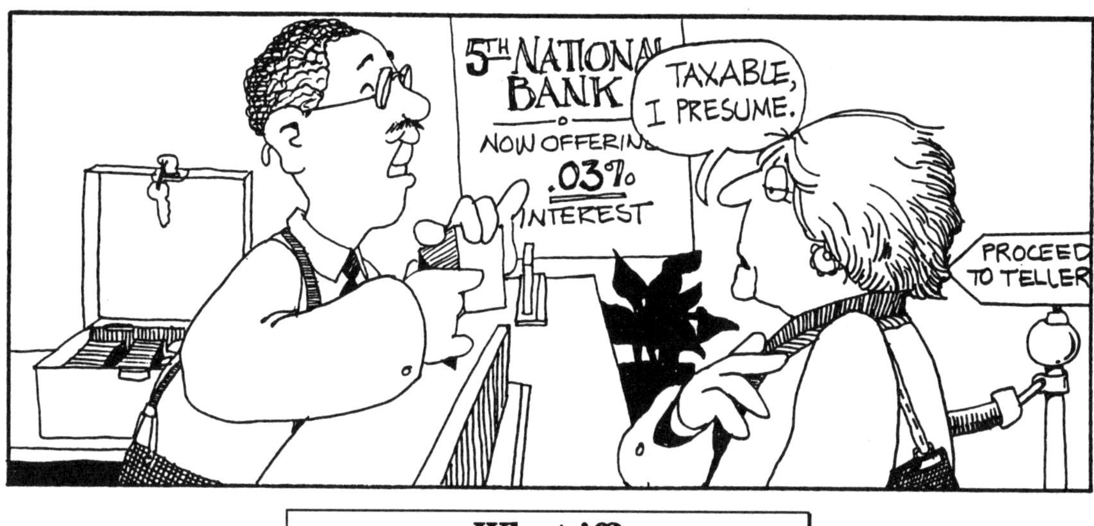

What if?

Q. My sister and I have a joint bank account but the *1099-INT* shows all the interest as being paid to me. Why should I have all the tax liability?
A. You don't have to. The banks are able to report only one Social Security number on each account, but you can then transfer your sister's portion over to her. On *Schedule B,* report the full amount because that is what the IRS matching program will be looking for. Then write "nomince distribution to..." and give your sister's name and Social Security number. Then subtract the amount that is her share. This accomplishes two things. It gets your sister's share out of your taxable income and it satisfies the IRS computer search for the full amount.

Q. I just discovered that I forgot to report some interest income on last year's return. What should I do?
A. Chances are good that the IRS is about to discover it, also. With continually increasing computer capability, the IRS is able to track more and more of our reportable income and expense. You probably received a *1099-INT* reporting the interest income and the IRS received a copy of the same form. You should call or write an IRS office and request a *Form 1040X,* which is the form to use to file an amendment to your original return. There is absolutely nothing to fear about telling the IRS that you didn't report your income. You will simply be assessed penalty and interest based upon that amount of additional tax due and the length of time from the due date of the original return. This is not unreasonable and you can expect that it will be quite painless, with the entire process taking place by mail. No revenue agent will come knocking at your door, nor will you be automatically singled out for future scrutiny because of this mistake.

Chapter Six

Line 9: Dividend Income

What you'll need

- *Forms 1099-DIV*
- *Form 1040*
- 1040 Booklet

Optional

- *Schedule B, Interest Dividend Income*
- *IRS Publication 550, Investment Income & Expenses*
- *IRS Publication 564, Mutual Fund Distributions*

What it's all about

Do you own shares of stock or mutual funds? If you have received dividends on these shares, report it here. Every share of stock represents a portion of ownership. If you received a dividend, you should receive a *Form 1099-DIV* from the corporation that paid the dividend. Your share of the earnings from the corporation's business activity that is paid to shareholders is treated as ordinary dividends. Your share of profits from the corporation's buying and selling of assets is treated as a capital gains distribution. Your share of the corporation's nontaxable activity is treated as nontaxable distributions (Box 1d on *Form 1099-DIV*). The combined total of all types of dividends is reported in Box 1a on *Form 1099-DIV*. So even though you received only one check and one *1099*, you may have up to three different tax scenarios.

Ordinary dividends are by far the most common type of dividend. They are fully taxable and reported on *Schedule B* if you receive more than $400. Capital gains are not unusual, especially with mutual funds. They are taxable, but can be offset by capital losses, and are limited to a top tax rate of 28 percent (other types of income are subject to a top rate of 39.6 percent).

Nontaxable distributions are more infrequent and may have no immediate tax consequences, but will certainly require special tracking to assure correct tax treatment. When you get back tax-free money, that actually reduces what the stock cost you. So when you sell the stock, these "nontaxable" distributions will need to be accounted for when computing gain or loss on the sale of these shares of stock.

When you buy shares in a mutual fund, your money is pooled with that of other investors, and the fund then buys and sells shares in many corporations. Mutual funds will issue just one *1099-DIV* reflecting all the activity within the fund for the year. You will not get a *1099-DIV* from every corporation in which the fund owns stock. You can understand that since mutual funds buy and sell shares in various corporations, it is not unusual to have a capital gain or loss, in addition to ordinary dividends.

Dividends are taxable even if reinvested. So don't think that just because you didn't receive a check in the mail you didn't get a taxable dividend. You did get it—and you are required to include it on your tax return. Just as nontaxable distributions reduce your cost (also referred to as "basis") of these shares, conversely, reinvested dividends increase your basis and will affect your gain or loss upon sale, so keep track of them carefully.

What to do with the forms

8a	**Taxable** interest income (see page 15). Attach Schedule B if over $400	8a	
b	**Tax-exempt** interest (see page 16). DON'T include on line 8a | 8b |		
9	Dividend income. Attach Schedule B if over $400	9	
10	Taxable refunds, credits, or offsets of state and local income taxes (see page 16) . .	10	
11	Alimony received	11	
12	Business income or (loss). Attach Schedule C or C-EZ	12	

Form 1040 Line 9. Total all the gross dividends you received (Box 1a on all *Forms 1099-DIV*). If this total is less than $400, you need only enter the amount on Line 9. If the total is more than $400, then you need to provide the IRS with some additional information. This information goes on *Schedule B,* and it is simply a listing of who paid you and how much was paid.

Now go to *Schedule B* if necessary.

Schedule B Line 5. Simply list all gross dividends (Box 1a of *Forms 1099-DIV*) here. We will back out any capital gains or nontaxable distributions in a minute.

Schedule B Line 6. Total amounts from Line 5.

Schedule B Line 7. Enter all amounts from Box 1c on *Forms 1099-DIV*, capital gains distributions. If you are using a *Schedule D* to report any capital gains other than these, then you will carry this figure over to Line 14 of your *Schedule D*. If, however, these are your only capital gains to report, then you can simply put this figure directly on Line 13 of *Form 1040*, skip *Schedule D* and write "CGD" on the dotted line next to *Form 1040* Line 13.

Schedule B Line 8. Enter amounts from Box 1d on *Forms 1099-DIV*, nontaxable distributions.

Schedule B Line 9. Total amounts from Lines 7 and 8.

Schedule B Line 10. Subtract Line 9 from Line 6. This is the total of your ordinary dividends, which is carried forward to Line 9 on *Form 1040*.

Now complete Lines 11 and 12 at the bottom of *Schedule B*. Everyone who is required to file a *Schedule B* is required to answer yes or no to these questions regarding foreign investments. If you have none, simply check the "no" box. If you do have any foreign bank accounts or trusts, check the "yes" box and read the IRS instructions for further direction.

Watch out!

If you receive nontaxable distributions on stock, referred to as return of capital distribution, you must reduce your basis in the shares of stock by such distributions. When the stock is sold, this reduced basis will result in a larger capital gain, or reduce the amount of your capital loss.

* * *

Typically, dividends are paid in cash by corporations or mutual funds, but they can be paid in stock or other property or services instead of cash. However, they're still taxable. They can also be paid to you through a trust, an estate or a partnership or association and still represent taxable income to you.

* * *

Distributions from S Corporations are generally not dividends.

What if?

Q. I just got a notice that my life insurance policy is paying a dividend. Is this taxable?

A. Most often, these are just nontaxable refunds of the premiums you've paid and are not really dividends at all. Generally, you do not need to include them in dividend income.

Q. My broker tells me I have a DRIP. What should I do about this?

A. Don't call a plumber, just a good bookkeeper! DRIP stands for Dividend Reinvestment Program. This means that instead of taking your dividends in cash, you have been using the funds to reinvest (buy more shares) in the corporation.

This is a great way to increase your investment, but it can cause headaches of migraine proportion when you go to sell the shares. With the declaration of each dividend, you actually have a stock purchase, so you need a record of how many shares were purchased with each dividend and what the price per share was. Thankfully, many mutual funds have recently begun reporting the cost basis per share along with the report of any sales or redemptions. So now, on one piece of paper, you may have all the information needed to report your sale to the IRS. From a tax preparer's standpoint, this is about the handiest thing since sliced bread!

Chapter Seven

Line 10: Taxable Refunds of State Tax

What you'll need

- *Forms 1099-G* received, or copy of last year's state tax return
- *Schedule A*, if any, from last year's federal tax return
- *Form 1040*
- 1040 Booklet

Optional

- *IRS Publication 525, Taxable & Nontaxable Income*

What it's all about

Did you receive a refund of last year's state income tax? Did you itemize deductions on last year's federal income tax return? If the answer to both questions is yes, you may need to include the refund in income this year.

Government in America operates on many levels, each with its own source of revenue and its own responsibility for providing services for the residents. Each state has a tax structure by which it raises the funds needed to operate. The most common forms of taxation on the state level are sales tax and income tax. All but five states (Alaska, Delaware, Montana, New Hampshire and Oregon) have a sales tax and all but seven states (Alaska, Florida, Nevada, South Dakota, Texas, Washington and Wyoming) have an income tax. Sales taxes paid are no longer of any consequence on your tax return, since they are no longer deductible unless paid as a business expense. State income taxes, on the other hand, may be deductible, and part or all of the refund may be taxable.

The federal government allows a deduction (if you itemize) for state income tax paid (note: *paid*, not owed!) and, likewise, many states allow some deduction for federal tax. If what you paid in state tax and deducted on *Schedule A* last year was actually more than what you owed, then you took an excess deduction that needs to be accounted for this year. This is an area of frequent misunderstanding and mistakes. We see many taxpayers claiming the entire refund as income when they don't need to, simply because they received a *1099* (from the *government,* no less). They report it because the IRS has been notified of a refund, and if the IRS knows about it, it must be taxable! Conversely, almost every client who does need to report it as income questions the logic of it: "Why should I have to pay tax on *that*?"

If you received no refund on your state taxes, you obviously do not have anything to report as income. If you did receive a refund but took only a standard deduction last year (did not itemize deductions on *Schedule A* of your federal return), then you received no tax benefit and therefore you do not need to include any refund amounts in with this year's income.

Any refunds you received from overpayment of last year's state income tax may be taxable to you the year in which you receive it. If you received a state tax refund, you should have received a *1099-G* indicating the amount of the refund and telling you that it may be taxable.

It is taxable *only* to the extent that you received a tax benefit for it *last* year. Even if you didn't receive a *1099-G*, or you can't find it, or you got mad and shredded it, you still may need to include it in income this year. Look at last year's state return (you *did* keep a copy, didn't you?) to find the amount of refund. Don't think that if you applied your refund to the next year's tax that you didn't really receive a refund. Theoretically, what happened is that you received it and just sent it right back as an estimated payment.

If you did itemize last year, you probably included a deduction on Line 5 of *Schedule A* for an amount of state income tax paid. This is where you enjoyed a tax benefit from the deduction. Now the trick is to determine just how much the benefit was, and how it compares to the amount of your refund.

What to do with the forms

b	Tax-exempt interest (see page 16). DON'T include on line 8a	8b	
9	Dividend income. Attach Schedule B if over $400	9	
10	Taxable refunds, credits, or offsets of state and local income taxes (see page 16) . .	10	
11	Alimony received	11	
12	Business income or (loss). Attach Schedule C or C-EZ	12	

Form 1040 Line 10. All taxable portions of state income tax refunds are reported here. If, on last year's return, your itemized deductions exceeded the amount of the standard deduction by more than the amount of state tax claimed as a deduction on Line 5 of *Schedule A*, then the full amount was a benefit to you and needs to be reported this year. If the difference between your itemized deductions and the amount of the standard deduction was less than the amount of state tax claimed on Line 5, then only that difference is reported on Line 10.

Clear as mud, right? The easiest way to figure the taxable portion is to use the IRS worksheet in the 1040 instruction booklet or a similar worksheet that we have included here. Just work through it, keeping in mind the general theory that what is taxable this year is only what you took last year as a deduction, but didn't really owe (remember *paid*, not owed). This amount is taxable only to the extent that your itemized deductions exceeded the standard deduction.

1. State income tax refund (from *Form 1099G*).	1.________
2. Amount from 1993 *Schedule A*, Line 26.	2.________
3. Amount corresponding to your filing status: • Single $3,700 • Married filing joint $6,200 • Married filing separate $3,100 • Head of household $5,450 • Qualified widow(er) $6,200	3.________
4. If you didn't complete Line 33a on your 1993 return, enter 0. Otherwise multiply amount on Line 33a by $700 ($900 if 1993 filing status was single or head of household).	4.________
5. Add Lines 3 and 4.	5.________
6. Subtract Line 5 from Line 2. Do not enter less than 0.	6.________
7. Smaller of Line 1 or Line 6. *This is the taxable portion of your refund that is reported on Line 10 of* Form 1040.	7.________

Working through a few examples may help demonstrate the way it all works:

1. Joe did not itemize last year and received a $500 refund of his state tax. No need to report the refund, even though he received a *1099-G*.

2. Jane itemized last year and received a $200 refund of her state tax. She is single and the total of her itemized deductions (Line 26 of *Schedule A*) was $4,000 and the amount of state tax claimed as a deduction (Line 5 of *Schedule A*) was $1,000. She needs to report all $200 as income this year.

$4,000	Total itemized deductions
3,700	1993 standard deduction amount
$300	More than refund received, so refund is taxable in full

3. Jim itemized last year and received a $500 refund of his state tax. He is single and the total of his itemized deductions (Line 26 of *Schedule A*) was

$3,800 and the amount of state tax claimed as a deduction (Line 5 of *Schedule A*) was $1,000. He needs to report only $100 as income this year.

$3,800	Total itemized deductions
3,700	1993 standard deduction amount
$100	Less than refund received, so only this amount is taxable, not entire refund

Watch out!

To complicate matters, beginning in 1991, Congress limited itemized deductions for high-income taxpayers. If your deductions were so limited, then your taxable refund is calculated proportionately. Obviously, this gets pretty complicated but can be handled by referring to detailed instructions in *IRS Publication 525*.

What if?

Q. I filed amended returns for last year and I just received both federal and state refunds. Are they taxable?

A. You report the state tax refund as income on this year's federal return, since this is the year you actually received it. Use the amended federal return to figure your tax benefit. Federal tax refunds are not taxable on your federal return, but may be on your state return.

Chapter Eight

Line 11: Alimony Received

What you'll need

- Record of amount of alimony received
- *Form 1040*
- 1040 Booklet

Optional

- *IRS Publication 504, Tax Information for Divorced or Separated Individuals*

What it's all about

Do you receive spousal support payments or alimony? If so, it is to be reported as taxable income. Conversely, the one paying alimony is allowed to take it as an adjustment (reduction) to income (See Chapter 20).

Alimony is payment under a divorce or separate maintenance agreement or court decree, including an award of temporary support. Child support and property settlement issues are *not* alimony, and you are not required to report these items as income. If you are receiving alimony, chances are that you can clearly identify what you receive. If not, read through your decree of divorce or separate maintenance, or ask your attorney to spell it out for you.

The alimony you report as income will be compared to the amount your ex-spouse is claiming as an adjustment to income, since the person making the payment (your ex-spouse) is required to report your Social Security number to the IRS. You are obligated to give your ex-spouse your Social Security number and if you don't, you will be subject to a $50 penalty by the IRS. If the payer claims a legitimate adjustment (reduction of income), then the person receiving it needs to claim it as income. Looking at it from that perspective, you can see that it actually is a shifting of income from one person to another.

The IRS looks very carefully at income-shifting issues and, therefore, you must insure that you are doing so under a divorce decree and the payments meet the standard definition of alimony. Say, for instance, that your divorce decree calls for you to receive $5,000 in annual alimony payments, but, because you were broke, your ex-spouse actually paid you $7,000. Your ex-spouse can only deduct the $5,000 and that is all you should claim as income. Without court authorization, the IRS just considers the additional $2,000 a loan or a gift. You can see why the IRS takes such a position.

Chances are that the person making the payments is in a higher tax bracket, and if the additional $2,000 is allowed as a shift in income to the person in the lower tax bracket, then the IRS receives less in tax revenues.

What to do with the forms

9	Dividend income. Attach Schedule B if over $400	9	
10	Taxable refunds, credits, or offsets of state and local income taxes (see page 16) . .	10	
11	Alimony received	11	
12	Business income or (loss). Attach Schedule C or C-EZ	12	
13	Capital gain or (loss). If required, attach Schedule D (see page 16)	13	

Form 1040 Line 11. Reporting alimony received as income is very simple. Just put the total amount received (up to the amount authorized) on Line 11. If you're on speaking terms with your ex-spouse, it's not a bad idea to make sure that you're reporting the same amounts. If you're not and the amounts reported differ, you can both be guaranteed a note from the IRS!

Watch out!

A marriage is a complex issue both financially and emotionally. When it is dissolved, there is no end of opportunity for making what is a fairly straightforward concept (support obligations and division of property) into confusing scenarios. If yours is a complicated situation or if you have items that you're not sure qualify as alimony, read through *IRS Publication 504*. You should contact your attorney or a tax professional if you cannot clearly identify your items of support.

* * *

Although a division of property pursuant to a divorce decree is a nontaxable event, there may be significant tax consequences to the recipient who sells the property subsequent to the divorce. Not all property is treated equally tax-wise, therefore, professional tax assistance is recommended when negotiating a property settlement.

What if?

Q. My ex-spouse fell behind in his alimony payments and I have some legal fees in connection with getting the payments resumed. Can I deduct them from the alimony I received?

A. Yes and no. You can deduct them, but only as a miscellaneous itemized deduction on *Schedule A*. So if you just use the standard deduction, you cannot deduct the expense at all. If you do itemize, miscellaneous deductions are subject to certain limits and may or may not be of much tax consequence depending upon your situation. You cannot deduct the legal fees or court costs for getting a divorce or for obtaining child support, only fees connected to obtaining alimony.

Chapter Nine

Line 12: Business Income or (Loss)

What you'll need

- *Schedule C or C-EZ, Profit or Loss from Business*
- *1099-Misc*, received from payer(s)
- *Form 1040*
- 1040 Booklet

Optional

- *Form 8829, Expenses for Business Use of Your Home*
- *Form 4562, Depreciation and Amortization*
- *IRS Publication 463, Travel, Entertainment & Gift Expenses*
- *IRS Publication 334, Tax Guide for Small Business*
- *IRS Publication 525, Taxable and Non-taxable Income*
- *IRS Publication 535, Business Expenses*
- *IRS Publication 587, Business Use of Your Home*
- *IRS Publication 917, Business Use of a Car*
- *Schedule SE, Self-Employment Tax*

What it's all about

Do you own and operate a business? If so and you are not a corporation or partnership, this is where you report the income and expenses from the business operation.

Small businesses, it is said, make up the backbone of our nation's economy, and sole proprietorship is the dominant business form in America. If you operate a business as a sole proprietor, you report income and expenses on a *Schedule C*. If you operate more than one business as a sole proprietor, you must file a separate *Schedule C* for each business. The combined net income/loss from all *Schedule Cs* is carried to Line 12 of *Form 1040*.

While owning and operating a small business carries with it additional tax reporting responsibilities, doing business as a sole proprietor, and not an employee, presents the taxpayer with significant tax-avoidance opportunities not available to the wage earner.

As a sole proprietor or independent contractor, your costs of doing business generally are fully deductible on *Schedule C*. If you were an employee reporting these same expenses as *miscellaneous itemized deductions*, part or all of these deductions might be lost. Additionally, sole proprietors may be able to contribute more to a self-employed retirement plan than they could to a simple IRA as an employee.

On the flip side of this coin, however, is the requirement that the self-employed individual is responsible for his or her own retirement and pays 100 percent of his or her Social Security contribution via self-employment tax. There is no 50-percent employer matching (see Chapter 24).

The key to taking full advantage of filing a *Schedule C* is setting up a good system of record-keeping to capture all expenses you incur in the operation of your business. You also want to have a system that will allow you to verify income received so that you do not rely upon *1099s* issued by payers, since these are often incorrect. The minimum necessary components of good record-keeping include a business checking account, business credit card and an automobile log. The busy entrepreneur is often well-advised to seek the services of a competent bookkeeper to insure accurate record-keeping.

As tax preparers, we have seen countless cases where clients have reduced their tax liability by hundreds, and even thousands, of dollars simply by keeping good records and preventing expenses from going unreported. Keep in mind that when federal tax, self-employment tax and state tax rates are combined, the self employed individual can pay as much as 60 percent of his/her net income in tax. Therefore, for every additional dollar of deduction you capture, your friendly government will pay you 60 cents in tax savings.

What to do with the forms

10	Taxable refunds, credits, or offsets of state and local income taxes (see page 16) . .	10	
11	Alimony received	11	
12	Business income or (loss). Attach Schedule C or C-EZ	12	
13	Capital gain or (loss). If required, attach Schedule D (see page 16)	13	
14	Other gains or (losses). Attach Form 4797	14	

The combined amount of net profit or loss from all sole proprietorships you or your spouse operate is reported on *Form 1040* Line 12. Information on each business (even if there is only one) is reported in detail on a separate schedule.

Most sole proprietorships will be required to file a *Schedule C* to report income and expenses for the business. There is a simpler form called a *Schedule C-EZ*. Please refer to the general information at the top of *Schedule C-EZ* to determine if this form is appropriate for you to file. Even if you qualify for the simpler form, you should still pay close attention to the following *Schedule C* discussion, since you still must know what expenses are deductible.

Schedule C is at once simple and straightforward, yet sometimes confusing and complex. With adequate records and the following instructions, however, preparation of your *Schedule C* will be as easy as falling off a log.

Schedule C Lines A-E. Fill in completely. See page C-6 of the *Schedule C* instructions for the Line B business code. Be careful to select the code that most closely fits your business. For instance, if you are a service provider, do not use a retailer code. To do so may trigger IRS scrutiny of your method of accounting as discussed later. If you do not have a separate employer identification number, leave Line D blank.

Schedule C Line F, Accounting method. If you do not maintain a set of books, *and* inventories are not an income-producing element of your business, then you must use the cash method of accounting. Unless required to use the accrual method of accounting, because of the existence of inventory in your business, you may use the cash or accrual method.

Keep in mind that if you are a cash-method *Schedule C* filer, income is recognized when cash is received, and expenses when cash is paid. The accrual method, on the other hand, recognizes income when earned, and expenses when incurred. Once a method is selected, you must use it consistently each year unless you obtain IRS approval to change.

Schedule C Line G. If your business has inventory, you must count and value the inventory on hand as of your business year-end. The method used to value that inventory should be indicated on Line G.

Most businesses will use either Items 1 or 2 (*cost* or *lower of cost or market*) to value inventory. Cost is simply what you paid to acquire the inventory. Lower of cost or market means the inventory is valued at what it is worth at year end, if that value is lower than your cost.

There are nuances to inventory valuation, such as last-in, first-out (LIFO) or first-in, first-out (FIFO). You should consult your bookkeeper, accountant or accounting textbook for a complete understanding of these concepts. For businesses that sell inventory, this year-end value is a most important number, since it directly affects the deduction you will claim on Line 4 (Cost of goods sold).

Schedule C Line I. A "no" answer to this question regarding material participation will set off one of those red flags the IRS is on the lookout for. If you don't materially participate in the operation of the business, it will likely be classified as a "passive activity," subject to special rules. If you operate on your own, you obviously are a material participant. If, however, you did nothing except invest money in a venture, your participation is questionable. See *Schedule C* instructions for a detailed explanation of material participation.

Every business is unique and, therefore, each will classify income and expenses differently. Most expense categories on *Schedule C*, such as advertising, are self-explanatory. Consequently, what follows is a discussion of the income and expense items, which may not be obvious from the descriptions.

Schedule C Line 1. Enter total sales.

Schedule C Line 2. If you had sales returns or allowances, enter the amount here.

Schedule C Line 4, Cost of goods sold. This should only be calculated when sale of inventory is an income-generating activity. If applicable, inventory should be counted and valued, per your valuation method, at the beginning and end of each year. The calculation for determining cost of goods sold is performed on page 2 of *Schedule C*, Lines 33 through 40.

Schedule C Line 9, Bad debts. These are applicable only to accrual taxpayers. For a debt to be written off as bad, it must be known to be worthless. Subsequent collection of a previously written-off bad debt is income in the year of collection. Cash method taxpayers have no bad debts since the income was never reported previously. Nonbusiness bad debts are reported on *Schedule D* as a capital loss (see Chapter 10).

Schedule C Line 10, Car and truck expenses. These can be computed by keeping a log of business miles traveled and multiplying this amount by the standard mileage rate of 29 cents per mile, or by keeping track of actual out-of-pocket expenses. In any event, commuting to and from work and your place of residence is *not* deductible. Only out-of-town travel or travel between two places of business is deductible. For instance, if you stop for supplies on the way to work, you cannot deduct any mileage expense. But if you go out for supplies during the course of the day and return to your place of work, that mileage is deductible.

You should use the method that results in the greater deduction. However, if you start out using actual expenses and depreciated the vehicle using a method other than the straight-line depreciation method, you cannot later switch to the standard mileage rate method. (See Appendix A, Section 4, Depreciation and Basis, for a discussion of various depreciation methods, including straight-line.) Also, if you lease your business vehicle, you *must* use actual expenses.

If you claim actual expenses, keep track of your oil, gas, repairs, insurance, etc. Your auto log will keep track of business and personal miles driven as a percentage of the total miles you drive during the year. The business percentage of your total auto expenses is the amount of your deduction. Also, you can claim a depreciation deduction for the business portion of your vehicle by filling out *Form 4562* (See Appendix A, Section 4, Depreciation and Basis).

If you rent or lease vehicles, however, you may have to reduce your deduction as a result of a set of complex rules that are fully explained in *IRS Publication 917, Business Use of A Car*. Before entering into a vehicle lease, you should understand the tax consequences as outlined in this publication. And remember...the car salesman is probably not a tax expert.

If you are not required to file *Form 4562* for depreciation and you claim vehicle expenses, then you must answer questions 41 through 45b in Part IV on page 2 of *Schedule C*.

Schedule C Line 13, Depreciation and Section 179 expense. See Appendix A, Section 4, for a discussion of depreciation and basis.

Schedule C Line 14, Employee benefit programs. These do not include any contributions made on the owner's behalf, only those made for employees. Benefits such as group term life insurance, dependent care assistance and accident and health plans are examples of employee benefit programs.

Schedule C Line 15, Insurance. This includes business premiums only, and not health insurance premiums. Casualty, bonding and professional liability are examples of insurance expenses reported on this line. Also, insurance that covers theft of or damage to office equipment would be included.

Schedule C Line 16a-16b, Interest expense. This includes interest on business-related debts only. There are detailed instructions in *IRS Publication 535, Business Expenses*, on allocating interest expense based on the use of the loan proceeds. In general, if all or part of a loan is used in your business, the interest is fully or partially deductible on *Schedule C*. Because *Schedule C* expenses reduce self-employment income and tax, it is very important to allocate interest expense to *Schedule C*. Only report on Line 16a the interest expense that was reported to you on *Form 1098*. If no form was issued, report the interest on Line 16b. Failure to report your interest expense in this fashion will likely result in the IRS sending you a troublesome matching notice, even though your return is completely correct.

Schedule C Line 17, Legal and professional services. Report on this line the cost of attorneys, accountants and other professional service providers. If these professionals perform business and nonbusiness consultation, be sure to ask them to issue a detailed billing outlining the portion of their bill that was business-related, so that you may claim the deduction on *Schedule C*.

Schedule C Line 19, Pension and profit-sharing deduction. This refers to contributions for employees only. The contribution made for the owner does not reduce *Schedule C* income, but must be reported on Line 27 of *Form 1040* as an adjustment to income. You should consult with your attorney or financial planner before the end of your tax year, as some plans must be adopted before year-end for contributions to be deductible.

Contributions to these plans typically must be made by the due date of your tax return, including extensions. Pension and profit-sharing plans, therefore, represent the rare tax-planning strategy that can be employed after the close of the tax year.

Schedule C Line 20a-20b, Rent or lease. Rent paid on business property, other than vehicles, is fully deductible. Examples include rents for office, storage, tools and machinery. Do not include any amounts here for the use of your own home. (See *Schedule C*, Line 30, next page.)

Schedule C Line 21, Repairs and maintenance. Only your out-of-pocket costs, and not the value of your own labor, are deductible on this line. The cost of improvements, which extend the useful life of or add value to an asset, are to be depreciated and are not currently deductible as repairs and maintenance. For example, if you pay a repairman to fix your copier, you can deduct the cost of parts. But if the parts include a sorter and an automatic paper-feed device, these are considered improvements and cannot be written off as a repair expense. Rather, these are taken into account when calculating depreciation on the copier.

Schedule C Line 23, Taxes and licenses. These include state and local tax imposed directly on your business. Property taxes (real and personal) on business assets are also reported on this line as is the employer portion of payroll taxes.

Schedule C Line 24a-24d, Travel, meals and entertainment. These expenses are reported as separate expenses on the appropriate lines. Your accounting and/or tax record-keeping system should be designed to separately account for travel as opposed to meals and entertainment.

For any of these expenses to be deductible, they must be ordinary and necessary to the active conduct of your business and not be of an extravagant nature. These expenses must be documented with receipts, which note the time, place, amount and the business purpose of the expense. For meals under $25, a separate receipt is not required but an entry in an entertainment log is sufficient. The log, however, must include the same information that would be required on a receipt.

While travel is fully deductible, the business meals and entertainment deduction is limited to 50 percent of your actual cost. In other words, half of your deduction is automatically disallowed. This is new for 1994.

When traveling away from home on business, it is possible to avoid having to keep track of actual meal costs by using a standard meal allowance. Refer to *IRS Publication 463, Travel, Entertainment, and Gift Expenses,* for information on the standard meal allowance rules.

Schedule C Line 25, Utilities. You may only deduct those utilities directly related to your business, such as office or warehouse gas, water, electricity and telephone. Utility expenses for a home office are reported on *Form 8829* as discussed later in this chapter. You can no longer allocate a portion of your personal telephone line to business use. You must maintain a second line into your residence in order to claim a deduction for anything other than long-distance calls.

Schedule C Line 26, Wages. These include amounts paid to employees. Sole proprietors often employ their children in the business and these wages are also reported on this line. Do not include amounts you pay yourself. A sole proprietor cannot be his or her own employee.

Schedule C Line 27, Other expenses. These go to Part V of page 2 and include any expenses not specifically listed elsewhere. Be careful not to raise any unnecessary red flags by lumping large expenses into "miscellaneous" categories. Break your expenses down as much as reasonably possible so the IRS has enough information to process your return without having to correspond with you or, worse yet, invite you to its office for a friendly chat.

Schedule C Line 30, Business use of your home. The rules for deducting a portion of home expenses as business expenses have become more stringent and more subject to scrutiny by the IRS. *IRS Publication 587, Business Use of Your Home,* contains a detailed explanation of these rules. If you use your home in connection with your business, you must attach *Form 8829* to your tax return. You may deduct business expenses for the use of part of your home only if that part is used exclusively for business and on a regular basis as your principal place of business or as a place used in the normal course of business by patients, clients, etc., or if it is a separate structure not attached to your home and is used in connection with business.

The nature of your business is critical in determining whether you qualify for a home office deduction. A teacher, for example, who spends the majority of time in a home office doing preparation for class cannot claim an office in home deduction. The main place of business is the classroom, not the home.

The deduction for use of your home is available to renters as well as homeowners. The exclusive business use requirement is relaxed somewhat for day-care providers in that they may be able to deduct business expenses even if the space in the home is used for nonbusiness purposes, as well.

You should consult a tax advisor, however, before converting a portion of your home to business use, since doing so may cause you to lose the tax benefits available to you upon the sale of your residence. For example, the tax deferral on the gain from the sale of your residence or the one-time exclusion of gains for those over 55 years of age may be partially lost, since these tax breaks apply only to residential, and not business property.

Schedule C Line 32a-32b. If you are economically at risk as a result of your participation in this business, you should check Box 32a. This means your loss, if any, is deductible.

If you are not at risk (you will not suffer economically from any or all loss), check Box 32b. You can only deduct losses to the extent you are at risk.

In other words, if you don't at some point have to personally write a check to cover your business losses, you may not get to deduct them.

Any losses not deducted due to at-risk limitations can be carried forward and may offset future income.

Schedule C Part III, Cost of Goods Sold

Schedule C Line 33, Inventory at beginning of year should agree with the ending inventory you calculated last year. For first-year businesses, this line is zero.

Schedule C Line 34, Purchases less cost of items withdrawn for personal use includes all items purchased for resale during the year. Be sure to subtract any goods you used for nonbusiness purposes. For example, the gadabout jewelry shop owner would not include the cost of the diamond rings given to each of his seven girlfriends.

Schedule C Line 35, Cost of labor would typically include the labor expense incurred in acquiring or producing property for resale (not including the owner's). All other labor would be included in Line 26.

Schedule C Line 36, Materials and supplies are those expenses incurred in acquiring or producing property for resale.

Schedule C Line 37, Other costs include freight and any other costs to acquire or produce goods for resale that do not fit into any of the above categories.

Schedule C Line 39, Inventory at the end of year is the inventory at year-end that you counted and valued in accordance with the valuation method noted on Line G. Notice that ending inventory is a subtraction in arriving at the cost of goods sold deduction. Higher inventory value equals lower cost of goods sold and vice versa, so be careful to accurately count and value inventory and keep good records.

Schedule C Part IV, Information on your vehicle. This is where you tell the IRS about the business use of your car if you use the standard mileage rate to calculate expense.

Schedule C Part V, Other Expenses. Use this section for expenses that do not fit into the preprinted categories on *Schedule C.*

Watch out!

If you have income from self-employment, you will likely be required to make estimated tax payments, especially since self-employment income over $400 may also be subject to self-employment tax in addition to ordinary income tax.

* * *

Club dues after 1993 are no longer deductible. This applies to clubs that operate for recreation or social purposes. Memberships in professional associations or civic groups are okay, but others, such as athletic clubs, country clubs, airline clubs and most luncheon groups, are not.

* * *

If the gross income reported on your *Schedule C* does not equal or exceeds the total of the *1099s* you received, you should reconcile this discrepancy. If your records, and not the *1099*s, are correct, attach a statement to your tax return explaining this. Remember, *1099s* are often incorrect, so keep your own records and do not rely solely on *1099s.*

* * *

If you are starting a business, the IRS provides two good publications you might want to read *Publication 334, Tax Guide for Small Business,* and *Publication 583, Taxpayers Starting a Business.*

* * *

Business losses may create a situation where you have overall negative income for the year. In this case you may have a "net operating loss," which can be carried back or forward to offset income in other years. NOLs are complicated calculations for which you will most likely need professional advice.

What if?

Q. I sold an asset used in my business. How and where do I report the gain?
A. Gain or loss on the sale of business assets is reported on *Form 4797* and is calculated by subtracting the adjusted basis in the asset from the sale price. Adjusted basis is the cost (what you paid), plus any improvements, less all the depreciation you were eligible to claim since the time the asset was placed in service. See Chapter 11 for a complete discussion of gain or loss on the sale of business assets.

Q. Why is "supplies" shown as an expense on both Lines 22 and 36?
A. Report on Line 22 supplies used in the operation of your business (office supplies or cleaning supplies, for example). But report on Line 36 only materials that become a part of goods sold to customers.

Chapter Ten

Line 13: Capital Gains and Losses

What you'll need

- *Schedule D, Capital Gains and Losses*
- *Forms 1099-B, Proceeds from Broker or Barter Exchange Transactions*
- *Forms 1099-S, Proceeds from Real Estate Transactions*
- *Forms 1099-DIV, Dividends* (if containing capital gains distributions)
- *Form 1040*
- 1040 Booklet

Optional

- *Form 2119, Sale of Residence*
- *Form 4797, Sale of Business Property*
- *Form 6252, Installment Sales*
- *Form 8824, Like Kind Exchange*
- *Schedules K-1* (if containing capital gain distributions)
- *IRS Publication 544, Sales and Other Dispositions of Assets*

What it's all about

As far as Uncle Sam is concerned, there are basically two types of income: ordinary income and capital gains. Capital gains is simply income you receive when you sell a capital asset for more than you paid for it. And just what is a capital asset? It is just about anything you own of a personal or investment nature.

The most common transaction reported as a capital gain is the sale of stocks or bonds. Those clearly fit the definition of property of an investment nature. When you sell stocks or bonds, you should receive a *1099-B* from the stockbroker. Hopefully, you will have a record of when you bought the stock and how much you paid for it. If so, reporting your capital gain or loss will be a snap.

One key rule of life is that nothing is ever as simple as it sounds. And so it is with calculating a capital gain or loss. For starters, more than just the purchase price of the asset needs to be considered. Sometimes there may not even be a purchase price. This is why the tax form asks you for what is called cost or other basis. This is generally your original cost plus any improvements or fees, minus any tax deductions for depreciation or casualty losses. Your basis can also vary depending upon how you obtained the asset. For example:

- **Purchase.** Your cost is what you paid for it and that is also your basis.
- **Trade.** Your basis is equal to your basis in the item given up in trade.
- **Gift.** Your basis is the same as the basis of the person gifting it to you.
- **Inheritance.** Your cost basis is generally the value at date of death.

Capital gains continues to be a controversial area of tax law. Until 1986, taxpayers with long-term capital gains received a tremendous tax break—only 40 percent of the gain was subject to tax! This was known as the capital gains exclusion, since 60 percent of any gain was actually excluded from income. There is no longer any such exclusion. Capital gains are 100-percent taxable, but the tax rate on long-term capital gains is limited to 28 percent. This is a distinct advantage, since the maximum tax rate on ordinary income is now 39.6 percent. Unfortunately for the little guy, this advantage is limited only to high-income taxpayers, those whose income pushes them above the 28-percent bracket.

Losses on investment property are generally deductible, but losses on personal items are not deductible. So, if you sell your car for a profit, you report the profit as a capital gain. But when you sell your car at a loss (as most of us do), you cannot deduct it as a capital loss. Fair is fair—and then there is the Internal Revenue Code!

What to do with the forms

11	Almony received	11		
12	Business income or (loss). Attach Schedule C or C-EZ	12		
13	Capital gain or (loss). If required, attach Schedule D (see page 16)	13		
14	Other gains or (losses). Attach Form 4797	14		
15a	Total IRA distributions . 15a | b Taxable amount (see page 17)	15b		

Most capital gain or loss is detailed on *Schedule D,* and the total is carried forward to Line 13 of *Form 1040*. But you may not need *Schedule D* at all. If your only capital gain is from a capital gains distribution (most likely from a mutual fund, reported on a *1099-DIV*) you do not need *Schedule D* at all. Just put the amount of capital gain directly on Line 13 of *Form 1040* and write "CGD" on the dotted line next to Line 13.

Schedule D serves the following functions:

- Details disposition (sale or trade or declared worthless) of capital assets. What the asset is, when you got it and when you got rid of it, how much it cost you (adjusted cost, that is!), what you got for it and what the resulting gain or loss is.

- Calculates limit on capital losses allowed and/or carried over. You can deduct only $3,000 in net capital losses each year, $1,500 if married filing separately. You can then carry over any unused amount and continue to deduct $3,000 per year until used up.
- Calculates tax so that capital gains are not taxed at more than 28 percent. Tax is calculated on a special worksheet to prevent tax rate on the capital gains portion of your income from going above 28 percent. This worksheet is included in the *Schedule D* instructions. It is for your records only and should not be attached to your tax return.

Schedule D Part I, Short-term gain or loss. Complete this section if you are reporting disposition of assets held for one year or less. If you need more room, go to page 2 of the form.

Schedule D Line 1

Column (a), Description of property. Just describe the capital asset you disposed of. The form does not allow much room and you will most likely have to abbreviate some words.

Column (b), Date acquired. When did you buy it, inherit it, receive it in trade or as a gift?

Column (c), Date sold. When did you sell it, trade it, give it away?

Column (d), Sales price. What did you get for it? Remember, if not cash, you have to report the value of whatever goods or services that you received instead.

Column (e), Cost or other basis. How much did you pay for it (adjusted per cost basis rules)? If you are selling stock, you can count broker's fees as part of your cost.

Column (f), Loss. Did you dispose of it for less than your cost basis? If so, subtract column (d) from column (e).

Column (g), Gain. Did you dispose of it for more than your cost basis? If so, subtract column (e) from column (d).

Schedule D Line 2. Enter total from Line 21 on page 2, if applicable.

Schedule D Line 3, Total of all sales price amounts. Add up all amounts in column (d) and enter here.

Schedule D Line 4. Report here any short-term gain (not loss) from the sale of your personal residence as calculated on *Form 2119, Sale of Your Home*, any short-term gain (not loss) from installment sales as calculated on *Form 6252*, any short-term gain or loss from taxable portion of like-kind exchanges as calculated on *Form 8824* or any gains or losses from *Forms 4684, Casualties and Thefts*, or *Form 6781, Gains and Losses From Sec. 1256 Contracts and Straddles*.

Schedule D Line 5. Enter here any short-term gain or loss from partnerships, S Corporations, estates or trusts as reported to you on *Schedules K-1*.

Schedule D Line 6, From last year's *Schedule D*. Report here any unused short-term loss from prior years that can be carried over to this year. You should have prepared a capital loss carryover worksheet for your records if you had unused capital loss last year. The amount of the unused loss entered on Line 6 will be taken from that worksheet.

Schedule D Line 7, Totals. Add the loss column (f) and the gain column (g).

Schedule D Line 8, Net. Net the gain against the loss on Line 7.

Schedule D Part II, Long-term gain or loss. Complete this section if you are reporting disposition of assets held for more than one year.

Schedule D Lines 9 - 11. These lines are the same as Line 1 through Line 3. The only difference is you are now reporting assets you owned for a longer period of time.

Schedule D Line 12. Enter any long-term gains from *Forms 4797, 2119, 2439* or *6252*. Also enter long-term gain or loss from *Forms 4684, 6781* or *8824*.

Schedule D Line 13. Enter here any long-term gain or loss from partnerships, S Corporations, estates or trusts as reported to you on *Schedules K-1*.

Schedule D Line 14, Capital gain distribution. Report here any such distributions reported to you on your dividend statements (*1099-DIV*). Remember, if this is your only entry on *Schedule D*, just put this amount on *Schedule B* and follow the instructions we gave you for *Schedule B*, Line 7.

Schedule D Line 15. Report here any unused long-term loss from prior years that can be carried over to this year. See Part V of last year's *Schedule D*.

Schedule D Line 16, Totals. Add the loss column (f) and the gain column (g).

Schedule D Line 17. Combine columns (f) and (g) from Line 16.

Schedule D Part III, Summary. Combine Parts I and II for the net gain or loss. Net long-term capital gains do receive some measure of preferential tax treatment.

Schedule D Line 18. Combine Lines 8 and 17. Enter the net gain or loss. If a gain, also enter the amount on Line 13 of *Form 1040*. If a loss, go to Line 19.

Schedule D Line 19. Enter the smaller of $3,000 ($1,500 if married filing separate) or the amount from Line 18 if a loss. Also enter this amount (as a negative to indicate a loss) on Line 13 of *Form 1040*. If the loss from Line 18 is greater than $3,000, then you will have an amount to carry over to next year. Use the capital loss carryover worksheet provided by IRS to keep track of any losses carried over. You will need this worksheet when you prepare next year's return, so keep it in your tax file for next year.

Schedule D Tax Worksheet. Tax on the capital gains portion of your income is computed at 28 percent rather than the top rate for ordinary income.

This worksheet is for the tax computation on capital gains as segregated from other income. It is self-explanatory and the bottom line is the amount of your tax. Enter this number on Line 38 of *Form 1040* and check Box C, which indicates that you calculated your tax using the *Schedule D* Tax Worksheet.

Watch out!

If you are selling investments at a loss in order to offset a capital gain on another sale, watch out for the "wash sale" rule. If you are planning to repurchase the stocks you just sold at a loss (because the price is low and you figure now is a good time to buy this particular stock), you must wait 31 days after the sale before buying the same stock. If you repurchase before that time, the IRS does not recognize the sale and repurchase, so it is as though you never did anything.

* * *

Be careful if buying, selling or trading property among family members. Strict IRS guidelines prevent you from structuring deals solely for tax avoidance. And who better to make such a deal with than your own family, or a family-owned business?

* * *

There is such an animal as a nontaxable trade. Most commonly, this takes place in a like-kind exchange of business or investment property. The rules for such transactions are spelled out in Section 1031 of the Internal Revenue Code. Hence, you may hear the term "1031 exchange" when referring to a tax-free exchange. These are very tricky and should not be considered without professional guidance through the maze of paperwork necessary to conform with IRS requirements. In the absence of any meaningful tax break on capital gains, many sellers of property are turning to like-kind (Section 1031) exchanges. How unfortunate it is that in this great bastion of capitalism, our elected officials fail to understand that the risk-takers who invest in capital assets should be given an incentive to take that risk. Taking 28 percent of an investor's profit in federal tax is hardly incentive!

What if?

Q. I loaned some money to a friend and realize now that I have no hope of ever collecting it. Can I take this as a capital loss on my tax return?

A. Yes, you can deduct it if certain requirements are met that certify it as an actual bad debt. To insure the deductibility, make sure that you can document the loan agreement in writing. Additionally, you have to prove the amount of the loan and prove that it is worthless by having taken reasonable steps to collect it. So, if you just gave this friend $500 cash out of your pocket during a poker game, you both forgot about it and he later moved away and now you remember it and want to take it as a loss because you've lost touch with him, *forget it!*

If, however, this was a formal loan to someone who signed a note, and from whom you have made efforts to collect and are reasonably sure that you never will be able to collect, then you have a deductible loss. Such a nonbusiness bad debt is deducted as a short-term capital loss on Part I of *Schedule D*. It is advisable to attach a statement to your return indicating the name of the debtor, date and amount of the debt, efforts you made to collect, and why you have decided that the debt is worthless. Attaching a short but complete explanation like this will reduce your chance of audit by showing the IRS that you have considered the situation and believe you are complying with the requirements for deductibility. This is a good procedure to follow whenever you are dealing with what could be a questionable deduction.

Chapter Eleven

Line 14: Other Gains or (Losses)

What you'll need

- *Form 4797, Sales of Business Property*
- Depreciation schedules (if applicable)
- *Form 1040*
- 1040 Booklet

Optional

- *IRS Publication 534, Depreciation*
- *IRS Publication 537, Installment sales*
- *IRS Publication 544, Sales and Other Dispositions of Assets*
- *IRS Publication 551, Basis of Assets*
- *IRS Publication 925, Passive Activity and At Risk Rules*

What it's all about

Have you disposed of property used in a business? If so, you report the sale and any gain or loss on *Form 4797*.

During your lifetime you will acquire and dispose of various types of property. The vast majority of these properties are personal items (residence, family car, stereo, those plastic pink flamingos that Grandma gave you and you couldn't wait to get rid of). You may have bought and held another type of property known as investment property, hoping to later sell it at a gain (stocks, bonds, mutual funds, bare land). Still another type of property may have been bought and used in your business (office equipment, rental house, business vehicles). These are referred to throughout this chapter as depreciable property.

Your intent in acquiring these various properties will determine if and where the sale or other disposition of them is to be reported on your tax return. Also of importance in reporting the disposition of property is *how* you dispose of it (sale, exchange or casualty, to name just a few).

Form 4797 is used to report the sale or exchange of business property. Generally, this is any property that is subject to depreciation (see Appendix A, Section 4, Depreciation and Basis). As a general rule, gain on the sale of business property, except for depreciation recapture, is capital gain, and loss is ordinary loss. Depreciation recapture is treated as ordinary income. Depreciation recapture usually occurs where business property is sold at a gain and:

1. It is depreciable "personal" property. The depreciation recapture is the lesser of the gain or the total depreciation you claimed or were allowed to claim since you used the asset in your business.

   -or-

2. It is depreciable "real" property and you used an accelerated method of depreciation in calculating your depreciation deduction. Therefore, if you used straight-line depreciation for real property, you probably won't have to recapture any depreciation upon sale. (Refer to Appendix A, Section 4, for an explanation of various depreciation methods.)

If business property was disposed of due to casualty or theft (involuntary conversion), use *Form 4684, Casualties and Thefts,* in addition to *Form 4797*. Keep in mind, however, that gains from involuntary conversions may not be currently taxable.

For instance, assume the office building you own burns down and the insurance company reimburses you based on replacement cost, which exceeds your tax cost, and you use the insurance money to rebuild the office. You can avoid tax on this gain, and rightly so, since the insurance money simply made you whole again and you put no cash in your pocket.

If you exchange your property for property of a like-kind, you may avoid current tax on any gain that results. Use *Form 8824* to report this transaction. These rules (under Internal Revenue Code Section 1031) are complex, however, and you should consult a tax professional since strict adherence to the tax regulations is essential to a successful like-kind exchange.

Finally, if you have previously claimed an investment credit on the property being disposed of, you may have to file *Form 4255, Recapture of Investment Credit,* and repay part, or all, of that credit.

What to do with the forms

12	Business income or (loss). Attach Schedule C or C-EZ				12		
13	Capital gain or (loss). If required, attach Schedule D (see page 16)				13		
14	Other gains or (losses). Attach Form 4797				14		
15a	Total IRA distributions	15a		b Taxable amount (see page 17)	15b		
16a	Total pensions and annuities	16a		b Taxable amount (see page 17)	16b		

In this chapter we will only address sales of depreciable business property. These are the most common types of sales reported on *Form 4797*. All other types of dispositions reported on *Form 4797* are beyond the scope of this book, since they would require the expert assistance of a tax professional to properly report them on this form. So much for tax simplification!

Form 4797 seems confusing at first. But, once broken down into its parts, it is really a fairly friendly form. This assumes, of course, you have kept good permanent records documenting your cost and depreciation of assets. The following is an explanation of each section of *Form 4797* and which sales get reported in each section.

Part I: Sales or exchanges of property used in a trade or business

This section is used to report sales of depreciable property used in your business. The IRS instructions refer to Section 1231 property. This is quite simply the section of the tax code that indicates what type of property is reported here. It includes depreciable real or other property that you have held for more than one year.

Gains in Part I are capital gains, while losses are ordinary. This is important since capital gains are taxed at a maximum federal tax rate of 28 percent, while the top tax rate on ordinary income is 39.6 percent. Ordinary losses, on the other hand, are fully deductible while capital losses are limited to $3,000 per year, $1,500 if married filing separate.

When depreciable property is disposed of at a gain, you first compute the ordinary income portion of the gain. This is done using Part III of *Form 4797*. The balance of the gain, if any, is Section 1231 gain and is reported here in Part I.

Part II: Ordinary gains and losses

This section is used to report any sales not reported in Parts I and III. Generally, this is any business property held one year or less, since any gain or loss then would be ordinary, in any event.

Part III: Gain from disposition of property

This section is used to separate the ordinary income portion of gains on the sale of depreciable property from the capital gains portion. This is because some depreciation, which you claimed in prior years, must be "recaptured" as ordinary income, while other depreciation does not require recapture and the gain can be reported as capital gains. Not all real property depreciation, for instance, must be recaptured.

Part IV: Recapture amounts

This section is used if you previously claimed a Section 179 expense deduction, or depreciated listed property (typically an automobile) in a year when its use exceeded 50 percent, and the business use has fallen below 50 percent this year.

With that overview in mind, let's look at the lines.

Form 4797 Line 1. If you received *Form 1099-S*, reporting the proceeds of real estate sales, and the real estate was used in your business, report the total proceeds here. The gross sale price will be reported in either Line 2, 11 or 22 of *Form 4797*.

Form 4797 Line 2. Briefly describe the property in column (a), enter the date it was acquired in column (b), the date sold in column (c) and the gross sale price in column (d). Even if no *1099* was issued, sales of business property must still be reported on *Form 4797*.

In column (e), enter the depreciation claimed on the property since it was acquired. This information will come from your permanent depreciation schedules. Even if you forgot or otherwise chose not to claim depreciation, you must report the correct depreciation that should have been claimed in column (e). In essence, this is what the term "allowed or allowable" refers to. Ideally, they are the same.

Report in column (f) your cost plus any improvements made to the property that you did not previously expense. The amount in column (f) also includes the expenses of selling the property.

If column (f) minus column (e) exceeds column (d), you have a loss and the amount should be reported in column (g). If, on the other hand, column (d) exceeds column (f) minus column (e), you have a gain and the amount should be reported in column (h).

Form 4797 Line 3. Gains computed on *Form 4684, Casualties and Thefts* (of business property), are reported here.

Form 4797 Line 4. Gain on business property sold on installment is reported on *Form 6252*. The gain on Line 26 or Line 37 of *Form 6252* is reported here on Line 4.

Form 4797 Line 5. Report gains or loss from like-kind exchanges of business property (from *Form 8824*) here.

Form 4797 Line 6. Pick up the recaptured depreciation from Line 34 on page 2 of *Form 4797*.

Form 4797 Line 7. Add Lines 2-6 of columns (g) and (h).

Form 4797 Line 8. Combine columns (g) and (h) of Line 7. See the Line 8 instructions for "all others" for where to enter this gain or loss.

Form 4797 Line 9. If you had prior year ordinary losses from sales of business property, you may have to treat Part I gains as ordinary, and not capital. These are referred to in the Line 9 instructions as nonrecaptured net Section 1231 losses. You should refer to *IRS Publication 544* for a full explanation.

Form 4797 Line 10. Subtract Line 9 from Line 8. See the Line 10 instructions for "all others" for where to enter this gain or loss.

Part II of *Form 4797* is used to report sales of property that are not capital assets and that are not reported in Parts I and III. See Chapter 10 for the definition of a capital asset.

Form 4797 Line 11. Here, you report ordinary gains and losses on property sold during the year, if the property was held by you for one year or less.

Form 4797 Lines 12-14. Enter any gain or loss from the applicable line.

Form 4797 Line 15. This picks up the gain or loss from casualty/theft as reported on *Form 4684*, Lines 31 and 38a.

Form 4797 Line 16. This line indicates gain from installment sales as reported on *Form 6252*, Lines 25 or 36.

Form 4797 Line 17. Here, you put gain or loss from like-kind exchanges as reported on *Form 8824*.

Form 4797 Line 18. Indicate recaptured Section 179 expense deductions for property disposed by partnerships and S Corporations of which you are an owner. You will receive a *Schedule K-1* detailing these amounts.

Calculating the amounts to be reported on Lines 15-18 will likely require the assistance of a tax professional.

Form 4797 Line 19. Add Lines 11-18 of columns (g) and (h).

Form 4797 Line 20. Combine columns (g) and (h) of Line 19. In most cases this amount will be carried forward to *Form 1040*, Line 14. But in some instances, the path to *Form 1040* is not quite so direct. For instance, there are more reporting requirements if you are dealing with casualty and theft items. Refer to *Form 4797* detailed instructions for where to report these items.

Part III is the section of *Form 4797* where depreciation recapture is computed. If you have business property that you have depreciated over the years and you dispose of that property at a gain, you may have to report part or all of your gain as ordinary income, not capital gain income. See Appendix A, Section 4 of this book for depreciation information, and *IRS Publication 544* for depreciation recapture information.

Form 4797 Line 21. This line is used to describe the property sold, the date acquired and the date sold.

Most taxpayers will be reporting Section 1245 property (depreciable personal property such as equipment) or Section 1250 property (real property).

You should consult a tax professional if Section 1252, 1254 and 1255 assets are disposed of, since these are obscure and complex code sections.

Form 4797 Lines 22-26. Use these lines to calculate the gain on real and personal property disposed of during the year upon which there may be depreciation recapture.

Generally speaking, there will be depreciation recapture if you have a gain on depreciable personal property, or a gain on real property that was depreciated using an accelerated method of depreciation.

Form 4797 Line 27. Here, you calculate depreciation recapture on personal property.

Form 4797 Line 27a. This is the same as Line 24.

Form 4797 Line 27b. This is the smaller of Line 26 or 27a. In other words, the ordinary income portion of your gain is the smaller of the gain or the depreciation allowed or allowable on the asset. Any excess gain is capital gain.

Form 4797 Line 28. This is a bit more complex, since the depreciation recapture amount on Section 1250 (real) property is not all the depreciation allowed or allowable—only what is referred to as "additional depreciation" on this property.

If you used straight-line depreciation, then there is no Section 1250 depreciation recapture and you will enter zero on Line 28g.

If you used any method of depreciation other than straight-line, you may have a recapture requirement. This calculation, if required, is performed on Lines 28a through 28g.

Form 4797 Line 28a. List the post-1975 additional depreciation on each asset here. Additional depreciation is the excess of actual depreciation over depreciation figured using the straight-line method.

Form 4797 Line 28b. This will be 100 percent, unless the property is low-income housing, in which case you may want to seek the advice of a tax professional.

Form 4797 Line 28d. This is the additional depreciation claimed after 1969 and before 1976.

You will need to keep good depreciation records throughout the time you own each asset. Also, when figuring depreciation recapture on real property, you will have to refigure the depreciation as if you used the straight-line method. The difference between actual depreciation and straight-line is the recapturable amount.

Form 4797 Line 28e. Enter the smaller of Line 28c or 28d.

Form 4797 Line 28f. This applies to corporations only.

Form 4797 Lines 29-31. These lines refer to items that are beyond the scope of this book.

Form 4797 Line 32. Add columns (a) through (d) of Line 26.

Form 4797 Line 33. This is the total of all recaptured depreciation per the instructions for that line. This portion of the gain (the ordinary income portion) should also be entered on page 1 of *Form 4797*, on Line 14.

Form 4797 Line 34. Subtract Line 33 from Line 32. This represents the capital gains portion of your gain. This amount should also be entered on page 1 of *Form 4797*, on Line 6.

If any portion of Line 34 is from casualty or theft, that portion should be entered on *Form 4684, Casualties and Thefts,* Line 33. The portion not from casualty or theft should then be entered on Line 6 of *Form 4797.*

Watch out!

A sale of property used in a trade or business may cause recapture of tax benefits claimed when the property was purchased. An example of such a benefit is the Section 179 expense election discussed in Appendix A, Section 4, Depreciation and Basis.

* * *

You will note that throughout *Form 4797,* depreciation is referred to as "allowed or allowable." This means that you must report the greater of actual depreciation claimed or the amount you were allowed to claim under the depreciation rules.

In other words, even if you failed for whatever reason to claim depreciation, you must still reduce the cost of any asset sold by the depreciation you should have claimed when calculating your gain on sale.

For example, assume you purchased a machine used in your business 10 years ago for $5,000. Since you had little or no income during those years, you decided not to claim depreciation deductions since you felt you didn't need them. In year 10 you sell the machine for $2,000 and assume you have a $3,000 loss.

Not so! You cannot elect to forego depreciation simply because you don't need the deduction. Even if you took no deduction, your gain is calculated as if you did. Since the property would have been fully depreciated by year 10, your gain is $2,000, calculated as follows:

Sales price	$2,000
Cost	5,000
Depreciation allowable	(5,000)
Adjusted basis	0
Total gain	$2,000

You may be able to go back and amend one or more prior returns and pick up the depreciation deduction. If not, you just picked up $2,000 of ordinary income while giving up $5,000 of prior year deductions.

What if?

Q. Can I delay gain recognition on the sale of business property by using an installment sale?

A. You may have to report the gain in the year of sale regardless of the installment sale rules, because of the depreciation recapture rules. Therefore, be careful if you are counting on installment sale relief when selling business assets. Best to consult a tax professional when contemplating the sale of depreciable property.

Chapter Twelve

Line 15: IRA Distributions

What you'll need

- *Forms 1099-R, Reporting IRA Withdrawals*
- *Form 1040*
- 1040 Booklet

Optional

- *IRS Publication 590, Individual Retirement Arrangements*
- *Form 8606, Nondeductible IRAs* (Contributions, Distributions, and Basis)

What it's all about

If you withdrew money from an IRA account, you must report it on your tax return even if part or all of it is not even taxable.

In a regular savings or investment account, you have already paid income tax on the money you invest. Then you pay tax each year on earnings of the investment, whether or not you take any money out. In an IRA account you may not have paid tax on the money invested and you do not have to pay tax each year on the earnings.

In an effort to encourage people to save for their retirement, the government, in 1974, authorized Individual Retirement Arrangements, popularly known as IRAs. An IRA sidesteps the normal tax routine and, under certain circumstances, allows pretax dollars to be invested with any earnings also untaxed until they are withdrawn.

This is not tax avoidance, but it is an excellent and fully legal method of tax deferral. Ideally, a taxpayer is in a higher tax bracket while in the work force, and it is then that the IRA contribution (reducing taxable income) is the most advantageous. When you are retired, chances are your income is less and IRA distributions are, therefore, taxed at a lower rate. But even if there is no difference in your tax rate when you retire, you will still have the advantage of IRA earnings accumulating faster than normal savings because the earnings aren't taxed each year.

In order to prevent IRAs from being used for something other than savings for retirement, the IRS imposes stiff (10-percent) penalties for premature (before age 59½) distributions. See Chapter 26, Other Taxes. Generally speaking, you can begin to withdraw your IRAs without penalty after age 59½. So any amount you withdraw from that point on is includable in your gross income but is not subject to any additional penalty.

You cannot keep funds in an IRA indefinitely—they must eventually be withdrawn. You are required to begin withdrawal of IRAs by April 1 of the year *following* the year in which you turn 70½. You can withdraw the entire amount or just a portion, but there is a minimum amount that must be withdrawn each year thereafter. This process continues until you withdraw the entire amount or you die (the death and taxes thing!). The amount you are required to withdraw is based upon life expectancy tables. These tables are available in *IRS Publication 590, Individual Retirement Arrangements.*

If you don't withdraw your IRA funds according to this recognized timetable, you are subject to another penalty. This one is an additional tax on excess accumulations...*and* if you withdraw too much (total retirement distributions for the year of over $150,000), you are subject to penalty on excess distributions. Most taxpayers will probably never be subjected to a penalty on excess distributions, excess accumulations or premature distributions (withdrawals that are too much, too little, too soon). Believe it or not, there is a fourth penalty associated with IRAs, and that is excess contributions, which we will discuss in Chapter 20, Adjustments to Income and Chapter 26, Other Taxes. You are well advised to keep these myriad penalties in mind when planning contributions to or distributions from your IRA.

What to do with the forms

13	Capital gain or (loss). If required, attach Schedule D (see page 16)			13	
14	Other gains or (losses). Attach Form 4797			14	
15a	Total IRA distributions	15a	b Taxable amount (see page 17)	15b	
16a	Total pensions and annuities	16a	b Taxable amount (see page 17)	16b	
17	Rental real estate, royalties, partnerships, S corporations, trusts, etc. Attach Schedule E			17	

Form 1040 Line 15a, Total IRA distributions. Report *all* IRA withdrawals here. No matter how old you are or what the circumstances are, you must report any IRA withdrawals here.

Form 1040 Line 15b, Taxable amount. Report only the taxable portion of your withdrawals here. What constitutes a taxable portion? Only those funds that you haven't paid tax on yet, or that are not eligible for IRA tax deferral via rollover.

Ordinary Withdrawals

The tax treatment is very simple for an ordinary situation where the taxpayer:

- Makes fully deductible contributions to an IRA during his or her working years.
- Does not withdraw anything from it (other than rollovers into other IRA investments) until age 59½.
- Begins withdrawals before age 70½.
- Does not withdraw more than $150,000 per year.

The amount withdrawn each year is simply reported on Line 15a and 15b of *Form 1040* as fully taxable. No other reporting is required.

Rollovers

Valid rollovers are not taxable. If you have simply transferred your IRA from one account into another (within 60 days) you have "rolled over" the IRA with no tax consequence. But because you and the IRS will both receive a *1099R* showing the distribution from the original account, you need to report the amount rolled over on *Form 1040* Line 15a, and show zero on *Form 1040* Line 15b (taxable amount). Remember, funds must be rolled over directly to another IRA account to avoid mandatory 20% withholding.

Withdrawal of Nondeductible Contributions

It is possible to make IRA contributions that are not tax-deductible. (See Chapter 20, Adjustments to Income.) When you withdraw these funds, the tax treatment is different because you have already paid tax on them. To now pay tax on the entire withdrawal would be to pay tax twice, something you don't want to do! You should pay tax only on the IRA *earnings* you are withdrawing. If you have made any nondeductible contributions, use *Form 8606, Nondeductible IRA Contributions, IRA Basis, and Nontaxable IRA Distributions,* to track the taxable portion of both contributions and withdrawals. To put it simply, if you did not get a deduction for the IRA contribution, you do not pay tax on the withdrawal of these funds.

Watch out!

Even though IRAs were designed to be simple, there are many complicating situations that can arise out of IRA distributions. Even many of the more simple ones involve additional taxes or penalties. If you have any questions on your particular situation, *IRS Publication 590, Individual Retirement Arrangements,* is highly recommended reading.

* * *

Do not report IRA earnings under tax-exempt interest! This is a common mistake and does sound logical, but it is wrong. You do not need to report IRA earnings, just IRA distributions. Better yet, do not report IRA earnings as taxable interest, dividends, capital gains, etc. Many IRA custodians (banks, mutual funds) issue year-end reports that look strikingly similar to reports on your taxable investments. Read year-end statements carefully before reporting the income on your tax return.

What if?

Q. I have made both nondeductible and deductible IRA contributions over the years. I have kept the nondeductible funds in a separate account. Can I now draw them out without having to include them in taxable income?
A. No, you must make an allocation according to the following formula:

$$\frac{\text{Total of contributions you made to IRAs that were not tax-deductible}}{\text{Total IRA funds you have}} \times \text{Amount you are now drawing out} = \text{Amount of withdrawal that you can exclude from taxable income now}$$

This allows the IRS to recognize and tax your withdrawals in proportion to the overall nature of your contributions. The IRS looks at your basis in your IRA funds as a whole, not just as separate accounts, with separate tax consequences. You will need to complete *Form 8606, Nondeductible IRAs*, and file it with your return.

Chapter Thirteen

Line 16: Pensions and Annuities

What you'll need

- *Form 1099-R*
- *Form 1040*
- 1040 Booklet

Optional

- *IRS Publication 559, Tax Information for Survivors, Executors and Administrators*
- *IRS Publication 575, Pension and Annuity Income*
- *IRS Publication 721, Tax Guide to US Civil Service Retirement Benefits*
- *IRS Publication 939, Pension General Rule*

What it's all about

Have you received a pension distribution, other than from your IRA account?

At first glance, reporting pension and annuity income would seem as straightforward as reporting wages. You receive a *1099-R,* showing your income for the year, just as the *W-2* reflects your wage income. You plug the income in on Line 16 of your tax return and you're through.

There is a little more to it than that, however. Carefully read this chapter and fill in the worksheet as directed, and you may find that part or all of your pension distribution is tax-free.

If you did not contribute, after-tax, to your pension or annuity, then the distribution you received will be fully taxable. If, on the other hand, part or all of the amount that has been distributed during the year represents prior after-tax contributions made by you, then you will not be taxed on the part of the distribution that represents a return of your cost.

In this chapter, we will explain *cost, general rule, simplified general rule, three-year rule, death benefit exclusion, lump sum distributions, rollover* and other terms. A thorough understanding of these terms and the worksheet that is included may help you avoid or reduce tax on pension and annuity distributions.

Cost is the amount you paid into the plan or that your employer withheld from your pay and still included in your *W-2* as taxable compensation. This represents an after-tax investment that you made into the plan. Taxing these amounts when distributed to you would obviously be double taxation.

Cost is reduced by any previous nontaxable refunds that you may have received before your annuity starting date or the date you received your first payment, whichever is later. The *1099-R* that you received should show your cost in the plan.

Annuity starting date is the first day of the first period that you received a payment from the plan, or the date on which the obligation of the plan became fixed, whichever is later.

How do you figure the taxable and nontaxable portions of your pension or annuity? Depending on your circumstances, you must use either the general rule, the three-year rule or the simplified general rule. These are the rules as to who qualifies for which method. As time goes by, fewer and fewer people will qualify for the three-year rule. General rule and simplified general rule are methods most used today.

Use the general rule if:

- The annuity starting date is after July 1, 1986.
- The annuity starting date is before July 1, 1986 and you do not qualify for the three-year rule.
- You do not qualify for or choose not to use the simplified general rule.

Use the simplified general rule if:

- You are a retired employee or survivor of a deceased employee.
- The annuity starting date is after July 1, 1986.
- The payments are for your life or your life *and* the life of your beneficiary.
- The payments are from a qualified employee plan, a qualified employee annuity or a tax-sheltered annuity.
- At the same time payments began, you were under age 75 or the payments were guaranteed for fewer than five years.

Use the three-year rule if:

- The annuity starting date is before July 2, 1986.

It may not be possible for you to determine on your own whether a retirement plan is "qualified" under the Internal Revenue Code. Your employer or the plan administrator will be able to give you this information.

Unfortunately, because of the complexity of using the general rule and the fact that this rule requires the use of actuarial tables, there is no simple worksheet available. Instead, you should refer to *IRS Publication 939, Pension General Rule,* or, better yet, seek the advice of a competent tax professional to figure your nontaxable pension under this rule.

Because it is simpler and probably results in lower tax to you, you will probably want to figure your taxable portion using the simplified general rule.

The worksheet appearing on the next page will make figuring your taxable pension under the simplified general rule quite simple. This worksheet is for your records only and should not be attached to your tax return.

Death benefit exclusion applies to beneficiaries of deceased employees. If you receive a pension or annuity under these conditions, you may qualify for this exclusion, up to $5,000.

The exclusion amount is added to the cost of the pension or annuity (Line 2 of the worksheet). The payer of the annuity will not add this exclusion to the cost for you. Therefore, if you qualify for this exclusion, you must attach a signed statement to your tax return stating that you are entitled to the death benefit exclusion in using the simplified general rule. This statement must be attached to your return each year until the cost in the pension or annuity is fully recovered.

Lump sum distributions are paid within a single tax year *and* include the entire balance from all the employer's qualified plans. A qualifying lump sum distribution must be paid for one of the following reasons:

- Because of the plan participant's death.
- After the participant reaches age 59½.
- Because of the participant's separation from service as an employee.
- If the participant is self-employed and becomes totally and permanently disabled.

Your cost in the lump sum is recovered tax-free. Additionally, there may be special tax-saving opportunities available on a qualified lump sum distribution. If the *Form 1099-R* you receive indicates that the distribution qualifies as a lump sum distribution, you would be well-advised to seek professional advice. Also refer to *IRS Publication 575, Pension and Annuity Income.*

What to do with the forms

14	Other gains or (losses). Attach Form 4797				14	
15a	Total IRA distributions .	15a		b Taxable amount (see page 17)	15b	
16a	Total pensions and annuities	16a		b Taxable amount (see page 17)	16b	
17	Rental real estate, royalties, partnerships, S corporations, trusts, etc. Attach Schedule E				17	
18	Farm income or (loss). Attach Schedule F				18	

Form 1040 Lines 16a and 16b are used to report pension and annuity distributions received during the year. Distributions are typically in the form of cash, but can also be noncash, such as a distribution of securities. Distributions from profit-sharing plans, retirement plans and employee savings plans are examples of the types of distributions reported on Line 16.

You will receive an information report from the plan administrator or your employer showing the distribution amount, any tax withheld from the distribution and other information referred to throughout this chapter. Do not attach *Form 1099-R* to your tax return unless you had tax withheld from the distribution.

If you receive Social Security or Railroad Retirement benefits, see Chapter 18 and refer to the instructions for Line 20. Do not report those distributions on Line 16.

Figuring Your Taxable Pension Using the Simplified General Rule

1. Total pension received this year. Also add this amount to the total for *Form 1040*, Line 16a or *Form 1040A*, Line 11a. ________

2. Your cost in the plan (contract) at annuity starting date, and death benefit exclusion.* ________

3.

Age at starting date:	**Enter this amount**
55 and under	300
56-60	260
61-65	240
66-70	170
71 and over	120

____

4. Divide the amount on Line 2 by the number on Line 3. ________

5. Multiply the amount on Line 4 by the number of months for which this year's payments were made. ________
   Note: If your annuity starting date is *before 1987*, enter the amount from Line 5 on Line 8 below. Skip Lines 6, 7, 10 and 11.

6. Any amounts previously recovered tax-free in years after 1986. ________

7. Subtract the amount on Line 6 from the amount on Line 2. ________

8. Enter the lesser of the amount on Line 5 or the amount on Line 7. ________

9. Taxable pension for year. ________
   Subtract the amount on Line 8 from the amount on Line 1. Enter the result, but not less than zero. Also add this amount to the total for *Form 1040*, Line 16b. ________

10. Add the amounts on Lines 6 and 8. ________
    Note: If your *Form 1099-R* shows a larger taxable amount, use the amount on Line 9 instead of the amount from *Form 1099-R*.

11. Balance of cost to be recovered.
    Subtract the amount on Line 10 from the amount on Line 2. ________

____

***Statement for death benefit exclusion** (Beneficiaries qualifying for this exclusion must sign, date and attach this statement to their tax return each year until their cost in the pension or annuity plan is fully recovered.

Cost in plan (contract) ________
Death benefit exclusion ________
Total (enter on Line 2 above) ________

If you did not contribute to the cost of your pension or annuity and the distribution does not qualify as a lump sum distribution, skip Line 16a and enter the total distribution on Line 16b since it is fully taxable.

Your pension or annuity may be partially taxable. If your *1099-R* does not show the taxable part, use the general rule to figure the taxable portion. If your annuity starting date is after July 1, 1986, you'll want to use the simplified general rule.

Even if your *1099-R* reports a taxable amount, do not automatically report this amount on Line 16b, although you may do so. You may be able to report a lower taxable amount by taking the time to use the appropriate rule to figure this amount. Only then should you report the taxable amount on Line 16b.

If you roll over part or all of your distribution, enter the total distribution on Line 16a, then enter *only* the portion not rolled over on Line 16b. If you rolled over your entire taxable distribution, then enter zero on Line 16b. *Rollover* is the term used to indicate a tax-free transfer from one retirement program to another.

Remember, you cannot roll over contributions that were not tax deductible when made (i.e. after-tax contributions). These must be held out of any rollover tax-free. Rolling them over will result in an additional excise tax.

Watch out!

If you receive a distribution from a qualified retirement plan before reaching age 59½ and you fail to properly roll over this amount, you may be subject to additional tax. Use *Form 5329* to figure this tax.

* * *

Some states do not provide for preferential tax treatment on lump sum distributions. You may be required in such states to add back your distribution in figuring taxable income on your state return. This is because the distribution was not included in your federal adjusted gross income—only the tax on the distribution as figured on *Form 4972* was included on your federal tax return.

* * *

Tax planning for annuity and pension distributions is complex, as are the withholding rules on distributions. Equally complex are the rules on rollovers of distributions. You should seek competent professional tax advice before you receive any such distribution in order to take advantage of the tax planning opportunities that may be available to you.

* * *

Even though a tax-free rollover sounds too good to pass up, never decide upon this course of action until you have consulted with your tax professional, since, by making the rollover, you may forgo valuable rights under the lump sum distribution rules.

* * *

New withholding rules apply to rollovers not made directly plan-to-plan. Failure to follow specific rules for a rollover may result in your having tax withheld from your distribution. Consult with the plan administrator and your tax advisor when contemplating a rollover.

What if?

Q: I have a life and I really don't want to spend a beautiful spring afternoon figuring the taxable part of my pension or annuity. Is there a way around this?

A. For $50, the IRS will figure the taxable part for you. That is if you're comfortable having a fox guard your chicken coop. You must request this assistance before the due date of your tax return (including extensions). See *Publication 939, Pension General Rule,* for details. The $50 is deductible as a miscellaneous itemized deduction in the year paid. Besides, you'll probably hustle twice that amount on the golf course during the time you would have spent doing the calculation.

Chapter Fourteen

Line 17: Rental Real Estate, Royalties

What you'll need

- *Schedule E Part I, Supplemental Income and Loss*
- *Form 1040*
- 1040 Booklet

Optional

- *IRS Publication 535, Business Expenses*
- *IRS Publication 527, Residential Rental Property*
- *IRS Publication 946, How to Begin Depreciation*
- *IRS Publication 534, Depreciating Your Property*
- *Form 6198, At Risk Limitations*
- *Form 8582, Passive Activity Loss Limitations*

What it's all about

If you own real property and rent it to others, you report the income and expenses for this activity on *Schedule E, Supplemental Income and Loss*. Special rules apply if, in addition to renting space, you provide services to your renters. This is the case with most motel operators, for example. In that case, the income and expenses are not reported on *Schedule E* but on *Schedule C, Profit and Loss From Business*.

As a landlord, you run a business. You have income from rents and deductions from operating expenses and depreciation. So far, so good. But as you might guess, there are some special rules in the tax code addressing this particular type of activity.

Rental activity is passive in nature. This is by definition, so it doesn't matter how hard you work—it is still a passive activity. Thus, you are subject to passive activity rules, which may limit any loss you can claim. There is, however, limited relief from the passive activity rules granted to rental real estate activities. This relief allows for deductibility of up to $25,000 of passive loss from this activity against nonpassive income for those who actively participate in the rental activity. See Appendix A, Section 3, Passive Activities. Investments in limited partnerships do not qualify for this break, and to take full advantage of this potential deduction, your adjusted gross income must be under $100,000.

Part I of *Schedule E* is used to report all income and expenses from rentals of real estate. Also reported are certain royalties received. The tax form itself is fairly uncomplicated. However, the underlying tax code is complex and your answers to questions and certain other entries on the form could present pitfalls to the unwary. On the brighter side, a careful reading of the *Schedule E* instructions will reward the astute taxpayer with an opportunity to earn tax-free income. (Hint: Think vacation home.)

What to do with the forms

15a	Total IRA distributions .	15a	b Taxable amount (see page 17)	15b
16a	Total pensions and annuities	16a	b Taxable amount (see page 17)	16b
17	Rental real estate, royalties, partnerships, S corporations, trusts, etc. Attach Schedule E			17
18	Farm income or (loss). Attach Schedule F			18
19	Unemployment compensation (see page 18)			19

Form 1040 Line 17, Rents, royalties, partnerships, estates, trusts, etc. The amount to be reported here will be determined by completing *Schedule E*, page 1 (for rental real estate and royalties) and page 2 for partnerships, S Corporations, estates and trusts (see Chapter 15).

When answering questions on *Schedule E, Supplemental Income and Loss*, take time to understand the implications of your answers. The rules of taxation, unlike the rules of golf, are not there to help you enjoy your taxpaying experience. The tax laws exist to allow Uncle Sam to extract his full measure from each and every dollar of your income.

Before filling out *Schedule E*, page 1, remember that generally only income and expenses from rental real estate are reported. Rental income from personal property, if you are in the business of renting equipment, is reported on *Schedule C* and may be subject to self-employment tax. Also, if a farm rental is involved, report that activity on *Form 4835, Farm Rental Income and Expenses*, not *Schedule E*. And if you provide significant services to renters, this income and the related expenses should be reported on *Schedule C, Profit and Loss From Business*.

Schedule E Line 1. Describe and list the location of each rental reported on *Schedule E*. Property A's income and expenses should be listed in Column A, Line 3-18, and so on.

Schedule E Line 2. Before answering for more than this question, understand the impact of your answer. If the property is used the greater of 14 days, or 10 percent of the total days, for personal use, you may not be able to deduct all your expenses. Interest and taxes will be deductible, in any event.

Other expenses, however, will only be deductible to the extent there is rental income in excess of interest and taxes. See the *Schedule E* instructions for the definition of personal use and include as personal-use days *only* those that fit this definition.

Remember the hint regarding tax-free income earlier in this chapter? Well, here's the payoff! Buried within the *Schedule E* Line 2 instructions is the sentence "If you checked 'yes' and rented the unit out for fewer than 15 days, do not report the rental income and do not deduct any rental expenses." You are, however, able to deduct interest and taxes on *Schedule A*, if you itemize. Residents of the Los Angeles area used this clause to their great advantage by renting their residences out for less than 15 days during the Olympics for as much as $1,000 per day. Residents of the Atlanta area may want to take note and plan their vacations during the Atlanta games while generating tax-free income on the rental of their residences. Congress has considered eliminating this break and in 1993 passed legislation restricting its applicability.

Schedule E Line 3, Rents received. This includes cash and/or the fair market value of goods and services received from renters.

Schedule E Line 4, Royalties. This includes those received from oil, gas and mineral properties (not operating interests) as well as from copyrights and patents. Rental expenses that may be deducted include any and all expenses that are ordinary and necessary to your conduct of this rental activity. Since many rental operators do not maintain a separate checking account and/or credit card for their rental business, it is very important that you save all receipts for rental-related expenses. This is particularly true if you pay such expenses with cash. The rental owner would be well-advised to set up a basic filing system for receipts and an automobile log, since doing so will help avoid the loss of valuable deductions.

Expenses

Certain expenditures for rehabilitation of low-income housing or to provide disabled access may qualify for tax credits. You should refer to the instructions for tax *Forms 8586* and *8526* respectively, for more information about these credits.

Schedule E Line 5, Advertising. Include any newspaper or other ads connected to your rental activity. Typically, these are ads placed in newspaper classifieds for the purpose of securing a renter.

Schedule E Line 6, Auto and travel. These expenses include only those that are ordinary and necessary. Auto expenses can include actual out-of-pocket expenses or, more commonly, the simpler standard mileage rate. To use the standard mileage rate, keep a log of your miles driven for rental purposes and multiply the total miles driven during the year by the standard rate of 29 cents per mile. To this amount, you can add parking and tolls paid to arrive at the total deductible amount.

If actual expenses are claimed, you must keep track of such expenses and have receipts to document them. A log will also be necessary since you will need to know the percentage of your auto use for rental activity purposes. That percentage of all gas, oil, repairs, insurance, licenses, tires, etc., may be deducted in addition to depreciation of the business use portion of your owned vehicle or lease payments on your leased vehicle.

If your rental property is located out of town and overnight travel is required, you may be able to deduct travel to and from the rental property, provided, of course, such travel is ordinary and necessary. A monthly trip to fluff the pillows at your Maui condo is probably not ordinary and necessary.

Schedule E Line 7, Cleaning and maintenance. Such expenses are only those that you pay out-of-pocket and do not include the value of your labor.

Schedule E Line 8, Commissions. Fees paid to rental agencies or travel agencies, in the case of resort properties, would be listed here.

Schedule E Line 10, Legal and professional fees. These are paid to attorneys, for instance, for consultation connected to the rental activity. Legal expenses paid to acquire the property must be capitalized as part of your cost and depreciated. If possible, have your attorney, CPA or other professional issue a detailed billing reflecting the cost of his or her services for rental activities so that you can claim the deduction here—and not on *Schedule A* as a miscellaneous deduction, where it would probably be lost.

Schedule E Line 11, Management fees. Be careful here, since payment of management fees may indicate that the rental property owner does not actively participate in the rental real estate activity. Please refer to Appendix A, Section 3 for a complete discussion of passive activities.

Schedule E Lines 12 and 13, Mortgage interest and other interest. On Line 12, include only interest reported to you by a bank or other lender or *Form 1098*. On Line 13, include interest expense paid on rental property loans that is not reported on Line 12. Interest expense not reported to you on *Form 1098*, which you put on Line 12 of *Schedule E* , will almost certainly result in an IRS matching notice. Save yourself some unnecessary hassle and report the interest on the correct line. In order for any interest to be deductible, you must be able to demonstrate that the proceeds of the debt were used in connection with the rental property. Specific rules pertaining to tracing the use of debt proceeds are included in *Publication 535, Business Expenses*.

Schedule E Line 14, Repairs. You should consider only those expenses that do not increase the value and/or useful life of the property, and include such items as painting, minor plumbing or electrical repairs and the like. Major improvements or additions should be capitalized and depreciated.

Schedule E Line 17, Utilities. These do not include telephone expenses paid for the first line into your residence. All other utilities related to your rental are deducted here.

Schedule E Line 18, Other expenses. These include all expenses that do not fit a category preprinted on *Schedule E*. Be careful not to lump expenses into a large miscellaneous category, thereby creating a red flag that may attract IRS attention.

Schedule E Line 20, Depreciation. See Appendix A and *IRS Publication 534, Depreciation,* for a discussion of depreciation rules.

Schedule E Line 23, Deductible rental real estate loss. See Appendix A, Section 3. Also refer to the instructions for *Schedule E* and *Form 8582, Passive Activity Loss Limitations*, to determine if your rental loss, if applicable, is limited.

Schedule E Lines 24-26, Income (loss). These three lines combine income and any allowable losses to arrive at a net figure. If the figure is a loss, be sure to enclose it in parentheses. If you have no need to complete *Schedule E*, page 2 (See Chapter 15), enter the amount from Line 26 onto *Form 1040*, Line 17. Otherwise you will include it with the total on *Schedule E*, Line 40.

Watch out!

If you are not a real estate professional, your loss from rental real estate may be limited to $25,000 in a year. This allowable loss may be reduced if your income exceeds certain limits. If you do not materially participate in the rental activity, the loss may not be deductible at all. See Appendix A, Section 3 for a full discussion of passive activities.

What if?

Q. I made substantial improvements to my rental. Can I create a large deductible loss due to the extraordinary repair expenses?
A. These repairs may actually be property improvements, which must be depreciated over the remaining life of the property and not deducted as repair expense in the current year. You can deduct repairs that do not increase the value of the property, make it more useful or lengthen its life.

Q. I charge first and last month's rent to new tenants. Do I have to claim that as income now, or can I wait until the "last month," which could be years from now?
A. You have to claim it as income now, even if you're keeping your books on an accrual basis. Advance rents are always income at the time you receive them.

Chapter Fifteen

Line 17: Partnerships, S Corporations, Trusts, Estates

What you'll need

- *Schedule E, Supplemental Income and Loss*, page 2
- *Schedule K-1* (Partnership Form 1065)
- *Schedule K-1* (S Corp. Form 1120S)
- *Schedule K-1* (Estate Form 1041)
- *Schedule K-1* (Trust Form 1041)
- *Form 1040*
- 1040 Booklet

(Note: Do not attach the K-1s to your tax return)

Optional

- *Form 4835, Farm Rental Income and Expense*
- *IRS Publication 448, Federal Estate and Gift Taxes*
- *IRS Publication 541, Tax Information on Partnerships*
- *IRS Publication 589, Tax Information on S Corporations*
- *IRS Publication 925, Passive Activity and At Risk Rules*

What it's all about

In the last chapter, we discussed the reporting of rents and royalties on *Schedule E*, page 1. Now we turn our attention to *Schedule E*, page 2. This is where you will report income or losses from partnerships, S Corporations, estates and trusts.

These four particular types of entities are required by law to maintain a separate set of books. For that matter, every business of any kind is technically required to maintain separate books and records. For example, if you own a shoe repair shop and a deli and operate both as sole proprietorships (you are the sole owner), you cannot combine the two businesses in one set of books. The accounting records must be separately maintained and you must file two *Schedule Cs*.

Partnerships, S Corporations, estates and trusts are separate tax entities and, as such, are required to file specific tax returns apart from the returns of the partners, shareholders and/or beneficiaries. These returns have varying due dates and must include very specific information as required by the tax code.

These entities are sometimes referred to as pass-through entities. This means that they generally do not pay tax. Instead, they report income and expenses to the IRS, and inform the IRS as to how the income and expenses are to be split among the owners.

The specific schedule, which tells the IRS how much the owners should report, is called a *Schedule K-1*. You, as a partner, shareholder or beneficiary, will also receive a copy of this schedule, which you will use to complete page 2 of *Schedule E*.

The 1980s witnessed the introduction of unprecedented complexity into the tax code. Few areas were more affected than these pass-through entities and the recipients of K-1s. Prior to this wave of legislation, the K-1 typically included two or three amounts, which you would plug into the appropriate line on your *Schedule E*.

Now, however, you may have 10 or more amounts listed on your K-1, which must be reported on various schedules attached to your tax return. For instance, if you are a partner, your K-1 may report ordinary income/loss, rental real estate income/loss, interest income, dividend income, charitable contributions made, equipment expensed under Section 179, investment income, investment expenses, and on and on.

Each separately stated item of income and expense on your K-1 is the result of tax legislation, mainly from the 1980s. Certainly you remember the '80s? That was when Congress "simplified" our taxes.

Fortunately, *Schedule K-1* does a fairly adequate job of telling you where to report these various amounts on your tax return. For the most part, you should have no problem.

Some amounts, however, deal with what are called the "passive activity loss rules." And unless you are a tax attorney or a CPA, you are probably going to struggle with these rules.

This chapter will focus on K-1 information from nonpassive activities. We will briefly explain the difference between passive and nonpassive activities. For information on how to report passive activity information, you should refer to Appendix A, Section 3, Passive Activities.

What to do with the forms

15a	Total IRA distributions .	15a		b Taxable amount (see page 17)	15b
16a	Total pensions and annuities	16a		b Taxable amount (see page 17)	16b
17	Rental real estate, royalties, partnerships, S corporations, trusts, etc. Attach Schedule E				17
18	Farm income or (loss). Attach Schedule F				18
19	Unemployment compensation (see page 18)				19

Form 1040 Line 17, Rents, royalties, partnerships, estates, trusts, etc. The amount to be reported here will be determined by completing *Schedule E*, page 2.

Before looking at the form itself, let's talk about passive and nonpassive activities. A passive activity is one in which you *do not* materially participate. A good example is a limited partnership in which you, as a limited partner, have no say in the management of the business. Also, your potential loss is limited to your investment in the business.

If you invest in a passive activity that generates a loss, you may not be able to deduct your share of the loss reported to you on *Schedule K-1*. First, your loss may be limited by the at-risk rules. Secondly, your deductible loss may be limited by the passive activity rules. At risk means your loss is limited to the amount you could potentially lose on the investment and the passive loss rules mean you can only deduct passive losses to the extent you have passive income.

Form 8582 is used to calculate the passive activity loss limitations. The instructions to *Form 8582* fully explain these rules as well as what constitutes material participation.

Schedule E Part II, Income or Loss From Partnerships and S Corporations

Schedule E Line 27 A-E. Here, you list the name of each entity from which you receive a K-1. In column (b) enter a "P" if a partnership or an "S" if an S Corporation. Check column (c) if the entity is a foreign partnership. Enter the employer identification number in column (d). This number is reported on the K-1 you received. Check column (e) if all your investment is at risk or column (f) if only some is at risk.

If your K-1 reports a loss, you must complete *Form 6198, At Risk Limitations*, to compute the amount of the loss that you can deduct on this year's return.

The at-risk rules limit the loss you can claim to the amount you can actually lose in the activity. For instance, assume you are a partner in a real estate partnership. You and a partner each invest $10,000 and secure a $100,000 nonrecourse loan in order to acquire a rental property for $120,000. Generally, a nonrecourse loan is one where you are not personally liable for repayment. In this case, you may only deduct up to $10,000 in losses from this partnership since that is the limit of your economic loss on this deal. If you invest additional sums or the partnership borrows additional sums that you are liable for, then your at-risk amount may increase.

Columns (g) and (h) pertain to passive investments.

The nonpassive loss reported on your K-1 should be entered in column (i).

If there was a Section 179 deduction on your *Schedule K-1*, this amount should have been entered on *Form 4562, Depreciation*, and then carried to column (j) on Line 27 of *Schedule E*.

Section 179 deductions are limited by law to $17,500. This is an annual limitation, regardless of how many business activities you conduct.

Nonpassive income from *Schedule K-1* should be reported in column (k).

Schedule E Line 28a and b. These are simply totals of the respective columns.

Schedule E Line 29. This shows the total of columns (h) and (k) of Line 28a.

Schedule E Line 30. This is the total of columns (g), (i) and (j) of Line 28b.

Schedule E Line 31. Put in the total of Lines 29 and 30. Line 30 is actually a loss line and should be subtracted from Line 29. Combine the Line 31 amount with the amounts on Lines 26, 36, 38 and 39 and enter on Line 40.

Schedule E Part III, Income or Loss From Estates and Trusts

Schedule E Line 32. Enter the name of the estate or trust in column (a) and the employer identification number in column (b).

Enter the nonpassive loss in column (e) and other income from *Schedule K-1* in column (f).

The K-1 you receive from the estate or trust will include directions as to where to report the various amounts on your tax return.

Schedule E Line 33a and b. These are totals of the respective columns.

Schedule E Line 34. Put the total of columns (d) and (f) of Line 33a.

Schedule E Line 35. Put the total of columns (c) and (e) of Line 33b.

Schedule E Line 36. This is the total of Lines 34 and 35. Line 35 is actually a loss line and should be subtracted from Line 34. Include this total in the Line 40 total as well.

Schedule E Part IV refers to Real Estate Mortgage Investment Conduits (REMICS). Since most taxpayers are not holders of REMICS, this part is not within the scope of this book. Holders of REMICS will receive a *Schedule Q (Form 1066)* with the applicable instructions.

Schedule E Part V, Summary

Schedule E Line 39. Enter any net farm rental income here as computed on *Form 4835* (not *Schedule F*).

Schedule E Line 40. This is the total of Lines 26, 31, 36, 38 and 39. This amount should be entered on *Form 1040*, Line 17.

Schedule E Line 41. This is a reconciliation figure for farmers and fishermen. Report here the total amounts you have reported on this return as gross income from farming or fishing. If the figure is less than what was reported to IRS on *Forms 1099*, expect a notice asking about the difference.

Schedule E Line 42. This is a reconciliation figure for Real Estate Professionals only. Report here all amounts on this return from rental real estate activities.

Watch out!

Before you can deduct losses from a partnership or S Corporation, you must have a sufficient at-risk amount to do so. If you have a loss on the K-1 from the partnership or S Corporation, refer to *IRS Publication 925, Passive Activity and At Risk Rules,* to determine your at-risk amount, or consult with a tax professional.

Income reported to you on *Schedule K-1* may subject you to underpayment penalties if you fail to make adequate estimated tax payments throughout the year. Refer to *IRS Publication 505, Tax Withholding and Estimated Tax,* for the estimated tax rules. Income from certain partnerships may be subject not only to regular tax but also self-employment tax. Income reported on Line 15a of your partnership K-1 as Net Earnings from Self-Employment means you probably have to pay self-employment tax as calculated on *Schedule SE.*

If you are a partner of an out-of-state partnership, you may be subject to the tax return filing requirements of that state. This is particularly so if the partnership generates income on property located in the other state. You should contact the revenue department of each state where the partnership conducts business to ascertain whether you are required to file a return.

Loans you make to an S Corporation that are used as a basis to give you an at-risk amount for loss deduction purposes may give rise to taxable income when the loan is repaid to you. Be careful when repaying S Corporation loans to shareholders, particularly if the corporation has passed through losses to shareholders. You may want to consult a tax professional before doing so.

Partnerships, S Corporations, estates and trusts may also report tax preference items that could subject you to the alternative minimum tax on *Form 6251.*

What if?

Q. What if I don't receive a *Schedule K-1* by the due date of my tax return?
A. File for an automatic extension of time to file by April 15. If you have not received a K-1 by August 15, request an additional extension by indicating that the reason is because you haven't received the necessary K-1. If you owe tax you should pay the amount owed, even if an estimate, with your first extension request.

Q. What if a partnership reports income and indicates that it is from self-employment?
A. Complete *Schedule SE, Self-Employment Tax,* and attach it to your income tax return. You may be subject to self-employment tax on this income. If you receive a K-1 from a partnership that reports a loss from self-employment you can use this loss to reduce your other income from self-employment. This will reduce your self-employment tax.

Chapter Sixteen

Line 18: Farm Income or (Loss)

What you'll need

- Books and records documenting income and expenses
- *Schedule F, Profit or Loss from Farming*
- *Form 1099-PATR, 1099-A, 1099-MISC, 1099-G or CCC-182*
- *Form 1040*
- 1040 Booklet

Optional

- *Form 4835, Farm Rental Income and Expense*
- *Form 4797, Sale of Business Property*
- *Form 8645, Soil & Water Conservation Plan Certification*
- *Form 6198, At Risk Limitations*
- *IRS Publication 225, Farmer's Tax Guide*
- *IRS Publication 538, Accounting Periods and Methods*
- *IRS Publication 917, Business Use of a Car*
- *IRS Publication 534, Depreciation*
- *Schedule SE, Self-Employment Tax*

What it's all about

Are you in the business of farming? We don't just mean gentlemen farmers who go about it for recreation or pleasure. If you make a living as a farmer or rancher and you operate as an individual, not as a corporation or partnership, you report your income and expenses on *Schedule F, Profit or Loss from Farming*.

Baseball, hot dogs and apple pie are among the most enduring icons of life in America. There is also something uniquely American about the beauty and bounty of America's countryside. Who among us has not dreamed of escaping the hassles of urban life to spend our evenings rocking on the porch overlooking peaceful countryside? Getting up at the crack of dawn and doing the chores will bring you back to earth. So, too, will preparing your tax return!

Operating a farm is not just hard work, it is a business. It is a special type of business and its uniqueness is reflected not only in the chiseled facial features of the farmer, but also in the tax code. Special considerations are allowed *Schedule F* filers that are to be found nowhere else in the tax regulations.

Even though you're self-employed, you don't have to make the same quarterly estimates that *Schedule C* filers do. In fact, you are required to make only one quarterly estimate (by January 15). You don't even have to make that one if you file your return by March 1 and pay any tax liability in full.

You can file using the cash method of accounting (count income when received and expenses when paid) even if you have substantial physical inventories (a barn full of hay or a field ready for harvest for example). Normally, such an inventory would require you to file on the accrual basis (count income when earned and expenses when incurred).

You can deduct prepaid expenses in the current year. This is really unheard of! It's true, though. You can deduct as a current expense any prepaid farm supplies, but they cannot exceed 50 percent of the other deductible expenses. Anything more than that must be expensed in the year of actual use. For instance, say Ed has a good year and ends up with money burning a hole in his pocket. He had gross income of $60,000 with expenses of only $20,000. The local feed store is offering a year-end special. Although Ed won't use anything he buys now until next summer, he can go on a shopping spree and spend up to $10,000 (half his other expenses for the year) on items that otherwise would be purchased and expensed next year.

Now comes the tricky part. Income (or loss) from sale of livestock purchased for resale is ordinary income and reported on *Schedule F*. Income from sale of livestock held for other purposes (milk cows, race horses, breeding stock to name a few examples) is a capital gain (or loss). This is because it is considered a sale of an asset used in your business. Such a transaction is reported not on *Schedule F*, but on *Form 4797, Sale of Business Property*. In order to qualify for this special capital gains treatment, you must hold the livestock for a year or more (two years for horses and cattle).

If you're following the logic of all this, you may have figured out that, just like any other business asset, your livestock gets depreciated! But this process doesn't begin until they reach maturity. So, in the case of a dairy cow, you can't begin depreciating her until she begins giving milk. This conforms to the tax code requirement that depreciation of a business asset begins when it is placed into useful service.

Just keep in mind that a farm is a business operation and it must conform to guidelines that apply to any other business. Just because we're dealing with chickens and tractors instead of computers and cars doesn't really change things. All expenses must still be ordinary and necessary to the business in order to qualify for deductions. The *IRS Publication 225, Farmer's Tax Guide*, is almost required reading.

What to do with the forms

16a	Total pensions and annuities 16a	b Taxable amount (see page 17)	16b
17	Rental real estate, royalties, partnerships, S corporations, trusts, etc. Attach Schedule E		17
18	Farm income or (loss). Attach Schedule F		18
19	Unemployment compensation (see page 18)		19
20a	Social security benefits 20a	b Taxable amount (see page 18)	20b

Form 1040 Line 18, Farm income or (loss). The amount to be reported here will be determined by completing *Schedule F*. *Schedule F* is a two-page form, but if you file on a cash basis you need only complete page 1.

Schedule F Line a. Describe in one or two words your principle crop or activity.

Schedule F Line b. See page 2 and select the three-digit code that most closely relates to your agricultural activity.

Schedule F Line c. Check the cash method if you report income when received and expenses when paid, and complete Parts I and II. Check the accrual method if you report income when earned and expenses when incurred and complete Parts II and III, and Line 11 of Part I.

Schedule F Line d. Enter your employer identification number, if you have one. Do not enter your Social Security number.

Schedule F Line e. Indicate whether you materially participated in this activity. See the material participation rules outlined in the instructions for *Schedule C*. Be careful, since lack of material participation may result in limitation of your ability to deduct your *Schedule F* loss.

Schedule F Part I, Farm Income, Cash Method

Schedule F Line 1. Enter the amount you received during the year from livestock sales as well as the sale of other items you bought for resale.

Remember that Part I is for cash method taxpayers so you should only report amounts actually received during the year.

Schedule F Line 2. Enter the cost of the livestock or other items sold during the year. Generally, cost is what you paid for the items.

Schedule F Line 4. This is for the sale of livestock or products that you "raised."

Schedule F Line 5a. Enter the total distributions you received from co-ops. You should have received a *1099-PATR*. But even if you did not, you must still report the total distribution here.

Schedule F Line 5b. Taxable patronage dividends do not include those from buying personal, capital or depreciable assets. Since you are not reporting these amounts as income, you should reduce your basis in the assets by the dividend amount.

Schedule F Line 6a. If you received government payments (even if you did not receive a *Form 1099-G* or a *CCC-182* from the Department of Agriculture), report the total amount received.

Examples of amounts reported on Lines 6a and 6b are price support payments, payments in kind (goods or services) and the value of commodity credit certificates.

Schedule F Line 6b. This reflects the taxable portion of the payments on Line 6a. Refer to *IRS Publication 225, Farmer's Tax Guide*, for examples of excludable payments.

Schedule F Lines 7a-7c. These lines pertain to the taxability of Commodity Credit Corporation loans. There are various elections that may be made with respect to these loans and/or the repayment of same. These elections affect how you report these loans for income purposes. You should refer to *IRS Publication 225, Farmer's Tax Guide*, for details.

Schedule F Lines 8a-8c. Enter the total crop insurance proceeds you received during the year on Line 8a. You may elect to treat these proceeds as income next year by checking the box at Line 8c. *IRS Publication 225* includes information on which proceeds may be deferred as well as details on a statement you must attach to your return when making this election. If you did not elect to defer to next year, enter the taxable crop insurance proceeds on Line 8b.

Schedule F Line 8d. Enter crop insurance proceeds you received last year, but elected to defer until this year.

Schedule F Line 9. Enter income received for doing machine work for other farmers.

Schedule F Line 10. Indicate income received during the year not reported elsewhere, such as bartering income, fuel tax refunds, gain or loss on commodity futures that provided a hedge against price changes.

Schedule F Part II, Farm Expenses: Cash and Accrual Method

Schedule F Line 12. Enter either actual costs of operating a car or truck or use the standard mileage rate. You must use actual expenses if you lease a vehicle or use more than one vehicle in your business. If you use the standard mileage rate for business miles traveled, to that amount you may add parking and tolls.

Be sure to complete Part V of *Form 4562, Depreciation and Amortization*, and attach this form to your return if you claim a deduction for auto expenses.

Schedule F Line 14. Conservation expenses (those to conserve soil or water or to prevent erosion) must be consistent with a plan approved by the Soil Conservation Service in order to be deductible. To claim this deduction, complete *Form 8645* and attach it to your tax return. Generally, your deduction cannot exceed 25 percent of your gross income from farming. If you received a tax-free government cost-sharing conservation subsidy, do not deduct as an expense anything you spend that money on. You can't have your cake and eat it, too!

Schedule F Line 16. See Appendix A or *IRS Publication 534* for a discussion of depreciation rules.

Schedule F Line 17. Enter payments made for employee accident and health plans, group life insurance plans and dependent-care assistance programs. Do not enter contributions to pension and profit-sharing plans, as these are entered on Line 25. Also, do not include payments made on your own behalf to accident and health plans, as these are deductible on Line 26 of *Form 1040* under the adjustments to income section of your tax return.

Schedule F Line 18. Enter feed expenses paid for in the current year, including allowable prepaids.

Schedule F Line 20. Freight does not include that which was paid for the transport of purchased livestock, which must be added to the cost of the livestock and deducted when the livestock is sold.

Schedule F Line 23a. Enter the interest paid on farm related loans from banks and other financial institutions here. This amount should agree with the *Form 1098* you received from the bank.

Schedule F Line 23b. Enter other interest paid that was connected to the farm activity but was not paid to a bank or other financial institution.

Schedule F Line 31. Taxes include real and personal property taxes on farm property, the employer portion of payroll taxes paid for employees, and highway tax. Do not enter on this line federal income, estate or gift taxes, taxes on personal assets, such as your residence, or sales tax on asset acquisitions, which must be added to the cost of the asset and depreciated.

Schedule F Line 32. Utilities include all farm, not personal, expenses. This includes telephone long distance for farm business and the cost of a second telephone line if it is for farm business.

Schedule F Lines 34a-34f. Enter expenses not deducted elsewhere, such as bad debts, legal and accounting fees, travel, entertainment and the business use of your residence. Also enter any loss from this activity that was not deducted last year due to the at-risk rules.

You may be required to include in inventory certain costs to produce property or to acquire property for resale. Instead of deducting these costs now, they are included in the inventory asset and deducted when the inventory is sold.

These "capitalized" costs are referred to as preproductive period expenses. You still may be able to deduct these expenses now, however, if the property produced has a preproductive period of more than two years. An election must be made on your tax return to currently deduct these expenses. This election also affects how the income is treated upon sale of the property. For more information on the election to deduct certain preproductive period expenses, see *IRS Publication 225, Farmer's Tax Guide.*

If you do not or cannot make this election, the preproductive period expenses you must add to the cost of the asset should be shown on Line 34f as a negative amount.

Schedule F Line 36. If a profit, enter this amount on Line 18 of *Form 1040.*

If a loss, go to Line 37a-b and check the appropriate box. If your investment is not all at-risk, your loss may be limited. If this is the case, you should complete *Form 6198, At Risk Limitations,* to figure your allowable loss.

The allowable loss should be entered here and on *Form 1040* Line 18. Any unallowed loss will carry forward to next year.

Schedule F Part III, Accrual Method

Schedule F Lines 38-51. These income items are essentially the same as those listed in Part I. The difference is that Part III is for accrual method taxpayers.

Watch out!

Farm income may be subject to self-employment tax and require that you file *Schedule SE, Self-Employment Tax.* See *Publication 225* and the instructions to *Form 4835, Farm Rental Income and Expenses*, since not all farm income may be subject to this tax.

* * *

If you pay wages and/or nonemployee compensation, you may be required to file various information returns. Failure to file these returns could subject you to significant penalties. Refer to the instructions for *Forms 1099, 1098, 5498* and *W-2G.*

* * *

You may have to make estimated tax payments based on your income from farming in order to avoid an underpayment penalty. See Appendix A Section 2, Estimated Taxes.

* * *

If you own farmland that you merely rent out to others, that activity does not get reported on *Schedule F.* This is actually rental income and is first reported on *Form 4835, Farm Rental Income & Expenses*, and from there carried forward to *Schedule E.*

What if?

Q. I'm a brain surgeon and I just built a house on 10 acres. Can't I plant some Christmas trees and deduct all the expenses of maintaining my property, and not just my mortgage interest and taxes?

A. Probably not. Unless an activity is "entered into for profit," deductions attributable to the activity are allowed only to the extent there is income. There is a presumption that the activity is "for profit" if it shows a profit for any three or more out of five consecutive years ending in the tax year. Otherwise, a taxpayer must be able to prove that profit was a primary motive for engaging in the activity.

Chapter Seventeen

Line 19: Unemployment Compensation

What you'll need

- *Forms 1099-G* from State Unemployment Agency
- *Form 1040*
- 1040 Booklet

Optional

- *IRS Publication 525, Taxable & Nontaxable Income*

What it's all about

Did you lose your job and collect unemployment benefits during the year? Believe it or not, you may owe additional tax as a result.

Unemployment compensation is designed to provide financial assistance to laid-off workers. Unemployment benefits are available in limited dollar amounts (based upon your earnings while employed) and for a limited time (hopefully, long enough to find another job). It is a government program administered by each state and financed by federal and state employment taxes. These taxes are paid 100 percent by the employer. There is no withholding from employee pay.

The most normal instance of what to report here is simply the unemployment benefits that you received from your state unemployment agency. It is possible, especially if you belong to a union, that you are receiving additional benefits that are *not* reportable on this line.

- Strike benefits are generally considered wages, not unemployment benefits. Report on Line 7.
- Benefits paid out of a union fund financed by regular dues are considered by the IRS to be neither wages nor unemployment benefits, but rather are reported as "other income." Report on Line 21.
- Benefits from a company-financed fund to which you did not contribute are wages, not unemployment benefits. Report on Line 7.

- Benefits from a private fund to which you *did* voluntarily contribute are taxable only to the extent that they exceed your contributions. This is a simple example of basis. You don't pay tax on your cost basis in anything because it is considered merely a return of what you paid and not an item of taxable income. The taxable portion is still not considered unemployment benefits, but is designated as "other income." Report on *Form 1040* Line 21.

This issue of taxing unemployment benefits is fairly new and controversial. They were not taxed at all until 1979, then partially taxed for several years, and fully taxed as of 1987. By including government benefits such as Social Security and unemployment compensation in taxable income, Congress has found a means of increasing revenues without raising tax rates.

Since there is no provision for income tax withholding upon payment of the benefits, the tax bite is especially tough come April 15. The great majority of people collecting unemployment are having trouble making ends meet, and the thought of making quarterly estimated tax payments on their benefits doesn't even occur to them.

What to do with the forms

17	Rental real estate, royalties, partnerships, S corporations, trusts, etc. Attach Schedule E	17	
18	Farm income or (loss). Attach Schedule F	18	
19	Unemployment compensation (see page 18)	19	
20a	Social security benefits 20a b Taxable amount (see page 18)	20b	
21	Other income. List type and amount—see page 18	21	

Form 1040 Line 19, Unemployment compensation. Report all state unemployment benefits here. You should receive a *1099-G* showing the total amount of state unemployment benefits paid to you.

If you paid back an overpayment of benefits, just subtract that from the total you received and show only the net amount on Line 19. The IRS will compare the amount you show on Line 19 to the copy of the *1099* it received from your state, and, if you subtracted a repayment amount, there will be a mismatch. To avoid problems, just write "repayment" and the dollar amount on the dotted line portion of Line 19. This lets the IRS know just what is going on and should avoid an annoying matching notice being sent to you.

Watch out!

It is possible to have benefits from many sources, some of which may overlap and require a special tax treatment. If you have anything other than government-issued benefits as reported on a *1099-G,* it would be advisable to consult the issuing agencies for a precise definition of just what it is you received.

What if?

Q. I have been notified that I have to repay some benefits I received last year. I have already filed my return for last year. Do I need to file an amendment?
A. No. Remember that you are on a cash basis as far as Uncle Sam is concerned. Because you actually received the money last year, that return is correct. This year, however, you have in effect a negative amount of benefits received. When preparing your return for the current year, just write "repayment for prior year" on the dotted line portion of *Form 1040* Line 19, and put the actual dollar amount in brackets to show that it is a negative amount. This will then reduce your current year income. See *Publication 525, Taxable and Nontaxable Income*, for details.

Chapter Eighteen

Line 20: Social Security Benefits

What you'll need

- *Forms SSA-1099, Social Security, and/or RRB-1099, Railroad Retirement*
- *Form 1040*
- 1040 Booklet

Optional

- *IRS Publication 915, Social Security Benefits and Equivalent Railroad Retirement Benefits*

What it's all about

Did you receive Social Security or Railroad Retirement benefits during the year? A portion of these benefits may be taxable.

The Social Security system was founded in 1936 during the Great Depression. It was set up by the Roosevelt administration as a self-financing, old-age insurance program. The program was intended to be "off budget" (not part of the U.S. general fund) and financed by payments from workers and employers into a Social Security Trust Fund. The surplus in this trust fund is required to be invested in U.S. Treasury notes. Thus, in a roundabout way the Social Security retirement fund has, over time, been mixed in with the general fund.

During the Johnson administration, the fund was actually put into a "unified budget" to help camouflage the growing national deficit. With the expansion of Social Security into more health and welfare programs and the commingling of funds with other government spending, the Social Security system found itself buried within the Department of Health and Human Services. But in 1994, Congress declared the Social Security Administration an independent agency. This move should provide more stable management and operation and remove it from the forefront of the political arena.

In 1984, Congress voted to tax some Social Security benefits and in 1993, they voted to raise the maximum amount of benefits taxed from 50 percent to 85 percent. This increase takes effect this year (1994).

How much is taxable?

This is no longer as easy a question to answer as it once was. If Social Security is your only source of income, your benefits are not taxed and you probably don't even have to file a return. If you had any income in addition to Social Security, then continue reading and fill in the worksheet.

How much of your Social Security benefit is taxable depends on your total income and your filing status. The easiest way to figure the taxable portion is to use the IRS worksheet in the 1040 instruction booklet or a similar worksheet, which is included on the next page.

Before filling in the worksheet, remember that Social Security benefits and Tier 1 Railroad Retirement benefits are treated in the same way. Retired railroad employees have a separate but similar retirement plan. Social Security benefits are referred to in the explanation contained here, but this explanation applies equally to Railroad Retirement benefits.

In general, Social Security benefits are not subject to tax unless your income, when computed in a special way, exceeds $32,000 for a married couple or $25,000 for a single individual. If your income falls between $32,000 and $44,000 for a married couple or between $25,000 and $34,000 for a single individual, then 50 percent of your social security benefits are taxable. If your income exceeds $44,000 for a married couple or $34,000 for a single individual, then as much as 85 percent of your benefits may be taxable. This recomputed income (called modified adjusted gross income) is calculated by taking the adjusted gross income from your tax return, adding tax exempt interest plus one half of your Social Security benefits received for the year. The worksheet provided here is similar to the IRS worksheet. Use either one to perform this required calculation and determine how much of your benefit is taxable.

What to do with the forms

18	Farm income or (loss). Attach Schedule F	18	
19	Unemployment compensation (see page 18)	19	
20a	Social security benefits 20a b Taxable amount (see page 18)	20b	
21	Other income. List type and amount—see page 18	21	
22	Add the amounts in the far right column for lines 7 through 21. This is your total income ▶	22	

Form 1040 Line 21a, Social Security benefits. Enter the total of your Social Security benefits here.

Form 1040 Line 21b, Taxable amount.

Now let's look at the worksheet. There is no required form that must be submitted with your return, but a little work is required to arrive at the amount to report on Line 21b of *Form 1040*. In order to facilitate the calculations, you should complete the entire front page of *Form 1040 except* for the Social Security amount on Line 21b. This identifies all the items of income and adjustments that you'll be asked for on the worksheet.

Social Security Worksheet

1. Enter total amount from Box 5 of all your *Forms SSA-1099* and *RRB-1099*. 1.______
2. Divide Line 1 above in half. 2.______
3. Add the amounts on *Form 1040*, Lines 7, 8a, 9 through 15, 16b, 17b, 18 through 20 and 22. *Do not include any Social Security benefit.* 3.______
4. Total tax-exempt interest and excluded foreign income. 4.______
5. Add Lines 2, 3 and 4. 5.______
6. Amount from *Form 1040*, Line 30. 6.______
7. Subtract Line 6 from Line 5. 7.______
8. Enter the amount shown below for your filing status:
   - Single, head of household or qualifying widow $25,000
   - Married filing jointly $32,000
   - Married filing separately $-0- 8.______
9. Subtract Line 8 from Line 7.
   If zero or less,
   Stop! None of your benefits are taxable.
   If more than zero, continue on. 9.______
10. Divide Line 9 above in half. 10.______
11. Enter the amount shown below for your filing status:
    - Single, head of household or qualifying widow $34,000
    - Married filing jointly $44,000
    - Married filing separately $-0- 11.______
12. Subtract Line 11 from Line 7.
    If zero or less, enter zero and go to Line 18.
    Otherwise, continue on to Line 13. 12.______
13. Enter the amount shown below for your filing status:
    - Single, head of household or qualifying widow $4,500
    - Married filing jointly $6,000
    - Married filing separately $-0- 13.______
14. Enter the smallest of Lines 2, 10 or 13. 14.______
15. Multiply Line 12 by 85%. 15.______
16. Add Lines 14 and 15. 16.______
17. Multiply Line 1 by 85%. 17.______
18. TAXABLE BENEFITS
    - If Line 12 is zero,
      enter the smaller of Line 2 or Line 10.
    - If Line 12 is more than zero,
      enter the smaller of Line 16 or Line 17. 18.______

You have now done the complicated job of determining how much of your Social Security benefit is:

- Exempt from federal income tax.
- Subject to the computation that 50 percent of your benefit is taxable.
- Subject to the computation that 85 percent of your benefit is taxable.

Watch out!

If you receive a lump sum amount that is actually a payment of benefits for prior years, you have a choice as to how to treat it on your return.

* * *

If you itemize deductions this year and have repaid more benefits (received in a prior year) than you received for this year, you may be able to take a deduction for any benefits claimed as taxable in the prior year.

* * *

Consult *IRS Publication 915, Social Security Benefits and Equivalent Railroad Retirement Benefits*, for explanations of these and other situations.

What if?

Q. How can I get answers to some questions I have about my Social Security benefits?
A. Call the Social Security Administration on its toll-free number. The number is 1-800-772-1213 and the lines are open Monday through Friday, 7 AM to 7 PM (ET).

Q. My spouse and I are both over 65. Our income consists of interest and dividends of $2,000, a capital gain of $34,000 and earned interest on tax-exempt bonds of $3,000. We also received $16,400 from Social Security. How much of this is taxable, if any?
A. Your taxable Social Security would be $8,720 in this case. A sample worksheet on the next page will show how we arrived at this figure.

Social Security Worksheet

1.	Enter total amount from Box 5 of all your *Forms SSA-1099* and *RRB-1099*.	$16,400
2.	Divide Line 1 above in half.	$8,200
3.	Add the amounts on *Form 1040*, Lines 7, 8a, 9 through 15, 16b, 17b, 18 through 20 and 22. *Do not include any Social Security benefit.*	$36,000
4.	Total tax-exempt interest and excluded foreign income.	$3,000
5.	Add Lines 2, 3 & 4.	$47,200
6.	Amount from *Form 1040*, Line 30.	-0-
7.	Subtract Line 6 from Line 5.	$47,200
8.	Enter the amount shown below for your filing status: • Single, head of household or qualifying widow $25,000 • Married filing jointly $32,000 • Married filing separately $-0-	$32,000
9.	Subtract Line 8 from Line 7. If zero or less, *Stop! None of your benefits are taxable*. If more than zero, continue on.	$15,200
10.	Divide Line 9 above in half.	$7,600
11.	Enter the amount shown below for your filing status: • Single, head of household or qualifying widow $34,000 • Married filing jointly $44,000 • Married filing separately $-0-	$44,000
12.	Subtract Line 11 from Line 7. If zero or less, enter zero and go to Line 18. Otherwise, continue on to Line 13.	$3,200
13.	Enter the amount shown below for your filing status: • Single, head of household or qualifying widow $4,500 • Married filing jointly $6,000 • Married filing separately $-0-	$6,000
14.	Enter the smallest of Lines 2, 10 or 13.	$6,000
15.	Multiply Line 12 by 85%.	$2,720
16.	Add Lines 14 and 15.	$8,720
17.	Multiply Line 1 by 85%.	$13,940
18.	TAXABLE BENEFITS • If Line 12 is zero, enter the smaller of Line 2 or Line 10. • If Line 12 is more than zero, enter the smaller of Line 16 or Line 17.	$8,720

Chapter Nineteen

Lines 21 & 22: Other Income and Total Gross Income

What you'll need

- Any record of income not already reported
- *Form 1040*
- 1040 Booklet

Optional

- *IRS Publication 525, Taxable & Nontaxable Income*

What it's all about

Do you have income that does not fall into one of the categories discussed so far?

The Internal Revenue Code states that *all* income is taxable, except that which is specifically exempted. Almost every type of income is reported on Line 7 (wages) through Line 20 (Social Security). But just in case, the IRS provides a catch all on Line 21, other income.

The most common examples of what constitutes other income are:

- **Prizes and awards.** Did you really think all those prizes Miss America wins are tax-free?
- **Lottery and sweepstakes winnings.** Many states are now using lotteries as a source of revenue. Remember when you win the million-dollar jackpot that you will report it on your tax return as "other income."
- **Gambling winnings.** You must report the gross amount of your gambling winnings. Losses are deductible (on *Schedule A*) only if you itemize deductions, and only to the extent of your winnings. In other words, you can never deduct a net gambling loss.
- **Jury duty fees.** Every juror is paid a small fee. This is a flat daily rate that varies among jurisdictions.
- **Barter income.** Being paid in services or merchandise instead of cash doesn't mean you can omit it from taxable income.

- ***Form 8814, Parents' Election to Report Child's Interest and Dividends.*** Line 5 is an election to include your child's investment income on your own return. See Appendix A Section 6, Kiddie Tax.

What to do with the forms

20a	Social security benefits	20a	b Taxable amount (see page 18)	20b
21	Other income. List type and amount—see page 18			21
22	Add the amounts in the far right column for lines 7 through 21. This is your **total income** ▶			22
23a	Your IRA deduction (see page 19)	23a		
b	Spouse's IRA deduction (see page 19)	23b		

Form 1040 Line 21, Other income. Report here all items of income not already reported elsewhere on your return. Write a brief description of the income on the dotted line. If there is not room for an adequate explanation, attach a separate statement and write "see statement" on the dotted line.

Form 1040 Line 22. Add the amounts of all income items from Lines 7 through 21.

Watch out!

Be sure to keep a record of where the deposits into your bank accounts come from. If you are audited and cannot identify the source of funds, the IRS could just label it "other income," even if these funds came from loans, gifts or other nontaxable sources.

What if?

Q. Is money I receive from an inheritance taxable as other income?
A. No, money you inherit is not taxable income to you. However, any income generated by your inheritance once you receive it is taxable. This would include interest, dividends and gains on sale of property you inherited. Say that Grandpa dies and leaves you $10,000 cash in April and you put $5,000 in the bank, $3,000 into a mutual fund, and spend $2,000 traveling to his funeral in Italy. None of this goes anyplace on your tax return. The $2,000 is not a deductible expense, because it was not for the purpose of generating taxable income. The only reportable activity will be the interest you received on the bank account (which goes on the top half of *Schedule B*) and the dividends you received on the mutual fund (which go on bottom half of *Schedule B*). In January, you will receive a *1099-INT* from the bank and a *1099 DIV* from the mutual fund. These will give you the correct amounts to report.

Q. I received jury duty pay, but had to turn it over to my employer in exchange for remaining on payroll. Why should I have to count my jury duty pay as taxable income when I didn't get to keep it?
A. You don't. You still must report it as income but you can deduct it under adjustments to income. Just write "Jury Duty Payback" on the dotted line portion of *Form 1040* Line 30 and include amounts in Total Adjustments.

Chapter Twenty

Lines 23 through 30: Adjustments to Income

What you'll need

- Statement or canceled check showing amount of IRA contributions
- Completed *Schedule SE, Self-Employment Tax*
- Receipts or canceled checks for payment of health insurance premiums, if self-employed
- Record of contributions to pension plan for year
- *Forms 1099-INT*
- *Forms 1099-OID*
- Record of alimony paid for the year
- *Form 1040*
- *Form 3903, Moving Expenses*
- 1040 Booklet

Optional

- *Form 8606, Nondeductible IRAs,* if making non-deductible contributions
- *IRS Publication 535, Business Expenses*
- *IRS Publication 560, Retirement Plans for the Self-Employed*
- Copy of divorce decree
- *IRS Publication 504, Tax Information for Divorced or Separated Individuals*

What it's all about

Up to this point, all you have been telling the IRS is who you are and how much your income was for the year. Now you get to start whittling away at that income. There are various ways the tax code allows you to do this. There are adjustments, deductions, exemptions and credits. Someday, there may be an overhaul of the system and there will be just one category called subtractions. But until then, you will just have to deal with each of these different categories on your return.

The most beneficial subtraction is a *credit,* because that is a reduction of the tax itself, not just of the income subject to tax. Next in importance come adjustments, because these are a direct reduction of your gross income with no strings attached. Deductions have more than a few gimmicks worked into qualifying for them, and many are restricted by your adjusted gross income. Exemptions are certainly more straightforward (simply $2,450 per person) but, again, are potentially limited by your adjusted gross income and may consequently be reduced to zero.

This next section of your return deals with adjustments. The nice thing about adjustments is that you can take advantage of them even if you don't itemize your deductions. Adjustments to income consist of the following:

- IRA contributions for yourself and your spouse.
- Moving expenses.
- One-half of self-employment tax.
- 25 percent of the cost of health insurance for self-employed persons.
- KEOGH or SEP contributions.
- Penalty on early withdrawal of savings.
- Alimony paid.

At the end of the adjustments section on *Form 1040,* there is a total line. Here you will add up all the adjustments. Don't forget to include in this total line any miscellaneous adjustments that don't really fit into any of the specific line items. This is where you toss in that jury duty fee that you gave back to your employer in exchange for remaining on payroll. Subtract the total adjustments from the total income and the result is a very important number called *adjusted gross income* (AGI). This will be referred to when calculating some itemized deductions, credits and even some adjustments.

IRA Contributions

An Individual Retirement Arrangement (IRA) is a very good retirement savings vehicle, whether or not your contributions to it are deductible on your current tax return. It is a one-person retirement plan established by opening an IRA custodial account with a bank, brokerage firm or a mutual fund. You can contribute to an IRA if you are under age 70½ (if you're 70½, it's time to stop putting in and start taking out) *and* have taxable compensation. You can deduct from taxable income up to $2,000 per year in IRA contributions, depending upon your filing status, earned income (including alimony) and eligibility for other retirement plans.

The maximum contribution allowed is $2,000 or 100 percent of your earned income, whichever is less. If you are filing a joint return and only one of you has earned income, then you can contribute a combined total of $2,250. This amount has to be set up in two separate accounts. You can split the contribution between the two accounts any way you like as long as no more than $2,000 goes into either account.

If you or your spouse were covered by a retirement plan (look on your *W-2* for verification), your IRA *deduction* may be reduced or eliminated, but this does not mean that you cannot contribute to an IRA—only that you cannot take it as an adjustment to your gross income. These nondeductible contributions are reported on *Form 8606* (a separate form is required for each spouse if both of you are making nondeductible contributions). NOTE: The nondeductible portion is your cost basis in the IRA, since you are investing already taxed money. Be very careful when you begin withdrawals that you do not report the nondeductible contributions as taxable also. Therefore, if you are making nondeductible IRA contributions, it is very important that you maintain accurate records so that you do not pay tax twice on the same monies. The *Form 8606* allows the IRS to track the same thing.

If you or your spouse were covered by an employer-sponsored retirement plan, you can contribute and deduct the full amount, if your AGI *before* IRA deductions is under $40,000 ($25,000 if single). The $2,000 IRA deduction is then phased out at a rate of 20 percent over the next $10,000 of AGI. Just multiply the amount that your AGI is over $40,000 ($25,000 if single) by 20 percent, and that is your *nondeductible* amount. Subtract that from $2,000, and you have your *deductible* amount. So if you're married earning $46,000 ($31,000 if single) and covered by your employer's pension plan, you can still deduct $800 in IRA contributions. But if your AGI is $50,000 ($35,000 if single), then you cannot deduct any part of the contribution. The 1040 booklet also has a worksheet for calculating this deduction.

The IRA contribution must be made by the due date of the return. This means April 15 (if the 15th is a weekend or national holiday, the due date is the next business day) and no later. So, how about if you file your return early, claim a deduction for an IRA contribution and then use your tax refund to actually make the contribution by April 15? This is perfectly okay!

Moving Expenses

The good news is that you no longer have to itemize deductions in order to claim moving expenses. The bad news is that there is not much left to deduct. Many moving expenses such as temporary living expenses and the cost of househunting trips are no longer deductible. You can still claim the expense of transporting yourself, your family and your household goods and you can claim it right here, as an adjustment to your gross income.

Moving expenses must be business or work-related. This means that you must be transferred by your employer or move to take a new job or to start a new business. Two additional tests must be met for a move to qualify:

- **A distance test.** To meet the distance test, your *new* job must be 50 miles farther from your *old* home than your *old* job is from your *old* home.

- **A time test.** To meet the time test, you must work in the area of your new job on a full-time basis for a minimum of 39 weeks during the first 12 months since your arrival. If you're self-employed, you must meet the 39-week test and, in addition, you must work full-time for 78 weeks during the first two years at the new location.

You may deduct the moving expenses on your return for the year of the move even though you haven't met the 39- or 78-week tests. If you fail the tests later, you must either amend your tax return for the year of the move or include the expense deduction as income on your return for the year you failed the test.

Form 3903 must be completed and filed with your return to support your moving expense adjustment. It is now a simple form:

Form 3903 Lines 1-3. This section performs the distance test calculation.

Form 3903 Line 4. Enter total of expenses for moving and storing your household goods.

Form 3903 Line 5. Enter total of expenses for moving (travel and lodging but *not* meals) you and your family.

Form 3903 Line 6. Enter total of Lines 4 and 5.

Form 3903 Line 7. Enter any reimbursements received from your employer.

Form 3903 Line 8. Subtract Line 7 from Line 6. This is your allowable adjustment to income. Note that if your reimbursements exceed your expenses, you must include the difference in income on *Form 1040,* Line 7.

One Half of Self-Employment Tax

This is one of those instances where you have to go forward on your return to get a number that you need for a calculation elsewhere. If you are self-employed, you will have a special tax that is calculated on *Schedule SE, Self-Employment Tax*. Refer to Chapter 24 for assistance in preparation of this schedule.

If you are an employee, you have a contribution made to Social Security on your behalf by your employer. This is where the funds come from to finance the various Social Security programs. One-half of this contribution is withheld from your pay and the other half is paid by your employer. But when you're self-employed, you are both employee and employer and your SE tax is the payment of both halves. In an effort to ease this double whammy, self-employed individuals are given back a small adjustment to their gross income to the tune of one-half of their self-employment tax. The amount is calculated on Line 6 or 13 of *Schedule SE.*

Self-Employed Health Insurance Deduction

If you are self-employed, you cannot deduct medical insurance premiums paid for you or your family as a *business expense*. You can, of course, deduct as a fringe benefit such expenses for employees. This is one of the hidden costs of being self-employed. To compensate for this inequity, you previously were allowed to take 25 percent of the cost of your insurance as an adjustment to your income. As of this writing, this deduction has expired and has not yet been reinstated.

KEOGH Retirement Plan and Self-Employed SEP Deduction

A self-employed individual has the option of establishing three different types of retirement plans. They vary in simplicity and dollar restrictions.

- *IRA* is the simplest plan. You can contribute up to $2,000 (or earned income, whichever is less) to an IRA account for yourself. Contributions must be made by the due date of the return with no extensions. You may or may not be able to claim the full amount as an adjustment to income. See Line 24, IRA Contributions, discussed earlier in this chapter.
- *SEP* stands for Simplified Employee Pension. It is sometimes called a Super IRA because it is almost as simple as an IRA, but has more generous limitations. Contribution amounts and due dates are specified in the tax law. The full amount is allowed as an adjustment to income regardless of whether you or your spouse are covered by another pension plan. You are required to make contributions for eligible employees in a nondiscriminatory fashion.
- *KEOGH* can be the most generous, as far as dollar amounts contributed, but requires a more formal structure and administration. You must have an actual written plan that conforms to IRS standards, and annual filings of *Form 5500, Return of Employee Benefit Plan*, must be made. Maximum contributions to a KEOGH and the due date for these contributions are specified in the tax law, which is strictly construed by IRS. The amount contributed is allowed as an adjustment to income regardless of whether you or your spouse are covered by a pension plan. You are required to make contributions for eligible employees in a nondiscriminatory fashion. Amounts contributed for employees are business expenses deductible on your business income schedule.

  These plans can take two forms: *defined benefit* and *defined contribution*. The defined contribution plans can be made up of a profit-sharing plan and/or a money purchase plan. Defined benefit plans allow for significantly larger contributions, but require actuarial computations and greater cost of administration. Perhaps it's time to call an accountant, a pension service or maybe just 911!

Penalty on Early Withdrawal of Savings

Some types of savings accounts (most typically CDs) are referred to as time deposits. This means they have a specific maturity date, a date upon which you can withdraw the original amount plus interest earned. If you need the funds before the maturity date, you may be charged a penalty for withdrawing the funds early. In effect, you receive a higher interest rate in exchange for a pledge to leave the funds for a period of time. The longer the time, the higher the interest rate. If, however, you withdraw your funds before the maturity date, you are assessed a penalty. This, in effect, just reduces the interest rate down to an amount paid for a shorter term.

Alimony Paid

If you're deducting alimony payments on your tax return, then your ex-spouse should be claiming the same payments as income. For that reason, you should first read Chapter 8.

Alimony does not include child support, cash or property settlements, or voluntary payments. Alimony is paid as a result of a court order or written separation agreement.

The person paying the alimony (and taking it as an adjustment to gross income on his or her tax return) must include the Social Security number of the person to whom the alimony is paid. If the Social Security number is missing, the adjustment may be disallowed and you may have to pay a $50 penalty. The alimony reported as income will be tied to the amount claimed by the ex-spouse as the amount paid under adjustments to income. We wonder how many ex-husbands claim to have paid thousands in alimony while the ex-wife claims only hundreds in income. The IRS wonders, too, and now has the computer capability to track and match up both claims via Social Security numbers.

What to do with the forms

23a	Your IRA deduction (see page 19)	23a			
b	Spouse's IRA deduction (see page 19)	23b			
24	Moving expenses. Attach Form 3903 or 3903-F . . .	24			
25	One-half of self-employment tax	25			
26	Self-employed health insurance deduction (see page 21)	26			
27	Keogh retirement plan and self-employed SEP deduction	27			
28	Penalty on early withdrawal of savings	28			
29	Alimony paid. Recipient's SSN ▶	29			
30	Add lines 23a through 29. These are your **total adjustments** . . . . ▶			30	
31	Subtract line 30 from line 22. This is your **adjusted gross income.** If less than $25,296 and a child lived with you (less than $9,000 if a child didn't live with you), see "Earned Income Credit" on page 27 ▶			31	

Form 1040 Line 23a. Report your deductible IRA contribution.

Form 1040 Line 23b. Report your spouse's deductible IRA contribution.

Form 1040 Line 24. Report your deductible moving expenses from *Form 3903.*

Form 1040 Line 25. Enter the amount from your *Schedule SE*, Line 6 (or Line 13 if required to use *Long Schedule SE*).

Form 1040 Line 26, Self-employed health insurance deduction. If this deduction is retroactively reinstated, enter the deductible amount (up to 25 percent) of the cost of health insurance premiums for yourself, your spouse and your dependents. Although this deduction expired at the end of 1993, IRS proofs of Form 1040 include this line in anticipation of reinstatement. Check the Form 1040 instructions before claiming this deduction.

Form 1040 Line 27. Enter the full amount of contribution to KEOGH or SEP on *your* behalf (not contributions for employees). If you are making an IRA contribution instead, use Line 23 to report the deductible amount, if any.

Form 1040 Line 28. Enter the amount reported to you on *Forms 1099-INT* or *1099-OID* for penalty on early withdrawal of savings.

Form 1040 Line 29. Enter the total amount of alimony paid for the year, but only up to the amount authorized by the divorce decree—*no more*. Include the Social Security number of the person to whom you are paying the alimony.

Form 1040 Line 30. Enter the total of all adjustments shown on Lines 23 through 29.

Watch out!

If you contribute too much to your IRA accounts, you report the excess contribution on *Form 5329, Additional Taxes Attributable to Retirement Plans Including IRAs.* This amount is subject to a 6-percent excise tax. Hopefully, you will discover the excess contribution before April 15 and withdraw it along with any earnings on those funds. The excess contribution is not income, but the earnings on the excess contribution are taxable to you. Each year you fail to withdraw the over-contributed amount, you are subject to a new 6 percent penalty on that amount.

* * *

If you made IRA contributions within the $2,000 limitation, but you find that they are not deductible, use *Form 8606* to report and track the deductible portion and the nondeductible portion.

* * *

The 15-percent SEP and 25-percent KEOGH contribution percentages are a little deceptive. For example, the 15 percent is to be calculated on net profit as reduced by your SEP contribution. Unless you're a mathematician, you probably wouldn't know that this translates to 13.0435 percent of net profit. So if your net profit is $20,000, your 15-percent contribution is $2,609.

* * *

SEPs can include a salary reduction plan, so if you have anything other than a simple SEP you should consult a tax professional well-versed in pension plans.

* * *

If you are establishing a KEOGH plan, or already have one in place, you would be well-advised to seek professional advice. Pension plans are an area of specialization that requires more than just casual attention. Tax consequences as well as fiduciary liability are substantial. Penalties for failure to file annual *Form 5500* series reports can be staggering.

* * *

If you are self-employed and you have a SEP or a KEOGH, you must be prepared to make contributions for employees as well as for yourself. For example, you can't exclude Lisa because you're angry at her, contribute only 5 percent of Joe's salary for him because he's a democrat, 8 percent of John's salary because he's broke and 12 percent of net profit for yourself because you deserve it. You must not discriminate.

* * *

If yours is a complicated divorce or separation scenario and support is taking the form of anything other than straightforward and clearly defined alimony payments, read *IRS Publication 504* and/or seek professional advice.

* * *

If your alimony payments decrease substantially or terminate during the first three years of payments, they are subject to recapture. This rule prevents people who are divorcing from structuring what is really division of property (no immediate tax consequence) as alimony (allows shifting of income to one with the lower tax rate). If your annual payments were reduced by more than $15,000 within the first three years for reasons other than death or remarriage, you are probably subject to recapture. This is a fancy word that means the IRS will not consider the full amount paid to be alimony. Calculating the recapture amount (amount you will have to take out of your alimony deduction) is no easy feat, and you should read through *IRS Publication 504* for additional information.

* * *

If you are getting a divorce and are contemplating some fancy maneuvers, make sure you have advisors well-versed in the tax law pertaining to divorce and alimony.

What if?

Q. I had every intention of making an IRA contribution by April 15. I never did get around to it, but I took a deduction for it on my tax return. Now what do I do?

A. This is an area where the IRS has an excellent matching program in place, so if you claim to have made an IRA contribution but don't actually make it, they will know. The solution to this problem is to file an amended tax return to remove the IRA deduction from your original tax return. To file an amendment, use *Form 1040X,* which is available from the IRS and is quite easy to follow.

Q. My *W-2* income exceeded the maximum amount subject to Social Security tax and my SE tax was zero. Can I still claim the full deduction on *Form 1040* Line 25?
A. No, since you only paid half the tax. Your employer paid the other half and already claimed a deduction for that portion.

Q. What's the deal with the health insurance adjustment. Is it back?
A. This is the on again-off again adjustment. First implemented in 1989, it has been authorized only for six months or a year at a time. It actually expired on June 30, 1992, and so 1992 returns (if they were prepared correctly) only considered health insurance premiums paid during the first half of the year. Then the Budget Reconciliation Act, which was not passed until August 1993, reinstated the credit retroactive to June 30, 1992. So if you want the benefit of an adjustment for the last half of 1992, you will need to file an amendment of your 1992 return. As of this writing, this adjustment expired again at the end of 1993 but may be reinstated for 1994. In fact, proofs of *Form 1040* for 1994 include Line 26 for claiming this deduction.

Q. I am not sure I can make a contribution to my business retirement plan each and every year. Should I just forget about it altogether?
A. You should consult a pension expert who will probably recommend a plan such as a SEP or a profit-sharing plan whereby contributions are discretionary on your part.

Q. I pay alimony to two ex-wives, but there is only room for one Social Security number on *Form 1040*. What do I do?
A. Write the words "see statement" in the space provided for the Social Security number. Then just attach a statement to your return with the breakout of the total alimony claimed showing the Social Security number and amount paid for each ex-spouse.

Chapter Twenty-One

Lines 31 through 34: Deductions, Standard and Itemized

What you'll need

- *Schedule A, Itemized Deductions*
- Statements & documents supporting your itemized deductions
- *Form 1040*
- 1040 Booklet

Optional

- *Form 2106 EZ, Unreimbursed Employee Business Expenses*
- *Form 2106, Employee Business Expenses*
- *Form 4684, Casualties & Thefts*
- *Form 4952, Investment Interest Expenses Deduction*
- *Form 8283, Noncash Charitable Contributions*
- *IRS Publication 463, Travel, Entertainment & Gift Expenses*
- *IRS Publication 502, Medical and Dental Expenses*
- *IRS Publication 508, Educational Expenses*
- *IRS Publication 521, Moving Expenses*
- *IRS Publication 526, Charitable Contributions*
- *IRS Publication 529, Miscellaneous Deductions*
- *IRS Publication 534, Depreciation*
- *IRS Publication 547, Nonbusiness Disasters, Casualties & Thefts*
- *IRS Publication 550, Investment Income & Expenses*
- *IRS Publication 587, Business Use of Your Home*
- *IRS Publication 917, Business Use of a Car*
- *IRS Publication 936, Limits On Home Mortgage Interest Deduction*

What it's all about

You can reduce your taxable income by certain expenses. This is called itemizing your deductions. You are automatically allowed an amount called a standard deduction. Over the years, this standard amount has grown and the amounts allowed as itemized deductions have become more restricted. The standard deduction varies with your filing status and is adjusted annually for inflation. Itemize only if your actual deductions add up to more than the standard amount.

Itemizing is not what it used to be. In years past, many personal expenses were deductible, but this is no longer the case. Over the past decade, itemized deductions have been whittled away by lawmakers scrambling to balance budgets with shrinking revenues. As a result, personal interest and state sales taxes are no longer deductible. Medical expenses, employee business expenses, mortgage interest, casualty losses and other miscellaneous deductions are allowed but are severely restricted. The most common of itemized deductions are now home mortgage interest, property tax, charitable contributions and, if you work in a state with an income tax, state taxes paid.

For high-income taxpayers (those whose adjusted gross income exceeds $111,800 ($55,900 if married filing separate), there is an additional limitation. The most common itemized deductions are reduced by 3 percent of adjusted gross income in excess of the $111,800 or $55,900 amounts. This limitation applies to a maximum of 80 percent of those deductions (so you never completely lose them). There is a worksheet included in this chapter to help you calculate your limitations.

What to do with the forms

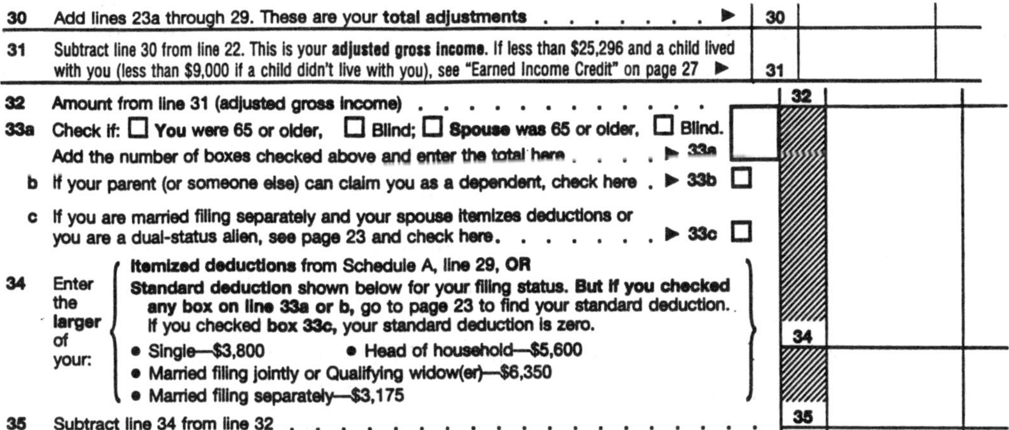

30 Add lines 23a through 29. These are your **total adjustments** . . . . ▶ 30

31 Subtract line 30 from line 22. This is your **adjusted gross income**. If less than $25,296 and a child lived with you (less than $9,000 if a child didn't live with you), see "Earned Income Credit" on page 27 ▶ 31

32 Amount from line 31 (adjusted gross income) 32

33a Check if: ☐ You were 65 or older, ☐ Blind; ☐ Spouse was 65 or older, ☐ Blind.
Add the number of boxes checked above and enter the total here . . . . ▶ 33a

b If your parent (or someone else) can claim you as a dependent, check here . ▶ 33b ☐

c If you are married filing separately and your spouse itemizes deductions or you are a dual-status alien, see page 23 and check here. . . . . ▶ 33c ☐

34 Enter the larger of your:
- **Itemized deductions** from Schedule A, line 29, **OR**
- **Standard deduction shown below for your filing status. But if you checked any box on line 33a or b, go to page 23 to find your standard deduction. If you checked box 33c, your standard deduction is zero.**
  - Single—$3,800
  - Head of household—$5,600
  - Married filing jointly or Qualifying widow(er)—$6,350
  - Married filing separately—$3,175

34

35 Subtract line 34 from line 32 35

Form 1040 Line 31. Subtract the total of any adjustments on Line 30 from your total income on Line 22. This gives you a very important figure called adjusted gross income (AGI).

Form 1040 Line 32. That AGI amount is *so* important that it is repeated here at the top of *Form 1040*, page 2. Just copy the amount from Line 31 onto Line 32.

Form 1040 Line 33a. Check any of the four boxes indicating if you or your spouse are over age 65 or blind. Enter the total boxes checked.

Form 1040 Line 33b. Can you be claimed as a dependent on someone else's return? If so, check this box, even if that someone else chooses not to claim you.

Form 1040 Line 33c. Are you married filing separate but your spouse itemizes, or are you a dual status alien? If so, check this box and be aware that you cannot use the standard deduction.

Standard Deduction

The standard deduction is a specific amount. The actual dollar amount changes every year based on inflation. These amounts are printed on Line 34 of *Form 1040*. Choose the one that corresponds to your filing status. The standard deduction is increased for taxpayers over 65 years of age or who are legally blind. These amounts are also indexed for inflation and change each year. If your itemized deductions total more than your standard deduction amount, don't enter anything on Line 34 yet, just continue reading.

The 1994 standard deduction amounts are as follows:

$6,350 for married/joint and surviving spouses
$5,600 for head of household
$3,800 for single filers
$3,175 for married/separate

If a person is 65 before the end of the tax year or blind, he or she is entitled to an additional standard deduction, $750 for a married person or surviving spouse and $950 for an unmarried person. If a person is over 65 *and* blind, the additional standard deduction is doubled.

Form 1040 Line 34, Standard deduction. Per above instructions, choose the amount that corresponds to your filing status and enter it here.

If you can be claimed on someone else's return (for instance, you are a student with a part-time job and are filing a return to report your *W-2* wages and some interest income), you *must* calculate your standard deduction in a special way. Generally, your deduction is limited to the greater of $600 or your earned income (do *not* count the interest income) up to the maximum standard deduction of $3,800 for a single person. The *Form 1040* instruction booklet includes a worksheet to calculate the standard deduction for a dependent filing his or her own return.

Itemized Deductions

Simply stated, itemizing your deductions means listing those personal expenditures that reduce your taxable income. Qualified deductions for itemizing fall into eight categories:

- Medical expenses
- Taxes paid
- Casualty losses
- Investment expenses
- Interest paid
- Gifts to charity
- Job expenses
- Miscellaneous

If itemizing, the form you must complete and include as part of your return is *Schedule A*. The total on *Schedule A*, Line 29 will be carried forward to Line 34 of *Form 1040* and used instead of the standard deduction amount. Don't forget to fill out the itemized deduction worksheet at the end of this chapter if you are a high income taxpayer as defined earlier.

1. Medical and Dental Expenses

You can claim as an itemized deduction certain medical and dental expenses paid for yourself, your spouse and dependents if—and this is a big if—those medical expenses exceed 7.5 percent of your adjusted gross income. You also must reduce the total of your expenses by the total of any insurance payments received during the year.

Rather than spending a lot of time compiling detailed lists of medical expenses, just multiply your adjusted gross income from Line 31 of *Form 1040* by 7.5 percent. The result is the amount you must exceed to benefit from this deduction. If you think your medical expenses (less insurance reimbursements) exceed this amount, then add them up for reporting on *Schedule A*.

Schedule A Line 1, Medical & dental expenses. Enter the total of all qualifying expenses for the year. Items that qualify as medical and dental expenses commonly include such things as doctor's fees, dentist's fees, hospital bills, lab fees, insurance premiums and transportation costs (including mileage at the rate of 9 cents per mile). A comprehensive list of allowable deductions can be found in the 1040 instruction booklet.

Schedule A Lines 2, 3 & 4. This is the calculation to back out 7.5 percent of your adjusted gross income from the total of your expenses. What remains is your deductible amount on Line 4.

2. Taxes You Paid

Certain taxes you pay throughout the year are deductible, but they must have been imposed on *you* and *you* must have actually paid them. Generally, the taxes that are deductible are state and local income taxes, property taxes and other taxes.

Schedule A Line 5, State & local income tax. Enter the total of state or local income taxes paid during the year. This may include the state tax paid for the prior year, state tax withheld from your paycheck (reported on your *W-2)* and any estimated state taxes you've paid. As a cash basis taxpayer, you may deduct what you actually pay during the year. *Do not* deduct Social Security, Medicare or federal tax withheld from your wages. One other state tax that is deductible here is the mandatory employee contribution to the California, New Jersey, New York or Rhode Island State Disability Funds. This will be reported on your *W-2* if such a tax is withheld. Do not reduce your deduction by any tax refund received or expected to be received.

Schedule A Line 6, Real estate taxes. Enter the amount of property tax paid on real estate that you own and maintain for either personal or investment use. If your property taxes are included in your mortgage payment (impound account), deduct the amount actually paid out of the escrow account, and not the amount collected from you.

If you pay real estate taxes on property other than your home, the nature of the property in your possession determines where you take the deduction. Taxes on rental property are deducted as rental expenses on *Schedule E*. Taxes on business property are deducted as a business expense on *Schedule C*. Taxes on farm property are deducted on *Schedule F*. Taxes on property held for investment or personal use are deducted here on *Schedule A*. Property that is partially business or partially rental and partially personal must be divided up among the schedules.

Schedule A Line 7, Personal property taxes. Enter here any personal property taxes that are based on the value of the underlying property. This type of tax is commonly paid in many states as a part of automobile registrations. The portion of the registration fee that is based upon your car's value is deductible as a tax paid.

Schedule A Line 8, Other taxes. Enter here any other taxes paid that are allowed as federal deductions. An example of such a tax is tax paid to a foreign country or U.S. possession. It may be to your advantage, however, to claim the foreign tax credit as opposed to this deduction, so refer to IRS Publication 514 for a complete discussion of foreign taxes.

Schedule A Line 9, Total. Enter here the total of Lines 5, 6, 7 and 8.

3. Interest you paid

Gone are the days when you could justify charge accounts or car loans by saying the interest was tax-deductible. Today, the only remaining interest deductions are for home mortgages, points paid to obtain a home mortgage and investment interest. All three of these are subject to specific limitations.

Schedule A Line 10, Home mortgage interest and points. Enter the amount of your deductible interest and points as reported to you on *Form 1098*.

In order to qualify for a home mortgage interest deduction, you must have a loan secured by your main home or a second home. A home is not necessarily a house, but it must provide basic living accommodations including sleeping space and toilet and kitchen facilities. Yes, a boat may qualify! The actual amount that you are allowed to deduct depends on the amount and date of the mortgages and how you used the loan proceeds. Here are the specific rules:

- If you obtained your mortgage on or before Oct. 13, 1987, *all* the interest you paid is deductible.

- If you obtained your mortgage after Oct. 13, 1987, in order to buy, build or improve your home, *all* the interest is deductible as long as the total mortgage balance does not exceed *$1 million*. For this purpose, total mortgage balance includes outstanding mortgage indebtedness obtained before Oct. 13, 1987. Interest paid for loans in excess of $1 million is *not* deductible.
- If you obtained your mortgage after Oct. 13, 1987 to do something other than buy, build or improve your home, you can deduct *only* the interest paid on the first $100,000. The mortgage must be secured by your residence. Any interest paid for loans beyond that amount is not deductible.

If you have refinanced several times, you may have what the IRS calls a "mixed-use" mortgage. You must trace the dates of the loans in question and determine how you used the proceeds in order to calculate the deductible amount. The flow chart below is provided to help you identify how much of the interest you paid is deductible.

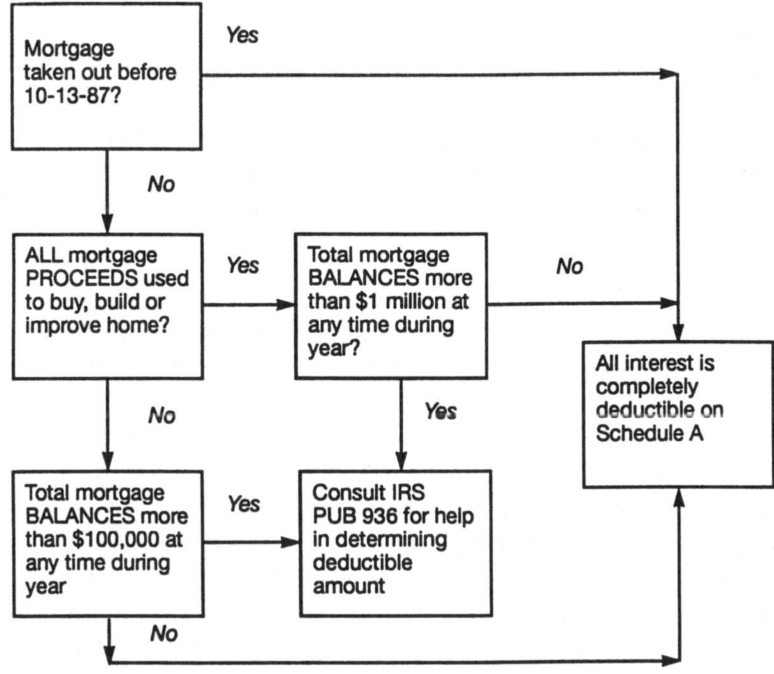

Schedule A Line 11, Home Mortgage Interest Not On *Form 1098*. Do you have a seller financed mortgage or some other loan on your home that is not through a financial institution? Unless the lender is actually in the loan business he may not be required to provide you (and the IRS) with a *Form 1098* reporting interest paid for the year. You are still entitled to deduct the interest but, of course, the IRS wants to make sure the deduction on your return gets reported as income on someone else's return. For that reason, you have to provide the name, address and federal ID number of the person you paid. Then simply write in the dollar amount of interest paid.

Schedule A Line 12, Points. Most instances of paying points will be reported to you on *Form 1098* and included on Line 10. Here you will report any points paid but not reported to you on *Form 1098*. You can look high and low on the escrow documents from the purchase or refinance of your home, but you will never find the word "points." You will find a loan origination fee or a loan fee listed as one of the charges paid at settlement. These loan fees are the points. The word "points" comes from the way the loan fees are computed, as percentage points of the amount you're borrowing. It really doesn't matter what you call them, they are amounts paid to acquire a loan. They represent interest since they are funds paid for the use of money. Points (loan fees) are generally deductible over the life of the loan. If you have a 10-year second mortgage on your home, you can deduct one-tenth of your loan fees each year as you pay off the loan.

There are two instances where loan fees can be deducted in full in the year you pay them:

- When you borrow money to buy your home.
- When you borrow money to improve your home.

The common denominator here is your *home*. You can't use the money for anything else. To qualify when you refinance, you must actually pay the loan fees from your own supply of money, not have them held back from the loan proceeds.

Schedule A Line 13, Investment interest. Enter the amount of deductible investment interest—interest paid on a loan that you've used to purchase investment property. Generally, this is property that produces income or grows in value over time. Examples are stocks, bonds and land.

Investment interest expense is only allowed to offset investment income. If you pay $5,000 of interest on investment loans and you have investment income of $3,000, you may deduct only $3,000 of your investment interest. The remaining $2,000 is carried forward for use in future years.

Investment income includes interest, dividends, annuities and royalties. If your expense is more than your income, the IRS wants more information. *Form 4952, Investment Interest Expense Deduction,* is provided for this purpose. Thankfully, any amount disallowed is carried forward and is available for deduction in subsequent years. Just don't forget about it next year!

Schedule A Line 14. Enter the total of Lines 10, 11, 12 and 13.

4. Gifts to Charity

Contributions made to qualified (in the eyes of the IRS!) charitable organizations are deductible. Most charitable organizations will tell you if they are qualified and, therefore, whether your contribution is deductible. Contributions can consist of cash or property. If you donate your time and energy to a qualified charity, you may deduct only your actual out-of-pocket expenses and automobile mileage at the rate of 12 cents per mile. You cannot deduct the value of your services or time.

There are limits on how much you can give away and deduct. The maximum amount can't exceed 50 percent of your adjusted gross income. Gifts to certain charities cannot exceed 30 percent of your adjusted gross income and gifts of certain types of property can't exceed 20 percent. If you're contemplating large contributions, check with the charity and the IRS publications to determine which limitations apply. Amounts not currently allowed can be carried forward for use in the next five years.

You can donate property to charity and take a deduction. The amount to deduct is the lesser of the value of the property when you give it, or its cost to you. So when you do your spring cleaning and haul all that stuff you paid thousands of dollars for over the years down to your local charity, you'll not be deducting those thousands of dollars on your tax return. Take some time to make a list of the items and estimate what you'd be able to sell them for in a garage sale, for example. This is the value for which you can take a deduction. Remember, you have to be able to substantiate your determination of the value if you are questioned, so be reasonable.

Some property, if donated, may give rise to a deduction equal to the property's value at the time donated, even if that value exceeds your cost. The type of property eligible is called capital gains property. This is property that, if sold, would generate capital gains, and not ordinary income.

The organization you chose to donate to and its use of the property may affect your deduction. So you may wish to seek professional tax advice before making a substantial contribution. Furthermore, property donations in excess of $5,000 require a written appraisal to support your deduction amount. Refer to *Form 8283, Noncash Charitable Contributions* instructions.

If the value of donated property exceeds $500, the IRS wants some additional information. You have to fill out *Form 8283*, giving the details of your donation.

If you received a benefit in connection with your gift (food, entertainment or merchandise), deduct only the amount of your gift that exceeds the value of the benefit you received. If a charity gave you goods or services in exchange for a contribution of $75 or more, that charitable organization must notify you of the value of what you received.

Gifts of $250 or more are deductible only if you have a statement from the charitable organization showing the following information:

- The amount of money contributed and a description (but not value) of any property donated.
- Whether or not the charitable organization provided any goods or services in return for the contribution. If there were goods or services given, then the statement must include a description and an estimate of value of these. If you received only intangible religious benefits (a front row seat at Easter Mass, for example), the statement must include this, but it does not have to include a description or value of this benefit.

You must obtain this statement by the date you file your tax return or the due date, including extensions, whichever is earlier. Keep this statement for your records and do not attach it to your tax return.

Schedule A Line 15, Contributions by cash or check. Enter the total of all contributions for the year made by cash or check.

Schedule A Line 16, Other than by cash or check. Enter *reasonable* value of all donated items. If the amount is over $500, you need to complete and attach *Form 8283*. On this form, you report what you donated, when and how you obtained it, when and to whom you donated it, and how you determined the value.

Schedule A Line 17, Carryover from prior year. Enter the amount you were not able to use in any of five previous years due to limitations. Do not enter the amount donated from a few years back that you forgot to report and now want to claim. That requires an amended tax return for the year you forgot the deduction.

Schedule A Line 18. Enter the total of Lines 15, 16 and 17.

5. Casualty and Theft Losses

Crack! Boom! That stately old oak tree that shaded your front porch is now an accessory in your master bedroom. In the blink of an eye, you have suffered a casualty loss—a sudden and unexpected occurrence that has damaged or destroyed your property. Losses due to casualty or theft are events that arise from vandalism, theft, fire, storm or similar cause. You may also be able to claim a deduction for money lost due to bankruptcy of your financial institution.

As you might expect, there are limits on the amount of loss you can claim. Your deductible loss is the total of the losses you've incurred during the year, minus $100 for each loss, and minus 10 percent of your adjusted gross income (Line 31 of *Form 1040*). The likelihood of deducting any loss is significantly reduced by this limitation. Only major casualties will result in a deduction.

Remember, the amount of the loss in each case is determined after any insurance reimbursement. If you receive, or are *eligible* to receive money from your insurance company, the amount lost is after the insurance reimbursement!

Schedule A Line 19, Casualty or theft losses. Enter the deductible amount of losses. You will determine this amount by completing *Form 4684, Casualties and Thefts*. This is a very straightforward form on which you give the description of the property and its fair market value both before and after the casualty. The form then leads you through subtracting out the $100 and 10-percent nondeductible portions of your loss. The result on Line 18 of *Form 4684* is carried forward to Line 17 of *Schedule A*.

6. Job Expenses and Most Other Miscellaneous Deductions

Miscellaneous expenses fall into two categories: those that are fully deductible and those to which an adjusted gross income limitation applies.

- **Fully deductible expenses.** There are few expenses that are deductible without reference to adjusted gross income. The most common of these are gambling losses, which are deductible only to the extent of the gambling winnings that you reported as "Other Income," Line 21 of *Form 1040*. For example, you win $1,000 gambling on Memorial Day. On Labor Day, you lose $1,200 gambling at the same casino. You report $1,000 as income and deduct only $1,000 of your loss. Other fully deductible miscellaneous expenses are listed in the 1040 instruction booklet.
- **Limited miscellaneous expenses.** Most of the deductions in the miscellaneous category are subject to an artificial limit based on adjusted gross income. Specifically, they must exceed 2 percent of adjusted gross income to be of any value in reducing your income tax.

The most complicated deduction in this section is that of unreimbursed employee business expenses. This is a deduction that was once allowed as an adjustment to income on the face of *Form 1040*. Since the Tax Reform Act of 1986, this deduction has been consigned to itemized deductions and is subjected to the 2-percent limitation discussed above. If you have business expenses that are not reimbursed by your employer, perform a simple test to see if it's worthwhile to fill out the forms. Multiply your adjusted gross income (*Form 1040* Line 31) by 2 percent. If your business expenses exceed this amount and you are itemizing your other deductions, go ahead and fill out *Form 2106, Employee Business Expenses.*

Some employers have what are termed "accountable plans" for expense reimbursement. This means that you submit the expenses and are reimbursed for them. In this case, assuming you were reimbursed in full, you don't have to do anything further. Other employers have "non-accountable plans." With this type of plan, you are given an expense allowance and no further accounting is done by your employer. The amount of the allowance has been included in your wages and reported on your *W-2*. In order to avoid paying tax on that allowance, you must keep all your receipts and be able to itemize your deductions. Adding up all your business expenses and entering them on *Schedule A* is not sufficient! The IRS wants specific information and *Form 2106, Employee Business Expenses*, is provided for you to report it.

The main focus of *Form 2106* is on travel and transportation expenses. The entire backside of the form is devoted to reporting and calculating the deductible expenses you are allowed for using your car for business. This includes everything from actual expenses for gas and oil to depreciation and miles driven.

The front side of the form picks up the vehicle expense from the back and continues with travel, lodging and meals. The line instructions are clear and can easily be filled in once you have gathered all your receipts.

The only caution relates to business expenses entered on Line 4. This includes any unreimbursed business expense other than travel, lodging and meals. The expenses that qualify are the ordinary and necessary costs appropriate and essential to maintaining job performance. This can include continuing education, professional dues, publications used in your work, tools, uniforms and cleaning. It can also include depreciation on equipment such as computers or cellular phones, if you are required to have them to keep your job.

There is a new form this year—*Form 2106 EZ*. It is easier than the regular *Form 2106* because it does not deal with any employer reimbursements. The main thrust of both forms is the same—to detail any expenses you had which were not paid for by your employer.

Schedule A Line 20, Unreimbursed employee expenses. You must detail any expenses you claim here on a separate form, which is attached to your return. Use *Form 2106* if you *did* receive expense reimbursements from your employer but still have additional expenses to claim. Use *Form 2106 EZ* if you *did not* receive expense reimbursements from your employer. Both forms are easy to complete and simply break out your expenses into vehicle expenses, transportation, travel and lodging, any other ordinary and necessary business expense (supplies, for example) and meals and entertainment (only 50 percent of actual cost is allowed). If you do claim any vehicle expense, the forms have a section for you to provide some additional information on the car and its use. Once you've assembled all your expenses and entered them on the appropriate lines of *Form 2106* or *Form 2106 EZ,* just follow the line instructions to compute the total deductible amount. Enter the total from Line 11 of *Form 2106* or Line 6 of *Form 2106 EZ* onto *Schedule A,* Line 20.

Schedule A Line 21, Tax preparation fees. You are allowed a deduction for any cost incurred in determining or defending your taxes. Tax preparation fees and the cost of this book are deductible, as well as legal and professional fees incurred for tax planning or dealing with the IRS. Remember, if you have a business, you can deduct as a business expense (on *Schedule C* or *Schedule E*) the portion of the cost attributable to the business. This will save on self-employment tax and avoid that pesky 2-percent limitation.

Schedule A Line 22, Other expenses. In addition to unreimbursed employee business expenses, you may deduct other expenses that have nothing to do with your employment. These are the expenses incurred in pursuing or producing other income. Examples are investment fees and expenses, safe deposit box fees rented to hold investment documents, IRA trustee fees and some legal fees. They must be the normal and reasonable expenses of producing income. There are a few other deductible expenses. If you have expenses not addressed here, refer to the IRS instructions for *Schedule A*.

Schedule A Line 23. Add Lines 20 through 22. Enter the total of these three lines for the total of your miscellaneous deductions subject to a limitation based upon the amount of your adjusted gross income.

Schedule A Line 24. Enter the amount from *Form 1040*, Line 32. This is the amount of your adjusted gross income.

Schedule A Line 25. Multiply Line 24 by 2 percent. This gives the amount by which you have to reduce your miscellaneous deductions. In other words, you will automatically lose the benefit of your miscellaneous deductions by the amount of 2 percent of your adjusted gross income.

Schedule A Line 26. Subtract Line 25 from Line 23. This backs out the 2 percent of your adjusted gross income, and what remains is your deductible amount.

Schedule A Line 27, Moving expenses incurred before 1994. It's possible that you had moving expenses in 1993, but didn't deduct them because you were receiving reimbursement from your employer in 1994. Since the expenses were actually in 1993, you are subject to the rules in effect at that time. Your employer should have included reimbursements in your W-2 and you should complete the back side (Parts II and III) of the *Form 3903*. The amount on *Form 3903* Line 19 will carry forward here to *Schedule A* as an itemized deduction. Remember, beginning in 1994, moving expenses are an adjustment to income, not an itemized deduction.

Schedule A Line 28, Other miscellaneous deductions. Enter any fully deductible expenses. The most common is gambling loss to the extent of gambling winnings. Consult the 1040 booklet for any other possibilities.

Schedule A Line 29, Total itemized deductions. Add up the total of all your deductible amounts shown on the right-hand side of the form (Lines 4, 9, 14, 18, 19, 26, 27 and 28). The majority of taxpayers will enter this sum total directly on Line 26. *But,* remember we said that high-income taxpayers have their itemized deductions restricted? Look at the worksheet on the next page to see if the restriction applies to you.

Watch out!

Most issues likely to emerge in the course of preparing this part of the average tax return have been discussed. If you have incurred an expense that has not been addressed in this chapter, you may want to do further research. Consult the instructions for *Form 1040* or the publications listed in the front of this chapter for a more detailed discussion of itemized deductions.

Here is a list of some common expenses that are *not* deductible.

NONDEDUCTIBLE EXPENSES

Life insurance premiums	Adoption expenses
Political contributions	Cosmetic surgery
Personal legal expenses	Funeral expenses
Nonprescription medicines	Commuting expenses
Expense of producing tax-exempt income	Fines and penalties

Itemized Deductions Worksheet

1. Enter total itemized deductions before limitation. 1.________
2. Add amounts on *Schedule A* Lines 4, 13 and 19, plus any gambling losses included on Line 25. 2.________
3. Subtract Line 2 from Line 1. If result is zero, *stop here,* enter amount from Line 1 above on *Schedule A* Line 29. 3.________
4. Multiply Line 3 above by 80 percent. 4.________
5. Enter amount from *Form 1040*, Line 32. 5.________
6. Enter $111,800 ($55,900 if married filing separately). 6.________
7. Subtract Line 6 from Line 5. If zero or less, *stop here*; enter amount from Line 1 above on *Schedule A* Line 29. 7.________
8. Multiply Line 7 above by 3 percent. 8.________
9. Enter *smaller* of Line 4 or Line 8. 9.________
10. *Total itemized deductions.* Subtract Line 9 from Line 1. Enter result here and on *Schedule A* Line 29. 10.________

What if?

Medical/Dental

Q. I spent a fortune on my daughter's doctor and dentist bills and then she got married in December. She and her husband are filing a joint return so I can't claim her as my dependent. Can I still claim her medical expenses?
A. Yes. If you're paying medical expenses for anyone you are *not* claiming as a dependent, consult the IRS instructions to see if you can deduct these expenses anyway. This is one instance where the IRS is lenient about who qualifies as a dependent.

Taxes You Paid

Q. My dad pays my property tax for me. Who gets the deduction?
A. No one! You must have some ownership of the property in order to deduct tax paid on it. So, only if your father's name is on the title along with yours, can he can deduct the taxes he paid. If not, he can either loan or give you the money so you can pay the tax personally and take the deduction.

Interest You Paid

Q. I have mortgages on my home, my beach house and my mountain cabin as well as loans on my RV and houseboat. Can I deduct it all as mortgage interest, since I divide my time among them?
A. You can deduct the interest on your main home and one other home. You do get to decide which is your second residence, so pick the one with the biggest mortgage.

Q. I bought a lot in a resort area that I hope to build on someday. Can I deduct the interest I pay on my mortgage for the land?
A. This is obviously not home mortgage interest because there is no home, just vacant land. So, until you build your vacation home, the lot may qualify as investment property and the interest paid as investment interest. Complete *Form 4952, Investment Interest Expense Deduction*, to determine how much if any is deductible in the current year.

Gifts to Charity

Q. We are taking up a collection to buy furniture for a neighbor family who lost everything in a fire. Can we tell people they can take a tax deduction for their contributions?
A. No, you do not have a nonprofit organization that has been qualified as such by the IRS. How about finding a church or qualified organization through which you can help these people?

Q. Can I deduct the price of tickets to a charity benefit dinner?
A. Yes, but the actual amount you pay for the tickets may not be the amount you can deduct. The deduction is limited to the excess of the ticket price over the value of the meal or entertainment provided.

Casualty Losses

Q. I had an auto accident and I paid to repair the car myself rather than report it to my insurance company and have them raise my premiums. Can I deduct the repairs?
A. No! Because you were entitled to reimbursement, you are deemed to have received the money whether or not you actually submitted a claim. You can count as a loss only the amount of your deductible, because that is an amount you would not have received from the insurance company.

Job Expenses

Q. I will be graduating soon and looking for a job. Can I deduct my expenses?
A. No, you cannot deduct expenses if seeking a first job, or a job in a new line of work.

Q. I was laid off early this year and am still not able to find a new job even though I've been actively looking. Can I deduct my expenses?
A. Yes, you do not have to get the job in order for the expenses to qualify.

Chapter Twenty-Two

Lines 35 through 40: Taxable Income and Computation

What you'll need

- *Form 1040*
- 1040 Booklet

Optional

- *Schedule D, Capital Gains and Losses*
- *Form 8615, Tax Computation for Children Under Age 14 Who Have Investment Income Over $1,200*
- Tax calculation worksheet from the *Schedule D* instructions.

What it's all about

In this chapter we will address two issues: the subtraction of the personal exemption amounts from gross income and the calculation of your tax liability. We have worked our way through the bulk of the *Form 1040* and reported income (in the form of just about anything you can think of) and outgo (in the form of allowable adjustments and deductions). There is one more reduction of income available before arriving at taxable income. This is the exemption amount. For most, this means reducing income by a specific dollar amount—a very clear-cut and easy calculation.

But what is a very simple procedure for most taxpayers has turned into a nightmare for high-income taxpayers. In years past, no matter what your income, you simply multiplied the number of exemptions by the dollar amount allowed. The year 1991 saw the advent of something called phase-out of personal exemptions. This involves reducing your normal exemption amount by 2 percent for every $2,500, or fraction thereof, that your adjusted gross income exceeds the following amounts:

- Married filing joint $167,700
- Qualifying widow(er) $167,700
- Head of household $139,750
- Single $111,800
- Married filing separate $83,850

Sound confusing? Well, it is. But, the following worksheet will lead you through the calculations. Use this worksheet only if the amount on *Form 1040*, Line 32, is more than the dollar amount shown on Line 3 of the worksheet. If the amount on Line 32 is equal to or less than the dollar amount shown on Line 3, multiply $2,450 by the total number of exemptions claimed on *Form 1040*, Line 6e, and enter the result on Line 36.

Deduction For Exemption Worksheet

1. Multiply $2,450 by the total number of exemptions claimed on *Form 1040*, Line 6e. 1.______

2. Enter the amount from *Form 1040*, Line 32. 2.______

3. Enter on Line 3 the amount shown below for your filing status. 3.______
   - Married filing separate, enter $83,850
   - Single, enter $111,800
   - Married filing joint or qualifying widow(er) enter $167,700
   - Head of household enter $139,750

4. Subtract Line 3 from Line 2. If zero or less, *stop here*; enter the amount from Line 1 above on *Form 1040*, Line 36. 4.______

   Note: If Line 4 is more than $122,500 (more than $61,250 if married filing separately), *stop here*; you cannot take a deduction for exemptions. Enter zero on *Form 1040*, Line 36.

5. Divide Line 4 by $2,500 ($1,250 if married filing separately). If the result is not a whole number, round it up to the next higher whole number. 5.______

6. Multiply Line 5 by 2 percent (.02) and enter the result as a decimal amount. 6.______

7. Multiply Line 1 by Line 6. 7.______

8. Deduction for exemptions. Subtract Line 7 from Line 1. Enter the result here and on *Form 1040*, Line 36. 8.______

Now that you have removed as much as possible from income, what remains is a very important figure labeled taxable income. This is the amount upon which the actual calculation of tax is made. There are four methods of calculating tax. The one you use will be dictated by the amount and source of your income.

1. **Tax table.** This is the easiest method and the one used by most taxpayers. If your taxable income is under $100,000 and you have no net capital gains or Kiddie Tax, then this is the one for you. You just follow the chart found in the 1040 instruction booklet.
2. **Tax rate schedules.** This is for those with taxable income over $100,000 who have no net capital gain or Kiddie Tax. It is just an extension of the tax table, but presented as a formula rather than as a chart. It is a series of four schedules that correspond to your filing status:

   - **Schedule X.** Use this if you're filing status is single.
   - **Schedule Y-1.** Use this if your filing status is married filing joint or qualifying widow(er).
   - **Schedule Y-2.** Use this if your filing status is married filing separate.
   - **Schedule Z.** Use this if your filing status is head of household.

3. ***Schedule D* Worksheet.** Use this if your marginal tax rate is over 28 percent and you had any net capital gain. The highest tax rate on a net capital gain is 28 percent, so the tax on any portion of your income that is capital gains will be held to that rate, while the rate on your ordinary income may be significantly greater. Use the *Schedule D* worksheet to compute tax only if you have capital gain income and your taxable income is above the following:

   - Married filing joint $91,850
   - Qualifying widow(er) $91,850
   - Head of household $78,700
   - Single $55,100
   - Married filing separate $45,925

4. ***Form 8615.*** This is the method used for the Kiddie Tax. It is a method of calculating tax for children under age 14 who have investment income of more that $1,200 and are filing their own return. The parents can include the child's investment income on their own return and not have to file this particular form. They will, however, have to attach *Form 8814, Parents' Election to Report Child's Interest and Dividends*, to their own return. See Appendix A for a more detailed explanation of Kiddie Tax.

In 1992, the top tax bracket was 31 percent. In 1993, this jumped to 36 percent for individuals with taxable income of $115,000 ($140,000 for married filing jointly, $125,000 for married filing separately). Those high-income taxpayers with taxable income over $250,000 are subject to an additional 10 percent surcharge. Combine this with the restrictions on exemptions and deductions for high-income taxpayers and it is possible to pay an effective marginal rate of 42 percent! Marginal tax rate is the rate of tax that you pay on your last dollar of taxable income. Of course, not all your income is taxed at that rate, just that above $250,000. That 28-percent maximum rate on capital gains looks attractive by comparison. There is no doubt that we will see some shifting of investments to create capital gains rather than ordinary income.

What to do with the forms

35	Subtract line 34 from line 32	35	
36	If line 32 is $83,850 or less, multiply $2,450 by the total number of exemptions claimed on line 6e. If line 32 is over $83,850, see the worksheet on page 24 for the amount to enter .	36	
37	**Taxable income.** Subtract line 36 from line 35. If line 36 is more than line 35, enter -0- .	37	
38	Tax. Check if from a ☐ Tax Table, b ☐ Tax Rate Schedules, c ☐ Capital Gain Tax Worksheet, or d ☐ Form 8615 (see page 24). Amount from Form(s) 8814 ▶ e	38	
39	Additional taxes. Check if from a ☐ Form 4970 b ☐ Form 4972	39	
40	Add lines 38 and 39. . . . . ▶	40	

Form 1040 Line 35, Subtraction of Line 34 from Line 32. This line is your adjusted gross income reduced by your deductions (standard or itemized).

Form 1040 Line 36, Exemption amount. The majority of taxpayers will simply multiply the number of exemptions (shown on Line 6e) by $2,450 and enter that amount here.

Remember that if you are claimed as a dependent on someone else's return, you cannot claim an exemption for yourself on your own return. In this case, you should put a big zero here.

If your adjusted gross income is high enough to require you to "phase out" your exemptions, you will need to use the chart and worksheet included earlier in this chapter to compute the amount put on Line 36.

Form 1040 Line 37, Taxable income. Subtract Line 36 from Line 35. If the result is a negative amount, just enter a zero.

Form 1040 Line 38, Tax. Check the box that tells the IRS which method you used to calculate your tax liability and then enter the amount of that liability here.

Form 1040 Line 38a, Tax table. Refer to the chart using your filing status and taxable income as a guide.

Form 1040 Line 38b, Tax rate schedules. Perform math calculations indicated within the schedule corresponding to your filing status.

Form 1040 Line 38c. Use *Schedule D* Tax Worksheet found in *Schedule D* instructions. This worksheet accompanying *Schedule D* instructions will lead you through step-by-step separation of income taxed at capital gains rates and at ordinary rates. The combined amount of total tax is carried forward from *Schedule D* Tax Worksheet to *Form 1040* Line 38.

Form 1040 Line 38d. *Form 8615, Tax for Children Under Age 14 Who Have Investment Income of More Than $1,200,* is used only when filing a return for your child under age 14 who has investment income of over $1,200. Line 1 through Line 18 of *Form 8615* will lead you through a calculation to insure that income over the $1,200 is taxed at the higher of the parent's or the child's rate. This larger amount is the end result on Line 18 of *Form 8615,* which is then carried forward to Line 38 of your child's *Form 1040*. Remember, this is a tax calculation for use only when filing a completely separate return for your child under age 14.

Form 1040 Line 38e. *Form 8814, Parents' Election to Report Child's Interest and Dividends,* is a form to attach to your own return to include the income of your child under age 14 on your own return. If you do this, your child will not have to file a return. The tax calculated on this form is to be included with your own tax as calculated on Lines 38a through 38c. Just indicate how much of your total tax on Line 38 of *Form 1040* is carried forward from Line 8 of *Form 8814*.

Form 1040 Line 39, Additional taxes. Check the box indicating what additional tax you're referring to and then enter the amount of that tax here. These are taxes on accumulation distribution of trusts or on lump sum distributions. Most likely, you will not have an entry for this line. If you do, you may wish to seek professional advice.

Form 1040 Line 40. Add Lines 38 and 39.

Watch out!

Lump sum distributions may qualify for special tax treatment. These taxes are reported on Line 39. There are, of course, restrictions upon just what qualifies these distributions for the special treatment. Seek professional advice!

What if?

Q. I'm not very good at math. What if I make a mistake and calculate my tax wrong?
A. Never fear. One of the first things the IRS does with your return is perform a math check. If you have made an error, your tax liability will simply be adjusted to the correct amount, and you'll be notified of the adjustment. You are not alone in your fear of math, and such adjustments take place frequently. In fact, the IRS instructions to *Form 1040* even explain conditions under which they will calculate your tax for you. One of the primary reasons the IRS is pushing electronic filing so hard is to eliminate math errors—those made by taxpayers when preparing their returns, as well as those made by the IRS when processing those returns.

Chapter Twenty-Three

Lines 41 through 46: Credits

What you'll need

- *Form 2441, Child and Dependent Care Expenses*
- *Schedule R, Credit for the Elderly or Disabled*
- *Form 1040*
- 1040 Booklet

Optional

- *IRS Publication 503, Child and Dependent Car Expenses*
- *IRS Publication 524, Credit for the Elderly or the Disabled*
- *IRS Publication 554, Tax Information for Older Americans*
- *Form 1116, Foreign Tax Credit*
- *Form 3800, General Business Credit*
- *Form 8396, Mortgage Interest Credit*
- *Form 8801, Credit for Prior Year Minimum Tax*

What it's all about

The mere mention of the word "credit" is enough to set a tax accountant's heart all aflutter. Why? Because a "credit," in tax parlance, means a dollar-for-dollar reduction in your tax liability.

The credits that are most likely to benefit the readers of this book are the *credit for the elderly or disabled* and the *child and dependent care credit*. This chapter will, therefore, focus on these two credits and the forms they require.

Credit for the elderly or the disabled

With the advent of more generous retirement plans and Social Security benefits, few taxpayers actually qualify for this credit. Most people whose income is low enough to qualify don't have a tax liability anyway. And, unlike the earned income credit, the credit for the elderly or the disabled is not a refundable credit. So if you don't owe any tax, the credit does you no good.

To be eligible for the credit, you must either be over age 65 by the end of 1994 or, if under age 65, you must be retired on permanent and total disability before reaching mandatory retirement age before January 1, 1994, according to your employer's retirement program (receiving taxable disability income). You must have a physician's statement certifying your disability. This statement is at the bottom of page 1 of *Schedule R*. This certification has to be made every year unless your doctor signs on Line B, which states that there is no reasonable probability that the disabled condition will ever improve. In this case, just the one-time certification will be sufficient for future years.

Generally, if you are single, head of a household or a qualifying widow(er), your AGI cannot be above $17,500 and you must have received less than $5,000 of nontaxable benefits. If your AGI is in this range, chances are good that none of your Social Security benefits are taxable. So you will completely miss out on the credit if you receive over $5,000 in benefits.

Credit for the elderly or the disabled is detailed on *Schedule R*. This is a two-page form that determines your eligibility for the credit on page 1 and calculates the amount of credit on page 2.

Basically, the credit is 15 percent of a base amount, which is determined by your filing status and, if married, whether one or both of you qualify and whether one or both of you are over age 65. This base amount is reduced by any nontaxable pension or disability benefits and any nontaxable Social Security benefits. Then it is further reduced by one-half the amount that your AGI is over yet a different base amount.

Does all this sound awfully confusing, especially for someone who is elderly or disabled? Thankfully, the IRS will compute the credit for you. Simply complete page 1 of *Schedule R* certifying to your eligibility and attach it to your return. Because this option is available and because the actual computation of the credit on page 2 of *Schedule R* is no bed of roses, we are not including line-by-line instructions.

Child and dependent care credit

The childcare credit is a tax break for those folks who have to pay for childcare in order to work. If you're married, you must both work in order to qualify. However, one of you can be a full-time student in order to satisfy this requirement. But don't expect a tax break for paying a babysitter so you can go shopping while your spouse is at work. This credit is strictly for those who are working but feeling the pinch when spending a chunk of their paycheck for childcare. In order to provide an incentive to remain working, the tax code provides a credit of inverse proportion to your earnings. If you earn under $10,000, your credit is calculated at 30 percent of your qualified childcare expense. For every increase of $2,000 in earnings, the rate of credit drops 1 percent until it is reduced to 20 percent for $28,000 and above in earnings.

We mentioned "qualified" childcare expense. As you might expect, there are restrictions not only on dollar amounts allowed, but also on who provides the care and who qualifies as a child. You can only declare expenses incurred for the care of a maximum of two children for a maximum amount of $2,400 apiece. So the maximum amount of qualified expense will be $4,800.

You cannot pay relatives to provide the care if they are your dependent or your children under age 19, whether or not they are your dependents. So don't try paying your 18-year-old daughter to watch your 5-year-old. Actually, you're more than welcome to pay her, just don't claim a tax credit for it!

And finally, the children cared for must be under age 13. This part of the tax code probably contributes greatly to the proliferation of latchkey children in America. Remember what we said about tax legislation effecting social change? This credit isn't strictly for care of young children, however. It also covers care provided to spouses or dependents who are physically or mentally unable to care for themselves.

What to do with the forms

Child and dependent care expenses are detailed on *Form 2441*.

Form 2441 Part I. This part of the form requests information on who you paid and how much you paid them.

Form 2441 Line 1. You must provide the name, address, Social Security number or employer identification number and the amount paid to each care provider. You would be amazed at the decrease in childcare credit claims since the IRS started demanding Social Security numbers of care providers. As you can well imagine, the IRS has a good matching program in place here.

Form 2441 Line 2. Add up amounts paid to all care providers listed.

Form 2441 Line 3. Enter the number of qualifying persons cared for during the year. Generally, a qualifying person is your child under age 13, your disabled spouse, or any disabled person you can claim as a dependent.

Does your employer help you out with childcare expenses? If he or she just increased your pay, then that has been included in Box 1 of your *W-2* as taxable income and is technically not childcare benefits, just an increase in gross wages. But you may have an employee benefit plan where you work to pay for dependent care. This is an arrangement that requires special reporting. Those payments have been deducted by your employer as a business expense, but they have not been taxed to you as income. Do you think the IRS is going to let you claim a tax credit for something paid out of tax-free dollars? Think again! So if you do receive such benefits, go to Part III before completing Part II. If you did not receive such assistance, go directly to Part II.

Form 2441, Part II. This section leads you through computation of the credit.

Form 2441 Line 4. Enter qualified expenses paid during the year. This is the lesser of actual expenses or a fixed amount of $2,400 for one child, $4,800 for two or more.

Form 2441 Lines 5-6. Enter your earned income and your spouse's earned income (if married filing joint). Earned income typically includes wages, tips and other employee compensation. If you or your spouse were a full-time student or disabled for all or part of the year, earned income for that part of the year is considered to be $200 ($400 if two or more qualifying persons were cared for) for each month you were a student or disabled.

Form 2441 Line 7. Enter the smallest of Lines 4, 5 or 6. This limits your credit to the lesser of qualified expenses, your earned income, or your spouse's earned income. In other words, if you earn less than you pay in childcare, you can only use the amount of your earnings to compute the credit.

Form 2441 Line 8. Enter your AGI from *Form 1040* Line 32.

Form 2441 Line 9. Enter the percentage amount from the chart provided here that corresponds to your AGI.

Form 2441 Line 10. This amount is generally Line 7 multiplied by Line 9. This is your allowable childcare credit and should be entered on *Form 1040* Line 41.

40	Add lines 38 and 39 . . . . ▶		40	
41	Credit for child and dependent care expenses. Attach Form 2441	41		
42	Credit for the elderly or the disabled. Attach Schedule R . .	42		
43	Foreign tax credit. Attach Form 1116	43		
44	Other credits (see page 25). Check if from a ☐ Form 3800 b ☐ Form 8396 c ☐ Form 8801 d ☐ Form (specify)______	44		
45	Add lines 41 through 44		45	
46	Subtract line 45 from line 40. If line 45 is more than line 40, enter -0- . . . . . . ▶		46	
47	Self-employment tax. Attach Schedule SE		47	

Form 2441, Part III. Complete this section (which is page 2 of *Form 2441*) if you received dependent care benefits from your employer. This section is a little confusing, but its purpose is to determine if any of your expenses will qualify for the credit. If they do qualify, then you will return to Part II to actually compute the credit.

Form 2441 Line 11. Enter the dependent care benefits you received for the year. This amount should have been reported to you in Box 10 of your *W-2*.

Form 2441 Line 12. If you did not use the entire amount of benefits you had your employer set aside for the year, you had a forfeited benefit. Enter this amount here.

Form 2441 Line 13. Subtract Line 12 from Line 11.

Form 2441 Lines 14-18. These are duplicates of Lines 4 through 7 in Part II. See instructions in Part II regarding qualified expenses and earned income.

Form 2441 Line 19. Enter the amount of excluded benefits. This is limited by law to $5,000. This means $5,000 is the maximum that your employer can provide in dependent care benefits without you having to declare it as income.

Form 2441 Line 20. Subtract Line 19 from Line 13. This is the amount of any dependent care benefit you received that is over the qualified expense to be considered for the credit. This amount needs to be included as income on *Form 1040* Line 7. What a drag, you start out thinking you're going to get this mondo credit and instead you end up with even more taxable income. Frustration...thy name be taxes!

Form 2441 Line 21. Enter amount of qualified expenses above and beyond any excluded benefits. In other words, do not count amounts on Line 19.

Form 2441 Line 22. Enter $2,400 ($4,800 for two or more qualifying persons).

Form 2441 Line 23. Enter excluded benefits (amount from Line 19).

Form 2441 Line 24. Subtract Line 23 from Line 22. If the result is zero or less, you have no expenses eligible for the credit, so stop here. Just because you can't claim a tax credit doesn't mean you shouldn't file the form with your return, however. Don't forget that the benefits you received from your employer have been reported in Box 10 of your *W-2* and so the IRS computers will be looking for it.

Form 2441 Line 25. Enter the smaller of Line 21 or Line 24. This is the amount of your qualifying expenses. Carry this amount forward to Part II, Line 4 and follow the above instructions for completing Part II to figure the credit.

Form 1040 Lines 41-45. All credits are computed on separate forms with the resulting amounts carried forward to Lines 41-44 of *Form 1040*. These are then all added together on Line 45.

Form 1040 Line 46. Subtract Line 45 from Line 40. This reduces your tax liability by the amount of credits you are claiming.

Watch out!

If you pay a care provider to work in your home, you are most likely subject to the rules governing household employees. Refer to *IRS Publication 926, Employment Taxes for Household Employers*.

* * *

Child support payments are *not* childcare expenses, nor are they alimony. Tough luck!

* * *

Other rarely used credits that we have not discussed are the foreign tax credit, general business credit, mortgage interest credit and credit for prior year minimum tax. If you feel you may qualify for one of these obscure credits, you will need to do some further research.

What if?

Q. Can I deduct as childcare the cost of summer camp for my kids?
A. No. Overnight camp no longer qualifies. The tax code considers that more recreation than *childcare*. A day camp where the kids return home every evening does qualify.

Chapter Twenty-Four

Line 47: Self-Employment Tax

What you'll need

- *Schedule SE, Self-Employment Tax*
- *Form 1040*
- 1040 Booklet

Optional

- *IRS Publication 517, Social Security & Other Information for Members of the Clergy*
- *IRS Publication 533, Self-Employment Tax*
- *Schedule K-1* from *Form 1065, Partnership Income Tax Return*

What it's all about

Do you have earnings from self-employment of $400 or more? If so, you are subject to a special tax.

Self-employment tax is the contribution to Social Security on behalf of the self-employed taxpayer. It is *not* an income tax. Unlike an employee who has Social Security and Medicare withheld from his or her paycheck, the self-employed individual adds amounts for these onto his or her income tax liability right here on *Form 1040*.

Because it is paid along with income tax, it isn't always clearly identified in taxpayers' minds. All the self-employed person knows is that his or her tax bite is horrendous. What is important to realize is that a portion of that bite is not income tax, but Social Security contributions. Unfortunately, the bite has grown so large, it threatens to flat-out devour some unsuspecting, self-employed taxpayers. This tax has grown so disproportionately over the past 15 years that it is not an uncommon occurrence when self-employment tax is more than double a taxpayer's regular tax liability. It is also not uncommon for our clients to abandon plans to start up a small business when confronted with the prospect of over 50 percent tax when self-employment tax is factored in. This is particularly true for spouses.

Generally, if you have net earnings from self-employment of at least $400 for the year, you are subject to this self-employment tax. Any *W-2* wages earned will be taken into account when calculating tax due. Self-employment earnings are generally from sole proprietorships (*Schedule C*) or farms (*Schedule F*). If you have more than one source of self-employment income, you combine the net earnings from each business. Therefore, a loss in one will reduce income in another for purposes of calculating your income subject to self-employment tax.

Most taxpayers can use the *Short Schedule SE* on page 1 of *Schedule SE.* Use the flow chart on the front of *Schedule SE* to determine if you have to use the *Long Schedule SE*, which is on page 2 of the form.

The *Long Schedule SE* is most commonly needed only if you had wages or tips, which, when combined with your self-employment earnings, were over the Social Security withholding limits. It is also required if you have unreported tip income or are calculating your earnings under an optional method.

Optional methods allow you to report more than your actual earnings for purposes of calculating the self-employment tax. Is this crazy or what? Who in the world would choose to increase their tax? People planning ahead might. Social Security benefits are based upon your earnings. If you have a year with exceptionally low earnings or a loss, it could have an adverse effect on your Social Security benefits down the road. This optional method increases your Social Security participation when profits are low or nonexistent, thereby insuring that you will maximize your retirement benefits. But can we be frank here? There is probably no more foolhardy investment on this planet than a voluntary contribution to Social Security. Unless, of course, you're contemplating buying the exclusive rights to sell hot dogs in October at Wrigley Field.

What to do with the forms

45	Add lines 41 through 44	45		
46	Subtract line 45 from line 40. If line 45 is more than line 40, enter -0- . . . . . . ▶	46		
47	Self-employment tax. Attach Schedule SE	47		
48	Alternative minimum tax. Attach Form 6251	48		
49	Recapture taxes. Check if from a ☐ Form 4255 b ☐ Form 8611 c ☐ Form 8828 . .	49		

Form 1040 Line 47, Self-employment tax. Enter the amount from *Schedule SE*, Line 5 if using *Short Schedule SE* or Line 12 if using *Long Schedule SE*.

Schedule SE Line 1, Net farm profit Enter *Schedule F* earnings plus any partnership earnings.

Schedule SE Line 2, Net profit from *Schedule C*. Enter *Schedule C* or *C-EZ* earnings plus any partnership earnings.

Schedule SE Line 3. Combine Lines 1 and 2.

Schedule SE Line 4, Net earnings from self-employment. Multiply Line 3 by .9235. This is a cushion to soften the impact of having to serve as both employee and employer when paying this tax. If the amount on Line 4 is less than $400, you do not have to pay any self-employment tax. You may want to, however...remember the optional method.

Schedule SE Line 5, Self-employment tax. If the amount on Line 4 is $60,600 or less, multiply Line 4 by 15.3 percent. If it is over $60,600 multiply the amount over $60,600 by .029, add $7,514.40 and enter the total on Line 5.

Schedule SE Line 6, Deduction for one-half of self-employment tax. Calculate one-half of Line 5 and enter here. This will be carried forward to *Form 1040*, Line 25.

Watch out!

Net income from self-employment also includes your share of ordinary income or loss as well as guaranteed payments from a partnership that is engaged in a trade or business. Such amounts will be reported to you as net earnings from self-employment on a *Schedule K-1* sent to you by the partnership.

* * *

Self-employment tax is computed separately for each spouse if married filing joint. Married taxpayers cannot combine their earnings to arrive at a net figure for self-employment income when calculating self-employment tax. However, both of you are jointly and individually liable for the payment of the tax!

* * *

If you have unreported tip income, you will need to complete *Form 4137, Social Security and Medicare Tax on Unreported Tip Income.*

* * *

If you are a member of the clergy, special rules apply. See *IRS Publication 517, Social Security and Other Information for Members of the Clergy.*

* * *

Don't forget self-employment tax when computing estimated tax payments for next year.

What if?

Q. When I started my small business in 1978, the maximum self-employment income subject to SE tax was $17,700 and the rate was 8.1 percent. Now the maximum Social Security income is $60,600 (Medicare income is unlimited) and the rate is 15.3 percent and going up. Why has my self-employment tax increased from $1,434 to more than $11,000 (over 700 percent) from 1978 to 1994?

A. Ask your Congressman!!!

Chapter Twenty-Five

Line 48: Alternative Minimum Tax

What you'll need

- *Form 6251, Alternative Minimum Tax for Individuals*
- *Form 1040*
- 1040 Booklet

Optional

- *IRS Publication 909, Alternative Minimum Tax for Individuals*
- *Form 8801, Credit for Prior Year Minimum Tax*
- *IRS Publication 534, Depreciation*

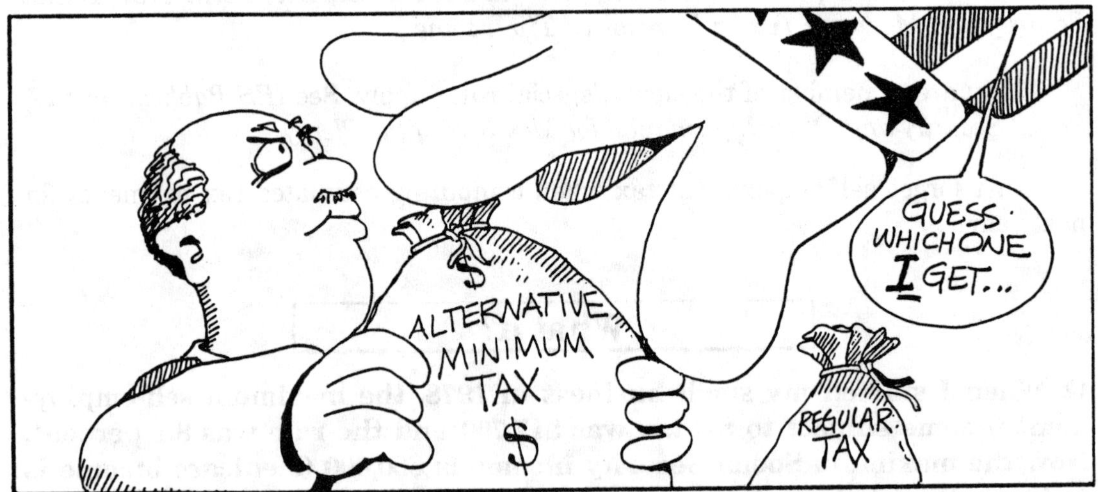

What it's all about

Just when you thought you could come up with some clever way to enjoy high income but pay little tax, along comes the AMT. It is a different method of calculating tax to insure that those high-income taxpayers who are able to avoid regular in-come tax *do* pay their fair share. Since the inception of the Internal Revenue Code back in 1913, special tax breaks have been granted to certain taxpayers. Over time, Congress added more breaks in the form of special deductions and credits.

Some taxpayers are better than others at taking advantage of all the tax breaks. Typically, those who benefit most are high-income individuals who use the services of CPAs, tax attorneys and financial planners (those who owe their livelihood to a tax code so complex, only *they* can figure it out).

When taxpayers and their advisors became too adept at avoiding tax by figuring out loopholes, Congress said enough! Instead of trying to close all possible loopholes, they created the AMT.

Most taxpayers are not subject to the AMT. For that matter, most taxpayers have never even heard of it. But since the AMT rate has risen steadily every year since its inception in 1986 (that wonderful year of tax simplification), it is ensnaring more and more taxpayers. So it is something you should at least be aware of. You should know that there is this special system operating side by side with our regular income tax, and that your actual tax liability is the greater of the two.

It works like this: If your income is over a certain amount after adjusting for some tax breaks, then you are subject to this tax. It's a straightforward concept akin to the flat tax that everyone says would never work. The AMT simply gives you a standard exemption amount based upon filing status, allows very few deductions and then assesses a flat rate. This single, flat rate did become two-tiered in 1993.

The starting point for AMT calculations is your taxable income, which may reflect some of those tax breaks we mentioned. From that you must take into account AMT adjustments and tax preference items.

And just what are AMT adjustments and tax preference items? They are generally items of income that go untaxed, or special deductions to your income. For instance, tax-exempt interest on private-issue (not government) bonds is taxable for AMT purposes, passive activity gains and losses are refigured, deductions for depreciation are refigured, value of stock options exercised is taken into account, and many itemized deductions are eliminated. These are just a few of the more common items considered for AMT purposes. Obviously, some adjustments will be additions to your income and some will be reductions in your deductions.

If you have a large number of deductions and credits, you may want to look a little further into this AMT business if your taxable income plus any AMT adjustments and tax preference items exceed the following:

- $45,000 Married filing joint or qualifying widow(er)
- $33,750 Single or head of household
- $22,500 Married filing separate

What to do with the forms

47	Self-employment tax. Attach Schedule SE	47		
48	Alternative minimum tax. Attach Form 6251	48		
49	Recapture taxes. Check if from a ☐ Form 4255 b ☐ Form 8611 c ☐ Form 8828 . .	49		
50	Social security and Medicare tax on tip income not reported to employer. Attach Form 4137 .	50		
51	Tax on qualified retirement plans, including IRAs. If required, attach Form 5329	51		
52	Advance earned income credit payments from Form W-2	52		

The calculation for AMT is performed on *Form 6251*. On this form you will complete a totally separate calculation of tax, utilizing different taxable income and different tax rates. This is not an easy form to complete and for this reason we do not provide line-by-line instructions. We offer the following general explanation instead.

The form begins with your taxable income from *Form 1040*, Line 35. It then makes all the adjustments needed to arrive at your taxable income for AMT purposes. It then reduces this by a standard exemption amount, which, to further complicate matters, is phased out for high-income taxpayers. Then the AMT tax itself is calculated. At the bottom of the form, you compare the AMT tax to the regular tax from *Form 1040*, Line 38. Uncle Sam wants the larger of the two amounts. So if the AMT tax is the larger, you will enter the difference between the two amounts onto *Form 1040*, Line 48 as the AMT amount. If the AMT tax is the smaller, forget everything. You don't need to file *Form 6251* after all!

Watch out!

Since completion of this form is beyond the scope of this book, we suggest that if you suspect you may fall under the AMT rules, you thoroughly read *IRS Publication 909, Alternative Minimum Tax for Individuals*. Chances are that if you have special income and deductions that throw you into the AMT trap, you are already making regular visits to a CPA. If not, you might want to consider doing so!

What if?

Q. I'm having a hard enough time figuring out my regular tax. How in the world can I be expected to understand all this?

A. Relax, most taxpayers don't even have to worry about AMT. The whole point of the alternative minimum tax is just to close some loopholes, not to confuse the ordinary taxpayer. Therefore, unless you have some substantial AMT adjustments or tax preference items, the AMT won't come into play on your return.

Chapter Twenty-Six

Lines 49 through 53: Other Taxes

What you'll need

- *Form 4137, Social Security and Medicare Tax on Unreported Tip Income*
- *Form 5329, Return for Additional Taxes Attributable to Qualified Retirement Plans*
- *Form 1040*
- 1040 Booklet

Optional

- *IRS Publication 531, Reporting Income from Tips*
- *IRS Publication 575, Pension and Annuity Income*
- *IRS Publication 590, Individual Retirement Arrangements*

What it's all about

In addition to the taxes we've already discussed, you may be subject to still more. As a general rule, if you ever claim a tax credit for business purposes, you may have to repay the credit if you cease the activity that gave rise to the credit in the first place. This repayment comes in the form of an additional tax, referred to as a recapture tax.

Another tax, the tax on tip income, is quite simply the collection of a tax on your income that was not collected during the year since your employer was not aware of the income.

A third tax is the tax code equivalent of a behavior modification technique. This is the tax on disallowed retirement plan contributions and withdrawals. If you decide to take your retirement funds out early, or put in too much, or take out too little, you're going to get whacked with regular tax *plus* an additional tax.

The fourth item included as another tax is advanced Earned Income Credit payments. This is technically not a tax, it is just an advance you may have received from your employer. This amount can be found on your *W-2* and entered directly onto *Form 1040*.

What to do with the forms

46	Subtract line 45 from line 40. If line 45 is more than line 40, enter -0- . . . . . . ▶	46	
47	Self-employment tax. Attach Schedule SE	47	
48	Alternative minimum tax. Attach Form 6251	48	
49	Recapture taxes. Check if from a ☐ Form 4255 b ☐ Form 8611 c ☐ Form 8828 . .	49	
50	Social security and Medicare tax on tip income not reported to employer. Attach Form 4137 .	50	
51	Tax on qualified retirement plans, including IRAs. If required, attach Form 5329	51	
52	Advance earned income credit payments from Form W-2	52	
53	Add lines 46 through 52. This is your total tax. . . . . ▶	53	

Form 1040 Lines 49-53. As a practical matter, most taxpayers will not ever be confronted with recapture tax. We will not discuss Line 49, since it applies to a very limited group of taxpayers. Nor will we address Line 52. We will, however, look at Lines 50 and 51, tax on tip income and tax on retirement plan distributions. These two taxes are far more common and more likely to be applicable to readers of this book.

To determine tax on tip income, you'll need to complete *Form 4137*.

Form 4137, Social Security and Medicare Tax on Unreported Tip Income. This form is used to compute the Social Security and Medicare taxes that would have been withheld, had you reported the tips to your employer. Since it wasn't done during the year, IRS figures now is as good a time as any to collect the funds.

If you work in an occupation where part of your compensation is in the form of tips and you received tips of $20 or more in a calendar month that you did *not* report to your employer, or if your *W-2* reports allocated tips, you must file *Form 4137*.

You may be able to report an amount less than shown in Box 8 (allocated tips) of your *W-2* if you maintain good records documenting that your actual tips were less than the amount of allocated tips reported by your employer. Likewise, if you had more tips than reported, you should report the larger amount.

Form 4137 Line 1. Report *all* tips received during the year. Include any allocated tips reported on your *W-2* unless you have kept records showing that you received less. If this is the case, attach a short statement with this form stating that you have such records and that is why you are reporting less.

Form 4137 Line 2. Enter tips you reported to your employer.

Form 4137 Line 3. Subtract Line 2 from Line 1. This amount must be included with your wages reported on *Form 1040* Line 7.

Form 4137 Line 4. Enter tips you were not required to report because they totaled less than $20 in a calendar month.

Form 4137 Line 5. Subtract Line 4 from Line 3. Also enter this amount on Line 2 of *Schedule U*.

Form 4137 Line 6. This is the Social Security wage maximum for 1994 preprinted.

Form 4137 Line 7. Enter total of all wages and tips reported on all *W-2s*.

Form 4137 Line 8. Subtract Line 7 from Line 6.

Form 4137 Line 9. Enter smaller of amounts on Lines 5 and 8. Also enter this amount down at the bottom of this same form on *Schedule U* Line 1.

Form 4137 Line 10. Multiply Line 9 by .062. This is the computation for Social Security tax.

Form 4137 Line 11. Multiply Line 5 by .0145. This is the computation for Medicare tax.

Form 4137 Line 12. Add Lines 10 and 11. Enter total on *Form 1040* Line 50.

Form 5329, Return for Additional Taxes Attributable to Qualified Retirement Plans (Including IRAs) Annuities, and Modified Endowment Contracts. If the title hasn't already caused you to slam the book shut, let's take a look at this form. Actually, *Form 5329*'s bark is worse than its bite. If you are subject to this tax, completing the form is really quite painless. The tax "bite," on the other hand, can be quite painful. The form is divided into four sections, each treating a different offense that will be punishable by an additional tax.

Form 5329 Part I, Tax on early distributions. Normally, you cannot begin to draw upon your retirement funds until age 59½. If you withdraw retirement funds too early, you will owe a 10-percent tax on the amount you withdraw. This is in addition to having to include it in your taxable income (it was never taxed, remember?). Add this to a state income tax if you have one and you could end up with only half your money left! That thought should help you resist the urge to dip into retirement funds unless absolutely necessary.

Form 5329 Line 1. Enter taxable distributions from retirement plans included in gross income.

Form 5329 Line 2. See *IRS Publication 575, Pension and Annuity Income*, for exceptions and/or IRS instructions to *Form 5329* for these special exceptions and the exception number if applicable. The most common exceptions are distributions from nondeductible contributions, distributions because of disability and distributions made after the owner's death.

Form 5329 Line 3. Subtract Line 2 from Line 1.

Form 5329 Line 4. Multiply Line 3 by 10 percent. This additional tax due to an early distribution should also be entered on *Form 1040* Line 51.

Form 5329 Part II Tax on excess contributions to Individual Retirement Arrangement. You have limits imposed on your IRA contributions. When you exceed these limits, you are assessed a stiff penalty equal to the lesser of 6 percent of your excess contribution or 6 percent of the value of your IRA on Dec. 31,

1994. The whole point of this tax is to get you to remove the extra funds. If you don't, you'll pay this same penalty again next year.

Form 5329 Line 5. Enter the excess contributions made to your IRA for the year. This is any funds contributed that are in excess of the limit allowed for your situation. See IRA contributions discussed in Chapter 20, Adjustments to Income.

Form 5329 Lines 6-11. Remember we said that if you don't withdraw the extra funds, you'll be taxed again the following year? This section of the form details any excess contributions from earlier years that have not been withdrawn.

Form 5329 Line 12. Add Lines 5 and 11. This is the total of excess contributions for both this year and earlier years.

Form 5329 Line 13, Tax due. Enter the smaller of 6 percent of Line 12 or 6 percent of the value of your IRA on Dec. 31, 1994. Also enter this amount on *Form 1040* Line 51.

Form 5329 Part III, Tax on excess accumulation in qualified retirement plans. If you have not received the minimum required distribution from your qualified retirement plan, you have an excess accumulation subject to an additional tax. And it is a stiff one! It is 50 percent of the difference between the amount that was required to be distributed and the amount that was actually distributed.

You must start receiving distributions from your IRA by April 1 of the year following the year in which you reach age 70½. At that time, you may receive your entire interest in the IRA, begin receiving periodic distributions calculated over your life expectancy (or the joint life expectancy of you and your designated beneficiary), or receive payments calculated over a shorter period.

Form 5329 Line 14. Figure the minimum required distribution by dividing the account balance of your IRA on December 31 of the year preceding the distribution by the applicable life expectancy. For applicable life expectancies, you must reference the charts in *IRS Publication 590, Individual Retirement Arrangements*.

Form 5329 Line 15. Enter amount you actually took out.

Form 5329 Line 16. Subtract Line 15 from Line 14.

Form 5329 Line 17, Tax Due. Multiply Line 16 by 50 percent. Also enter this amount on *Form 1040* Line 51.

Form 5329 Part IV Tax on excess distributions from qualified retirement plans (including IRAs). If you took out more than $150,000 from your retirement plan during the year, you may be subject to a 15-percent penalty. This is a much more complicated issue than the situations covered by the first three sections of this form. There are special exceptions, special rules for lump sum distributions, a special grandfather provision allowed back in 1987 and 1988 that, if made, will affect tax treatment of this distribution, and so on and so forth. If you took such a sizable sum from your retirement plan or IRA, you most definitely should seek the advice of a tax professional.

Form 1040 Line 53. Add Lines 46 through 52 to determine your total tax.

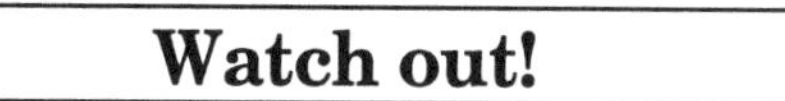

The dollar amount of retirement accumulations can be substantial and so, too, can the tax consequences. You may want to seek the advise of a tax and/or pension expert to see if there are any tax-planning strategies you should keep in mind.

What if?

Q. Why is there a place for my signature at the bottom of *Form 5329*?
A. It is possible that you have an IRA penalty, but you are under the income limits for having to file a tax return. In this case, you can file *Form 5329* all by itself. Just be sure to sign it and enclose a check.

Chapter Twenty-Seven

Lines 54 through 65: Payment and Refund or Amount Due

What you'll need

- *Form 1040*
- 1040 Booklet

Optional

- *Schedule EIC* and worksheets
- *Form 8841, Deferral of Additional 1993 Taxes (if election made last year)*
- *Form 2210, Underpayment of Estimated Tax by Individuals*
- Checkbook at the ready!

What it's all about

Line 53 on *Form 1040* is just what it says—this is your total tax, *not* what you owe. From this amount you will subtract any payments made from:

- Withholding for federal income tax (on your *W-2*)
- 1099 withholding
- Quarterly estimated tax payments
- Overpayment from last year applied to this year
- Payments sent in with extension requests

You will also subtract any other credit toward tax paid. These are:

- Excess Social Security or Railroad Retirement Tax withheld. Did you have more than one job with combined Social Security withholdings in excess of $3,757? If so, you can claim a credit toward your income tax for the excess amount.
- In extremely rare instances you will have a Regulated Investment Company Credit (*Form 2439*) or a Credit for Federal Tax on Fuels (*Form 4136*). Don't get excited. This does not mean you get a credit for all the tax you

pay when filling your tank at the local station. This applies only to certain fuels used in farming or aviation.

The Earned Income Credit is sometimes referred to as a negative income tax. It is what is called a refundable credit. This means that you can actually reduce your tax liability below zero and get a refund of money that you haven't even paid. Initially introduced in the 1970s, Congress seems unable to resist constant tinkering with it. Up to now it was available only if you had a dependent child, but beginning in 1994 the basic credit is now available even to those without qualifying children. Also gone now are the extra credits for health insurance and newborns, which greatly simplifies filling out the forms.

- **No children.** The maximum possible credit is $306. You must have earned income less than $9,000 and you (or spouse) must be over 24 and under 65 years of age.
- **With children.** The maximum possible credit is $2,038 with one qualifying child and $2,527 with two or more.

For those of you who may be overwhelmed by trying to figure out just how much you are eligible for, the IRS will calculate the credit for you. You do have to give them some basic information on *Schedule EIC* (only if you have children qualifying you for the credit) and attach it to your return.

If you prefer to do the calculations yourself, there is a two page Earned Income Credit Worksheet to lead you step by step through the process. The 1040 booklet contains tables to look up the amount of credit based upon your situation and income. The worksheet does *not* go to the IRS as part of your return. It is designed simply to assist you in your calculations and is for your records only. Afraid you'll make a mistake? Don't worry, the IRS will calculate the correct amount and notify you of any difference.

What to do with the forms

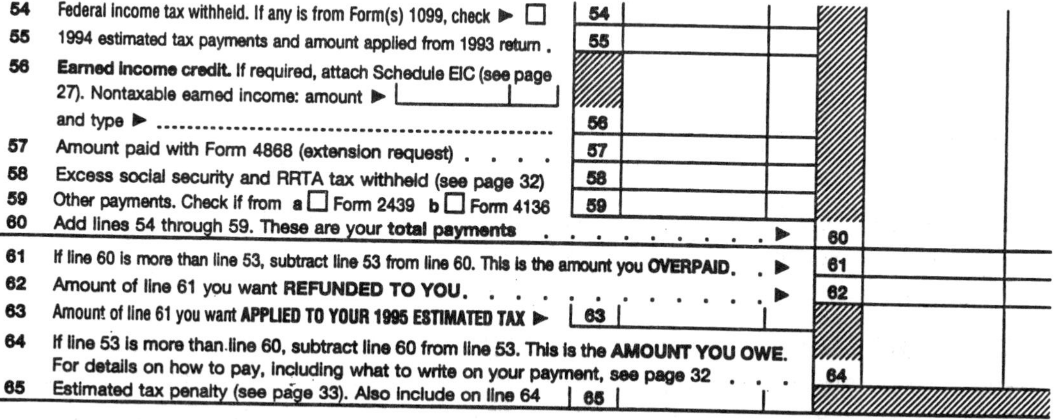

54 Federal income tax withheld. If any is from Form(s) 1099, check ▶ ☐ | 54

55 1994 estimated tax payments and amount applied from 1993 return . | 55

56 **Earned income credit.** If required, attach Schedule EIC (see page 27). Nontaxable earned income: amount ▶ and type ▶ | 56

57 Amount paid with Form 4868 (extension request) . . . . | 57

58 Excess social security and RRTA tax withheld (see page 32) | 58

59 Other payments. Check if from a ☐ Form 2439 b ☐ Form 4136 | 59

60 Add lines 54 through 59. These are your **total payments** . . . . ▶ | 60

61 If line 60 is more than line 53, subtract line 53 from line 60. This is the amount you **OVERPAID**. . ▶ | 61

62 Amount of line 61 you want **REFUNDED TO YOU**. . . . . ▶ | 62

63 Amount of line 61 you want **APPLIED TO YOUR 1995 ESTIMATED TAX** ▶ | 63

64 If line 53 is more than line 60, subtract line 60 from line 53. This is the **AMOUNT YOU OWE**. For details on how to pay, including what to write on your payment, see page 32 . . . | 64

65 Estimated tax penalty (see page 33). Also include on line 64 | 65

Form 1040, Line 54, Federal income tax withheld. Report the total amounts of federal tax withheld from all *W-2s* and *1099s*.

Form 1040, Line 55, 1994 estimated tax payments & amount applied from 1993. Report the total amounts of quarterly estimates and any overpayment on last year's return you did not have refunded but rather applied to this year's liability.

Form 1040, Line 56, Earned Income Credit. Indicate and describe any nontaxable earned income and then (if you figured the amount yourself) enter the EIC credit. Or leave it blank for the IRS to compute.

Form 1040, Line 57, Amount paid with *Form 4868*. Enter the amount of any payments you made at the time of filing your application for extension.

Form 1040 Line 58, Excess Social Security. Enter the amount of any Social Security or RRTA tax withheld in excess of the limits discussed earlier in this chapter. This will occur only if you have wages from more than one job.

Form 1040 Line 59, Other payments. Enter the amount of any credits from *Form 2439, Regulated Investment Company Credit*, or *Form 4136, Credit for Federal Tax on Fuels*.

Form 1040 Line 60, Total payments. Enter the sum of Line 54 through Line 59.

Form 1040 Line 61, Amount of overpayment. If Line 60 is greater than Line 53, subtract Line 53 from Line 60. This is the amount you paid above and beyond what you owed.

Form 1040 Line 62, Amount to be refunded. Enter the amount from Line 61 that you want refunded to you. You can choose to have all, some or none of it refunded. See the next line.

Form 1040 Line 63, Amount to apply to 1995 tax. Enter the amount of your overpayment that you want to apply to next year's tax liability. You can apply your entire refund in this manner, or split the amount of your overpayment between here and a refund on Line 62. In any case, Line 62 and Line 63 have to equal Line 61. See "What if" at the end of this chapter if you elected to defer 1993 additional tax on *Form 8841* last year.

Form 1040 Line 64, Amount you owe. If Line 53 is greater than Line 60, subtract Line 60 from Line 53. This is the amount of tax you still owe. This does not include any penalty or interest. See next line.

Form 1040 Line 65, Estimated penalty. Attach *Form 2210*, which shows your computation of underpayment penalties. Include this amount on Line 64, because this is the total amount you will be paying. If you want, the IRS will calculate the penalty for you. In that case, just leave Line 65 blank and put the amount owed without regard to penalties on Line 64, then sit back and wait for that most pleasant of correspondence, the IRS notice of tax due.

Watch out!

It is possible to receive advance payments of your Earned Income Credit through payroll. You must complete a *Form W-5* for your employer. The amount of advance payments will be shown on your *W-2* and reported on Line 52 of *Form 1040* under Other Taxes. These payments are referred to as Advanced Earned Income Credit Payments.

* * *

If the amount owed with your return is over $500 and more than 10 percent of your total tax liability, you probably owe a penalty for underpayment. You can let the IRS compute the penalty and just pay that bill separately when it arrives. Or you can complete *Form 2210,* which walks you through the calculation of the underpayment penalty. There are special circumstances that may exempt you from any penalty. The one that most frequently applies is if you have paid in at least as much as your total tax from last year. Do complete the questions on page 1 of *Form 2210* to see if you might qualify for an exception. Go ahead and file the *Form 2210* with your return so the IRS will know what you're thinking. Don't worry about trying for it if you're not sure. The IRS will not be shy about telling you that you don't qualify and will just bill you for any interest or penalty.

* * *

If your refund amount is under $1 don't hold your breath waiting for your refund check. The IRS will issue a refund only upon written request. On the other hand, if you owe less than $1 you don't have to pay!

* * *

The safe-harbor to avoid the underpayment of estimated tax penalty for certain high income individuals was changed in 1994. See Appendix B, "New for 1994," for an explanation.

What if?

Q. I think I may be eligible for the Earned Income Credit but I didn't claim it on my return because I didn't understand it. Can I still get it?
A. Yes. Eligibility for the Earned Income Credit is something the IRS computers are programmed to check for. You most likely will be receiving an IRS notice saying that you appear eligible, and asking for some additional information. The IRS is not always trying to squeeze blood out of a turnip. And the tax code giveth, as well as taketh away!

Q. I only had one job and my employer withheld too much Social Security and Medicare tax. Should I report this amount of *Form 1040* Line 58?
A. No. Contact your employer in order to seek reimbursement for this over-withholding.

Q. The increase in 1993 tax rates caused additional tax last year which I elected to pay in three equal installments by filing *Form 8841* with my 1993 tax return. How do I make these installment payments?
A. If you elected to pay the additional 1993 taxes solely due to the rate increases reflected in the 1993 tax rate schedules in three equal annual installments, these installments are due by April 15, 1994; April 17, 1995; and April 15, 1996. The April 15, 1994, installment was part of the tax you paid with your 1993 return. You still have the 1995 and 1996 installments left to pay. Failure to make these payments by the respective April due dates will result in the remaining balance becoming immediately due and payable. You will not be billed for interest as long as your payments are on time. Mail the April 17, 1995, payment separately from your tax return. You should have received (in January 1995) a payment voucher from the IRS to send along with your payment.

If you filed *Form 8841, Deferral of Additional 1993 Taxes,* with your 1993 tax return, you may be able to apply part or all of your refund to your installment due by April 17, 1995. The most you can apply is the amount of your refund, reduced by any payments made after April 17, 1995. Also, you must file your 1994 return on or before its due date, including extensions.

Caution: If you have any other outstanding Federal tax liability (including any other 1993 Federal income tax liability), any refund on your 1994 tax return will first be applied to such a liability before being applied to the installment due. This is true regardless of how you indicate to apply your refund. If the remaining refund is not sufficient to cover the installment due, your installment payment election will be terminated. Any unpaid installments of the additional 1993 Federal income taxes will be due upon notice and demand from the IRS. In addition, you will owe interest and the failure to pay penalty on any remaining balance from the due date of the installment. Therefore, it may be to your advantage to use the separate payment option explained above.

To apply part or all of your refund, on the dotted line next to line 62 write the words "93 OBRA Install." and the amount you want applied. *Do not* reduce the amount on line 62 by the amount applied. If the amount you apply is less than the installment due, you may send a separate check for the balance. *Do not* include a check for the balance with your return.

Q. I am unable to pay the full amount of the tax I owe. Should I delay filing my return until I get the money?
A. Delaying filing your return will only result in additional interest and, possibly, penalty assessments. File your return on time with *Form 9465 Installment Agreement Request* attached. See the forms section of this book for a copy of this form.

Chapter Twenty-Eight

Assembly and Filing Instructions

What you'll need

- Any required attachment schedules
- Any statements of explanation for unusual items on your return
- *Form 1040*

Optional

- Check or money order if tax owing
- Copy of any extension requests or approvals

What it's all about

Now that you have completed the preparation of your return, there are a few very important details to attend to before mailing it off.

- Put the forms in proper sequence. Look at the upper right-hand corner of each form and schedule. There will be a small number just below the large 1994. This is called the attachment sequence number. Simply put all the forms in numerical order using that number. If there is no number, just put that form at the end.

- Make a copy of the return for your records. You can always get a copy back from the IRS, but it will cost $14 and take several weeks.
- Sign and date the return. If it is a joint return, both spouses must sign.
- Attach any *W-2* forms to the face of the return.
- Enclose (do not attach) a check or money order for any tax owed. Always write your Social Security number on the check or money order.
- Attach a copy of any extension request or approval.
- Put sufficient postage on the envelope. Do not trust your judgment on this. Go to the post office and have it weighed. Even if you mail your return on time, it may end up being filed late if it is returned to you for insufficient postage. If a return is filed late, it may result in late filing penalties or cause you to lose certain tax elections that must be made by the due date.
- Mail return and attachments to the address listed at the end of this chapter.

The due date for individual income tax returns is April 15, or the next business day if April 15 falls on a weekend or holiday. If you have a refund coming, it stands to reason that the earlier you get your return in, the earlier you will get your refund check. If, however, you owe money with your return and you are not subject to any underpayment penalty, why rush into things? Might as well have the use of the money for as long as possible. So the rule of thumb is: File early if expecting a refund, and wait until April 15 if you have to pay.

If you are not able to file your return on time, there is help available. File *Form 4868, Application for Automatic Extension of Time to File*, by April 15. Be sure to keep a copy to attach to your return when you do file it. Beware: An extension of time to file is *not* an extension of time to pay. So if you think that you will owe tax, you should send a payment along with the extension request. Although this is an automatic four-month extension (yours just for the asking), it should not be used carelessly because it does not stop the clock from running on interest and penalties.

If at the end of the four-month extension, you still don't have your return completed, you can apply for an additional two months. File *Form 2688, Application for Additional Extension,* by August 15. This one is not automatic and you have to provide a legitimate reason for not filing your return. A legitimate reason might be "awaiting K-1 information." "Just haven't got to it yet" is not a legitimate reason.

Watch out!

If you owe tax but don't have the money to pay it, file your tax return by the due date. Owing the IRS is unpleasant enough without incurring a late filing penalty on top of it! You can expect correspondence from an IRS computer for awhile concerning your unpaid tax, and to be assessed late payment penalties and interest. Generally speaking, you can expect five notices about three weeks apart before you will be turned over to an agent for more intensive collection procedures. If you just send as much money as possible with each billing notice, perhaps you will be all paid up before the computer spits you out.

If you cannot pay the tax due upon receipt of these notices, you may want to contact collections at your local IRS office to arrange a payment plan. Remember, however, that taxpayers have certain rights, even those who are delinquent in their tax payments. Depending on the amount you owe, the years involved when you filed your return and the particular notices sent by IRS, you may want to consult with a CPA or tax attorney to discuss exactly what your rights are.

What if?

Q. I lost my refund check. How can I get another check issued?
A. Call your nearest IRS office and request that they send you *Form 3911, Taxpayer Statement Regarding Refund.* Complete the form and sign it (both you and your spouse sign the form if the refund was for a joint return). Mail the completed form to the IRS Service Center where the return was filed. You should receive a duplicate check within four to six weeks.

Q. I just received a notice from the IRS that I owe more tax. They're charging me penalties and interest. Do I have to pay that?
A. The IRS is quick to assess penalties, but is also agreeable to forgiving them for reasonable cause. If you feel you have reasonable cause, write to the IRS explaining the circumstances and request that they waive the penalty. The IRS rarely excuses taxpayers from paying interest on late payments, so you may want to submit payment for any interest (not penalty) charges with your letter as a show of good faith.

Q. I know I am supposed to attach W-2s to my return, but are there any other information reports that get attached?
A. Generally speaking, you must attach any other statements that show a withheld tax on them. For instance, if you had tax withheld on dividends or bank interest payments, the 1099 you received in January will report the amount of tax withheld and should be attached to your return. Be sure to carefully review all 1099s for such withholding that you may not have been aware of. Be sure to place an "x" in the box on Line 54. See the chart at the end of this chapter for a listing of forms on which tax withholding may appear.

Appendix A

Other Considerations

We will now address a few of the more commonly encountered situations that, while they do not merit a line of their own on *Form 1040*, are fairly common occurrences. Chances are good that you will encounter at least one of these situations sometime in your taxpaying life. They are *Sale of Residence, Estimated Taxes, Passive Activities, Depreciation and Basis, Installment Sales* and *Kiddie Tax*. While we will not attempt an in-depth discussion of these concepts, we will present an explanation of what is involved and what forms are necessary to satisfy IRS reporting requirements.

1. Sale or Purchase of Residence

Have you bought or sold a home this year? Whether or not you owe tax on the transaction, you need to report it to the IRS.

A home is a capital asset and every time it is sold at a profit, there is a capital gain subject to income tax. But if you stay within certain guidelines, you may never have to pay the tax on your gains. Not everyone is in the right place at the right time and you may have to sell your home at a loss. Unfortunately, you are still required to report the sale, but you *cannot* deduct it. When you sell at a loss, the basis of your new home is its cost, since there is no gain to be deferred.

The sale of your home is an event that is rarely without tax consequences. One of four situations will be created when you sell your home for a profit:

- The gain will be taxable.
- The gain will be deferred or postponed.
- The gain will be excluded and never taxed.
- The gain will result in a combination of the above.

Taxable Gain

Any gain realized when you sell your residence is fully taxable as a capital gain if you do not replace the residence within a period beginning two years before and ending two years after the sale. The amount of gain is the difference between the *amount realized* from the sale and the *adjusted basis* of your home. This is a costly end to your days as a homeowner.

Deferred Gain

The gain from the sale is automatically postponed when you purchase a replacement residence if:

- The new home costs as much or more than the adjusted sales price of the old one.
- You buy or build your new home and move into it within a time period beginning two years *before* and ending two years *after* you sell the home. It's not enough to just buy it; you've got to actually move in and live there within the replacement period.

Because the payment of tax is postponed under these rules, a system had to be devised that would allow the untaxed gains to be carried forward to future years. The most expedient way to accomplish this was to simply reduce the basis, or tax cost, of your new home by the amount of gain that was not taxed when the old home was sold. Remember! The taxes are deferred—not forgiven. All deferred gains are carried forward and accounted for in future transactions involving your personal residences.

Excluded Gain

One of the few remaining tax shelters is the over-55 exclusion. If you are over age 55 on the date you sell your home, you can elect to exclude up to $125,000 of gain, and never pay any tax on it!

This exclusion is an election. This means that if you qualify, you can choose to exclude the gain—or not. You may want to wait for a future sale to claim the exclusion. This isn't a use-it-now-or-lose-it situation. Your choice should be determined by your financial and tax situations. To qualify for the exclusion, three tests must be met:

- You (or your spouse, if a joint return) must be age 55 or older on the date of the sale. This means that the earliest possible date you can sell your home and exclude the gain is your 55th birthday.
- You (and/or your spouse, if a joint return) must own the home for at least three years, and you must occupy it as your main home for at least three years during the five-year period immediately preceding the sale. Interestingly enough, the three years of ownership and the three years of occupancy do not have to coincide for you to qualify for this exclusion. Nor do the three years have to be continuous. However, both tests must be met within the five-year period preceding the sale.
- You or your spouse cannot have excluded the gain on any other residence before. If you've been married before to someone else and excluded the gain on the sale of a prior residence by virtue of your spouse meeting these requirements, you are deemed to have taken your once-in-a-lifetime exclusion. Further, if and when you remarry, your new spouse will not be allowed

to use this exclusion. The tax code may encourage home ownership, but it sure doesn't encourage marriage!

Combination

All three of the preceding circumstances—taxable gain, deferred gain and excluded gain—could exist in a single sale. Suppose, for example, you sell your home for $325,000, you're over age 55 and you qualify for the exclusion. The adjusted basis of the home is $100,000 and you pay $150,000 to purchase a small retirement home. You have taxable gain, deferred gain and excluded gain all in the same sale as shown below:

Selling price	$325,000
less adjusted basis	(100,000)
Gain realized	225,000
less gain excluded	(125,000)
less gain deferred by reinvestment	(50,000)
Taxable gain	$50,000

Many possible situations can arise when you sell your home, and it may appear to be a very complicated transaction, but don't lose hope. The IRS forms and worksheets provided for reporting the sale of your home are well-designed and operate to calculate the necessary factors regardless of the situation.

What to do with the forms

The sale of your principal residence is reported on *Form 2119, Sale of Your Home*. On this form, you calculate the amount of gain you may defer, the amount to exclude, the amount of gain to be taxed, and the adjusted basis of any new home. This form is required to be filed whenever you sell your home. The IRS needs to know the details of the entire transaction from the original sale of the home to its eventual replacement. If all the events relating to the sale of your home have not transpired by the time your tax return is due, then a second *Form 2119* will have to be filed to report the completion of the events.

Form 2119 is unique in that you can file it all by itself in order to report activity. Say, for instance, that you sell a home, but have not replaced it by the time to file your tax return rolls around. You can file a *Form 2119* with your return with the box checked that you intend to reinvest in another home. When you actually do invest in the other home, you should then file a new *Form 2119* (all by itself) to give details of the reinvestment. If, however, there is a taxable gain, you will have to file an amended return for the year of sale.

Form 2119 Part I, General Information

Line 1. Enter the date of sale as stated on the escrow document.

Lines 2 and 3. Answer yes or no. If you have used a portion of your home for business or rented it out during your ownership, the portion used in these activities *does not qualify* for the deferral of gain. You must treat this sale differently. See *Publication 523, Selling Your Home*, for the details of how to report this sale.

Form 2119 Part II, Gain on Sale

Line 4. Enter the selling price of the home from the escrow document.

Line 5. Enter the total expenses you paid to sell your home. Most of these expenses will be listed on the escrow document, but you may have expenses that you've paid separately. Selling expenses include commissions, advertising, legal fees, appraisal fees, inspection fees, title insurance, transfer taxes, recording fees and any loan charges you are required to pay.

Line 6. Subtract Line 6 from Line 5.

Line 7. Enter the adjusted basis of your home. If you sold a home and deferred a gain when buying the residence you are presently selling, you can obtain the basis from the *Form 2119* you filed for the year you bought this home. Now is the time you will realize the value of keeping old tax returns! Be sure to add to your basis the cost of any improvements or remodeling you did while you owned it. A worksheet is provided at the end of this chapter that will help you keep track of improvements.

Lines 8 and 9. By subtracting Line 7 from Line 6, you will have arrived at the gain on your sale. You then follow the instructions to proceed:

- If no gain, you are finished with *Form 2119*. Just be sure to attach it to your return.
- If there is a gain, you now tell the IRS if you're going to exclude it (Part III) or defer all or part of it (Part IV). In most cases, however, if you buy or build within the replacement period, you *must* postpone the gain. Deferral, in other words, is mandatory, not elective.

Form 2119 Part III, One-Time Exclusion of Gain

Lines 10-14. Determine here if you qualify for the once-in-a-lifetime exclusion of gains. Answer each question and follow the instructions. The amount to be excluded is entered on Line 1.

Form 2119 Part IV, Adjusted Sales Price, Taxable Gain & Adjusted Basis of New Home

Lines 15-23. Calculate, here, the taxable gain, if any, and the adjusted basis of your new home. There are only two lines that require new information in this part. The remainder of the section is devoted to adding or subtracting and is self-explanatory. Enter on Line 16 any fixing-up expenses you incurred. On Lines 19a and 19b enter the date you moved into the replacement residence and its cost, respectively. Cost is calculated from the escrow documents from the purchase. It includes the purchase price as well as the recording fees, title search and title insurance fees, and any other costs you incur in purchasing the home—*except for* interest, property taxes, hazard insurance, mortgage insurance, rent or charges for utilities.

The following is a list of common items found on escrow or closing statements, and how they affect your tax return or the tax basis of your home. Take your escrow documents and consult the chart. It will tell you how to classify each expenditure.

	Seller	**Buyer**
Attorney fees	Selling expense	Add to basis
Commissions	Selling expense	Add to basis
Document preparation fees	Selling expense	Add to basis
Recording fees	Selling expense	Add to basis
Stamp taxes	Selling expense	Add to basis
Surveys	Selling expense	Add to basis
Title insurance	Selling expense	Add to basis
Title search	Selling expense	Add to basis
Transfer fees	Selling expense	Add to basis
Appraisal fees	Selling expense	No effect
Credit checks	Selling expense	No effect
Inspection fees	Selling expense	No effect
Loan origination fees	Selling expense	*Schedule A*
Prorated interest	*Schedule A*	*Schedule A*
Real estate taxes	*Schedule A*	*Schedule A*

When *Form 2119* has been completed, any taxable gain from Line 21 is carried to *Schedule D*. If there is no taxable gain at this point, then there's nothing more to do except include this form with your tax return. Do keep a copy for future reference, however, since the adjusted basis of new home on Line 23 will be needed to calculate gain or loss when that home is sold.

Watch out!

The purchase or sale of a residence is usually a straightforward event. However, there are many ways to acquire or dispose of property and, depending on how the transaction is structured, it can become a very complicated situation. There are a number of issues that can surface, any one of which will send you to the instructions for additional help. Below is a list of topics or circumstances beyond the scope of this guide. If any apply to your situation, consult the IRS instructions or applicable IRS publications (such as *Publication 523, Selling Your Home*, and *Publication 530, Tax Information for Homeowners*). There are also specific rules in the tax code and regulations pertaining to the time elections must be made and/or revoked. If in doubt about these or any other situations when selling a residence, you should seek the advice of a tax professional.

- Sale and purchase of more than one home within the replacement period, new rules apply.
- Business or rental use of your home.
- Installment sale of your home.
- Home of "over 55" taxpayer destroyed or condemned.
- Home acquired from spouse.
- Home acquired other than by purchase.
- Trading homes for other property or another residence.
- Condemnation of home.

2. Estimated Taxes

Do you have income other than wages? If you do and you owe more than $500 with your return, chances are you should have been making estimated payments toward your tax liability. Chances are better yet that the IRS will want you to start making them now!

Uncle Sam doesn't want to wait until April 15to get your money into the system. Ours is a pay-as-you-go tax. If you wait until April 15 and send along a big fat check with your return, you will be assessed a late payment penalty even if you're paying in full. In fact, you can have a refund coming and *still* be subject to the penalty!

Income tax is collected throughout the year, either in employee withholdings or in quarterly payments. Both methods are based on estimates of what your tax liability will be. Your employer is required to withhold income tax from your wages according to a formula based upon your income and exemptions. These withholdings are then deposited in your name and Social Security number with the IRS. If you're self-employed or have much investment income, you make these deposits yourself.

The deposits are like installment payments on your tax debt for the year. They are due quarterly on April 15, June 15, September 15 and January 15 (of the next year). If you file your return by January 31 and pay any tax due, you don't have to make the fourth payment due on January 15.

If you're a farmer or fisherman, not only does your work come in bunches, your income does, too. So if at least two-thirds of your gross income is from farming or fishing, you qualify for special consideration. You are required to make only one estimated payment by January 15. You can even skip this one if you file your return by March 1 and pay any tax due.

Generally, you should make quarterly estimated payments if you expect to owe more than $500 with your return. If you do owe that much, you are considered to have underpaid and will be subject to a penalty. The penalty is calculated on the tax due from each quarter. So if you skipped your first estimate but doubled up on the second one, you will still have an underpayment penalty for the first quarter.

But there are exceptions, known as safe harbors, which protect you from the penalty.

- If you paid an amount equal to 100 percent of last year's tax and your return last year showed a tax liability, you are exempt from penalty. If your AGI is over $150,000, it is 110 percent of last year's tax that must be paid in to avoid penalty.
- If you paid in at least 90 percent of your total tax liability. So, if your total tax bill is $10,000, you are safe from penalty if you have paid in $9,000. Remember, it's not going to fly you haven't paid it in equal installments throughout the year.

For 1994, everyone can use the 90 percent of current tax as a safe harbor. The 100 percent of last year's tax safe harbor is available to those with an AGI under $150,000. Higher-income taxpayers must use 110 percent of last year's tax. Remember, you only have to qualify for one exception, not both, in order to avoid underpayment penalties.

Estimated payments are made via *Form 1040ES*. It's actually a series of four payment coupons, one for each quarter. Each coupon asks for your name, address, Social Security number and the amount of your estimated payment. If you make estimated payments one year, IRS will send you a *1040ES* with your identifying information preprinted.

Simply fill in the amount you are paying and send it in with check enclosed. Do be sure to put your Social Security number on the check. Unlike a tax return, there is no reason to send a coupon without payment enclosed. So if you are unable to make a payment, don't announce it!

There is also a *1040ES* worksheet to help you calculate your anticipated tax liability. It is a one-page summary of what you expect to have on next year's tax return. You aren't required to complete it and it does *not* get filed with the IRS. It is purely for your own use as a guide.

Form 2210 is used to calculate underpayment. You are not required to complete or file this form. The IRS is more than happy to do the calculations for you. For your own information, completing Part II of *Form 2210* will tell you if you qualify for the exceptions to penalty.

Watch out!

The quarterly estimates do not get mailed to the same location as your tax return. So be sure *not* to include your first estimate coupon and payment with the filing of your tax return. Check your *1040-ES* instructions for the mailing address to use.

* * *

There is a rather complicated calculation available to avoid penalties if your income took a big jump at the end of the year. You can't be expected to make the earlier estimates on an unpredicted upswing in your finances. The annualized in-come method spreads your deductions evenly to quarters where income is distributed as it was received.

* * *

Applicable IRS publications include *Publication 505, Tax Withholding and Estimated Tax.*

3. Passive Activities

The purpose of this section is only to familiarize you with the general concept of passive activities. The likelihood is that if you are reporting passive losses on your tax return, you will require the assistance of a tax professional. The rules, calculations and carryovers are so complex that even many professionals find them nearly impossible to comprehend without the assistance of sophisticated computer software.

Prior to the introduction of the passive activity rules, taxpayers were able to invest in activities for the sole purpose of buying tax benefits. In some investments, the tax savings were the only source of return to the investors. The promoters of these abusive tax shelters were merely taking advantage of the tax law then in existence to create a guaranteed return on investment via tax benefits. Congress recognized this and passed legislation designed to limit such tax breaks. Now, losses from passive activities are deductible only to the extent of any income from other passive activities. And these losses may be further limited by the at-risk rules. This means, simply, that you must have some personal economic risk involved in the activity generating the loss.

And just what is a passive activity? It is defined as a trade or business in which you do not materially participate—or any rental activity, whether or not you participate. This sounds easy enough, but how do you define material participation? There are several different ways to meet this test, the most common is having worked more than 500 hours during the year on the activity or having performed substantially all the work done for the year. Remember, though, it doesn't matter if you work full-time at rental activities, they are passive by definition.

The intent of this law is to discourage abusive tax shelter activity, not to punish the little guy with some rental real estate. So there is a *little guy allowance* that allows you to deduct up to $25,000 of rental losses against regular income. To qualify for this, you must actively participate in the activity. This means merely that you must be at least a 10-percent owner and participate in management decisions or arrange for others to provide services. This allowance begins to phase out when your AGI reaches $100,000. From that point on, you lose $1 in deductions for every $2 that your AGI exceeds $100,000. At an AGI of $150,000 the deduction is gone entirely.

Gone, but not forgotten! All passive activity losses that you cannot deduct now are not lost forever, they are just suspended. This means you need to keep track of any disallowed loss so that you can dip into it if and when you have passive income. You also get to recognize all the suspended losses when you dispose of the investment.

Form 8582, Passive Activity Loss Limitation, is used to compute your deductible loss from passive activities. The form itself comes with six worksheets designed to allocate and track allowed and suspended losses. Does this give you some idea of the complexity of passive activity rules? The forms were supposed to be simplified for 1994, but it didn't happen.

Here is another advantage to being one of the little guys. If your only passive losses are under $25,000 and from real estate rentals that you actively manage and your AGI is under $100,000, you don't need to bother with this difficult form.

Watch out!

Income from publicly traded partnerships is defined as portfolio (investment) income instead of passive income. So you might think that you wouldn't have to worry about all this passive activity stuff if you have a loss. Not so! Losses from publicly traded partnerships can only be used to offset income from the *same* partnership. So you must suspend any loss and carry it forward to future years. You can use the loss either when you have income from the partnership or when you dispose of your entire (not just a portion) interest in it.

* * *

We have not even begun to scratch the surface of passive activity rules. They are exceedingly complex and almost definitely call for the guidance of a tax professional to accurately track and recognize suspended losses. Failure to keep track of these losses will result in your losing valuable tax benefits when you sell or dispose of the investment.

* * *

Applicable IRS publications include *Publication 925, Passive Activity and At-Risk Rules.*

4. Depreciation and Basis

If you use property (real or personal) to produce income, you cannot claim the cost of the property as an expense in the year of purchase. But you may be able to deduct the cost of the property over a specific period of time. Deducting the cost of such property over this period of time, known as the recovery period, is what is called depreciation.

We will now take a look at how to determine the basis for depreciation, the recovery periods for different types of property, and some of the methods used to calculate the amounts allowed as a deduction. In general, property you own is depreciable if it meets the following requirements:

1. It must be used in business or held for the production of income.
2. It must have a determinable useful life longer than one year.
3. It must be something that wears out, decays, gets used up, becomes obsolete or loses value from natural causes.

Property that you cannot depreciate includes inventory, land, property you rent from others, repairs and replacements.

You begin to depreciate your property when you place it in service for use in your trade or business. You stop depreciating it when your property is disposed of or otherwise taken out of service, or when you have taken 100 percent of the depreciable basis as an expense.

To determine the amount of depreciation that you can claim as expense, you simply multiply your basis times the percentage of your business use times a percentage that will be determined by the type of property and the year of depreciation.

Basis

Basis is simply a measure of your investment in a property. When you depreciate property, you are deducting as an expense a certain percentage of your basis. For property that you buy, your original basis is usually your cost. If the property you are going to depreciate came to you in some other fashion, such as trade, gift or inheritance, you may need help determining your basis. See *IRS Publication 551, Basis of Assets*.

When you convert personal-use property to business-use property (room in your home converted to an office for example), the basis for depreciation purposes is the lesser of fair market value on the date of conversion, or your basis in the property on that date.

Recovery Periods

The recovery period is the length of time over which you depreciate the asset. In effect, you are spreading the cost of the asset out over a number of years.

The length of the recovery period varies with the type of asset involved. The following is a list of the recovery periods now in effect for property placed in business use after 1986:

- 3-year property — Horses over 12 years old, racehorses over 2 years old, breeding hogs and over-the-road tractor units. Obviously, farmers and truck owners will be most likely to have property in this class.

• 5-year property	Trucks and cars, computers and peripheral equipment, office machinery such as typewriters, calculators and copiers. Lots of small business owners have property in this class.
• 7-year property	Office furniture and fixtures, business equipment not specifically assigned as 5-year property. Lots of small business owners have property in this class, as well.
• 10-year property	Water transportation equipment, certain agricultural structures, fruit or nut bearing vines or trees. Farmers and fishermen will be most likely to have property in this class.
• 15-year property	Municipal waste water treatment plants.
• 20-year property	Municipal sewers.
• 27.5-year property	Residential rental real estate. Owners of rental houses or apartments will use this class.
• 31.5-year property	Commercial rental real estate placed in service after 1986 and before May 12, 1993. Owners of commercial structures such as office buildings will use this class.
• 39-year property	Commercial rental real estate placed in service after May 12, 1993. (Where does Congress come up with these dates?)

Calculation Methods

The Modified Accelerated Cost Recovery System (MACRS) generally is used to calculate depreciation for property placed in service after 1986. This system uses five different methods. The method most often used for 5- and 7-year property is the *double declining balance method*. For the sake of simplicity, we present a chart that gives the applicable percentages to use for calculation for most common situations:

	5-year property	7-year property
Year 1	20.00%	14.29%
Year 2	32.00%	24.49%
Year 3	19.20%	17.49%
Year 4	11.52%	12.49%
Year 5	11.52%	8.93%
Year 6	5.76%	8.92%
Year 7		8.93%
Year 8		4.46%

If you're really paying attention, you will notice that 5-year property is depreciated over 6 years and 7-year property over 8 years. This is due to a further twist in the law called the half-year convention. This treats all property as being acquired midway through the year. So you are allowed only a half-year's worth of depreciation in the first year and you get the other half at the tail end. If you purchase over 40 percent of your assets during the last 3 months of the year, then you have to go into something called the mid-quarter convention. This is a more complicated computation and just another example of why accountants love computer software.

If you are depreciating real property, you must use the *straight-line method* rather than the *double declining balance method*. The straight-line method is very easy to figure out. It simply spreads the expense out evenly over the assigned life of the asset. The hitch comes when you realize that the tax code applies a mid-month convention here. This means that you can only take depreciation for the exact number of months you had the property in service, not for the entire year. The charts for percentages to apply to real property are of fluctuating detail month by month for the first and last years of the recovery period. They remain constant for the intervening years. The charts to use for calculating depreciation for both residential and commercial rental property can be found in *IRS Publication 534, Depreciation*.

Section 179 Deduction

If you stay within certain guidelines, you can choose to expense up to $17,500 of asset purchases in one year. This completely sidesteps any calculations or limitations we've just discussed...just depreciate 100 percent of the asset right off the bat. You can use this only on tangible personal property, not real estate. You cannot use this special form of depreciation to throw you into a loss situation...it can only go against taxable income. Also, if you purchase more than $200,000 in assets during the year, your Section 179 deduction begins to whither away.

Depreciation is reported on the two-page *Form 4562, Depreciation and Amortization*. Page 1 summarizes the expense amounts from the different classes of property. Page 2 is devoted to questions regarding use of automobiles and other listed property (property that lends itself to personal use). The bottom of the form is a section for reporting amortization expense. Amortization is simply depreciation of intangible assets. A common example is organization costs incurred (such as attorney fees) when starting a business.

Watch out!

You are limited on the amount of depreciation allowed for automobiles used in business. This is known as the luxury auto limitation and was designed to prevent people from quickly writing off the cost of expensive cars. The maximum amounts allowed for 1994 are: $2,960 for year 1; $4,700 for year 2; $2,850 for year 3; and $1,675 for succeeding years.

Say you have a $20,000 automobile used 75 percent for business. Using the MACRS percentages, the first-year allowance would normally be $3,000 ($20,000 x 75 percent business use x 20 percent MACRS formula). Because of the luxury auto limitation, you can only claim $2,220 ($2,960 maximum x 75 percent business use). Because of limitations, you'll depreciate the car beyond the normal recovery period.

* * *

The sale of a business asset that has been depreciated requires special treatment, because you have to take into account and recapture all the years of tax benefit you had via depreciation. A frequent example for sole proprietors is the sale of a car used for business. Much like the sale of your home, the gain on the sale of your car (and there probably will be one with depreciation recapture rearing its ugly head) can be deferred into the basis of your replacement vehicle.

* * *

You might be surprised what constitutes depreciable property eligible for depreciation deductions. In 1994, the tax court ruled in favor of an exotic dancer who claimed a depreciation deduction for the cost of breast implants. The court found that due to the extraordinarily large size of the implants that they constituted stage props and not a personal expenditure. As such, they were useful only in her business, said the court in its opinion. While the opinion of the tax court was a summary opinion and, therefore, not a precedent setting opinion, it does offer proof that everything you ever wanted to know about your taxes (but were afraid to ask) may not necessarily be found in the IRS instructions.

* * *

There is seemingly no end to the series of rules and regulations concerning basis and depreciation. This seems to be a prime area for legislators to make adjustments and there have been frequent changes in recovery periods and depreciation systems, methods and conventions. If you have anything but the simplest of depreciation situations, it is recommended that you consult a tax professional to ensure that you are performing any calculations correctly.

Applicable IRS publications include *Publication 534, Depreciation, Publication 551, Basis of Assets* and *Publication 946, How to Begin Depreciating Your Property*.

5. Installment Sales

An installment sale is a sale of property where one or more payments are received after the close of the tax year. When you sell an asset for a profit, a portion of the sales price is capital gain and a portion is just return of your original investment. But what if, when you sell, you don't get paid in full, but rather you carry back a loan on which the buyer makes payments? If you do negotiate some type of contract, chances are you are charging the buyer interest. So each payment you receive is going to be comprised of three elements:

- Return of investment (no tax consequence).
- Interest income (reported on *Schedule B*).
- Gain on sale (reported on *Form 6252, Installment Sale Income*).

Recognizing that it doesn't seem fair to assess tax on profit you haven't yet received, the tax code allows you to report the gain as income in the years you actually receive it.

A certain percentage of each payment (after subtracting out the portion that is interest) is reported as gain from the sale. This percentage usually remains the same for each payment you receive. It is called the gross profit percentage, and is figured by dividing your gross profit by the contract price.

For example, say you sell property at a contract price of $2,000 and your gross profit is $500. Your gross profit percentage is therefore 25 percent. After subtracting interest, 25 percent of each payment, including the down payment, is the taxable gain portion to be reported as income. If your sale does not result in a profit; you have no need to use the installment method on your tax return. You have no gain on which to pay tax, so there is nothing to spread out over the years. If you have a loss on business property, you deduct it only in the year of sale. You don't get to deduct losses on personal use property.

You can elect not to have the installment sale rules apply to your sale. If you so choose, report your entire gain in the year of sale, even though you will not be paid all of the sales price until later. You then do not have to report any gain as you receive the payments. Installment sales are reported on *Form 6252*. Only in the year of sale will you need to complete Part I, which calculates your gross profit percentage.

Every year you receive any payments, you will complete Part II where you apply the gross profit percentage to the payments received. Remember, you are working with the principal portion of the payment only. You should already have put the interest portion onto *Schedule B*. The taxable amount of the portion of gain received will then be carried forward from Part II of *Form 6252* to either *Schedule D* or *Form 4797* in route to *Form 1040*.

Watch out!

While the general concept of installment sales is pretty straightforward and easy to understand, it is not unusual to have something go wrong or to find yourself with circumstances that call for special tax treatment. For instance, what if you want to sell to a related party, or you don't want to charge interest, or you have some depreciation recapture, or you have to sell your contract to a third party, or the buyer defaults and you have to repossess the property? The possibilities are limitless!

Applicable IRS publications include *Publication 537, Installment Sales*.

* * *

Depreciation recapture can result in the recognition of gain in the year of sale even if you are using an installment sale to spread the gain out over time. When selling depreciable personal property or real property depreciated under an accelerated method, beware the dreaded recapture!

* * *

Property expensed under the $10,000/$17,500 Section 179 expense election may also create recapture gain upon disposition.

6. Kiddie Tax

Do you have a child under age 14 who has investment income of more than $1,200? If so, you must compute this tax in a special way, applying what has been dubbed the Kiddie Tax rules. The objective of the Kiddie Tax is to tax any investment income over $1,200 at the parents' marginal tax rate (probably high) rather than at the child's rate (probably low). What about the first $1,200? The first $600 is tax-free and the next $600 is taxed at 15 percent. After that, it's all taxed at the parents' top rate. These $600 increments are based on the standard deduction for someone claimed as a dependent on another person's return.

Shifting income to children has long been an easy way to earmark funds for their expenses—college tuition, for example. At the same time, the savings grow faster because you have minimized the tax bite on the investment income. As usual, the tax code stays just one step behind the quick-thinking taxpayer. In 1986, Congress came up with the Kiddie Tax, which precisely defines limits on such tax breaks. The Kiddie Tax requires the child to file his or her own return, but to compute the tax at the parents' rate. In 1988, Congress devised a way to make reporting a little easier—allow parents to include their child's investment income on their own return. So you now have two choices of how to report your child's investment income and calculate the Kiddie Tax:

- Report the income on the child's own return. Complete and attach *Form 8615*.
- Report the income on your own return. Complete and attach *Form 8814*.

You can include the income of your child under age 14 on your own return, and the child is, therefore, not required to file a return, only if:

- Child's gross income is over $500 but under $5,000.
- Child's gross income consists only of interest and dividends.
- Child has no withholding or estimated tax payments made.

Which method should you choose? It all depends on the particulars of your tax return. Reporting on the child's own return obviously requires the filing of a separate return, completing a fairly complicated form, and possibly making estimated payments in the child's name. Including the income in your own return sounds pretty good at this point. But all is not sugar and spice with this method either. It does increase your AGI and can, therefore, have a ripple effect all throughout your return.

Use *Form 8814* when including the child's income on your own return. Only the amount over $1,000 is actually added to your income. The first $500 is excluded from tax and the additional tax on the next $500 is computed at 15 percent and entered on your return as an other tax.

Use *Form 8615* when filing a separate return for the child. Remember that this is a form used to calculate tax in a special way only for the child's *own* return. The first $600 is excluded from tax and the tax on the next $600 is computed at 15 percent. Anything over this first $1,200 is taxed at the parents' rate.

More than one child under age 14 with investment income over $1,200? You have to combine the income and compute the tax you would pay on the total. Then you must prorate each child's share based upon their share of the combined total of children's income. Sounds tough, but *Form 8615* walks you through it step by step.

Watch out!

The choice to report the income with your own return is what the IRS calls an "irrevocable election." This means you elect to include it when you file *Form 8814* with your return, and you cannot change your mind.

* * *

The computations become a little more complicated if anyone involved is eligible for the net capital gain tax rate. And just because this is a child's return doesn't mean that the alternative minimum tax surprise cannot pop up. Special rules do apply however. They are covered in *IRS Publication 929, Tax Rules for Children and Dependents*.

Appendix B

New for 1994

Miscellaneous Provisions

Increase in Medicare hospital insurance tax. Starting in 1994, the $135,000 cap on earnings subject to Medicare tax is repealed and there is no limit on wages and self-employment income that is subject to the tax.

Estimated tax. After 1993, individuals with adjusted gross income of more than $150,000 shown on the return for the preceding year can avoid the estimated tax underpayment penalty by paying in 110 percent of the preceding year's tax or 90 percent of the current year's tax. See Appendix A.

Tax on Social Security benefits. As much as 85 percent of Social Security benefits may be subject to taxation for certain taxpayers after 1993. If your modified AGI plus half of your Social Security benefit exceed $34,000 for single taxpayers and $44,000 for married taxpayers filing jointly, this new rule applies. See Chapter 18, Social Security Benefits.

Passive loss of real estate professionals. Losses from rental real estate that have been realized by individuals involved in "real property trades or businesses" are no longer subject to the restrictions imposed by the passive activity loss rules. Taxpayers who meet certain requirements are now able to use losses from rental real estate to offset nonpassive income. An individual will be treated as being in the "real property trade or business" if:

1. More than 50 percent of the individual's personal services during the tax year are performed in real property trades or businesses in which the individual materially participates.
2. The individual performs more than 750 hours of service in the real property trades or businesses in which the individual materially participates.

The term "real property trade or business" means any real property development, redevelopment, construction, reconstruction, acquisition, conversion, rental operation, management, leasing or brokerage trade or business. "Material participation" means that the taxpayer must be involved in the operations of the activity on a regular, continuous and substantial basis. Limited partners are generally not considered as material participants in limited partnerships. This passive loss relief is effective for tax years beginning after 1993. See Appendix A.

New depreciation lives for nonresidential real estate. For nonresidential real property placed in service after May 12, 1993, the regular tax depreciation period is lengthened from 31.5 years to 39 years. See Appendix A.

Earned Income Credit. If you don't have any qualifying children, you earned less than $9,000, and you or your spouse were at least age 25, you may be able to take this credit. If you have one qualifying child and you earned less than $23,755, you may be able to take a larger credit. If you have two or more qualifying children, you must have earned less than $25,296. If you can take the credit, you *must* attach *Schedule EIC* to your return. Also, the extra credit for a child born during the year and the health insurance credit are no longer allowed.

Self-Employed Health Insurance Deduction. This deduction expired December 31, 1993. However, at the time *Form 1040* was printed, Congress was considering legislation that would allow a deduction for 1994. For later information about this deduction, get *Publication 553, Highlights of 1994 Tax Changes*.

401(k) Deduction Limit. The maximum deductible contribution is $9,240.

Capital Gain Distributions. The separate line for reporting capital gain distributions when *Schedule D* is not filed has been removed. Instead, capital gain distributions are now reported on Line 13. If you have capital gain distributions and don't need to file *Schedule D*, enter those distributions on Line 13. Write "CGD" on the dotted line next to Line 13 to indicate that you don't need to file *Schedule D*.

Payment of Deferred Additional 1993 Taxes. Some higher-income taxpayers owed additional 1993 Federal income taxes due solely to the 1993 income tax rate increases. If you were one of these taxpayers and elected to defer these taxes and pay them in installments by filing *Form 8841, Deferral of Additional 1993 Taxes*, with your 1993 return, you have an installment due on April 17, 1995. The installment due is one-half of the amount shown on Line 16 of *Form 8841*. There is no interest on the installment payment if it is made on time. But if you do not make the installment payment by April 17, 1995, the entire amount you deferred will become due and payable upon notice and demand from the IRS. You should receive a reminder notice early in January 1995 showing the installment amount due by April 17, 1995.

You have two options to pay the installment:

- Send a separate check or money order to the IRS by April 17, 1995. The notice you receive in January will include a tear-off voucher for you to send back with your check or money order payable to the Internal Revenue Service. Clearly write your SSN and "1993 OBRA Installment" on your payment. Send your payment with the tear-off voucher in the return envelope included with the notice. If you don't have the tear-off voucher or envelope, send your payment by itself to the Internal Revenue Service Center for the place where you live. IRS will apply this payment to your deferred 1993 taxes regardless of any other outstanding debts you may have.

Do not send this payment with your tax return. Also, do not make this payment using a payment voucher other than the one attached to the reminder notice.

- Apply part or all of any refund on your 1994 tax return toward the installment payment.

Deductions

Charitable contributions documentation. After 1993, no deduction is allowed for charitable contributions of $250 or more, unless the charitable organization provides a written receipt. A cancelled check is no longer enough. Also charities must notify you of the value of goods and services you receive in exchange for gifts of $75 or more.

Meal and entertainment expenses. After 1993, the business meal and entertainment expenses deductible portion is reduced to 50 percent. The deductible portion prior to 1994 was 80 percent.

Club dues. After 1993, no deduction is allowed for club dues for any club organized for business, pleasure, recreation, social, athletic, luncheon, airline frequent flyer, etc., purposes.

Travel expenses for spouses and other dependents. After 1993, no deductions are allowed for spouses, dependents or other individuals accompanying a person on a business trip *unless* the other person is an employee of the person paying the expenses, the travel is for legitimate business purposes and the expenses of the other person would otherwise be deductible.

Moving expenses. After 1993, house-hunting trips, temporary living expenses, home buying and selling expenses, and lease acquisition and settling expenses are no longer deductible nor are meal expenses while traveling to the new location. Also, to be eligible to deduct allowed moving expenses, the new job location must be 50 miles farther from the former residence than the old job location, as opposed to the old 35-mile limit. After 1993, the moving expense deduction is taken into account in calculating AGI—which generally works to the taxpayer's benefit. Previously, moving expenses were an itemized deduction. Finally, after 1993, qualified moving expense reimbursements received from your employer are excludable from taxable income. Amounts that are not qualified reimbursements will be treated as compensation.

Tax Law Changes Not Listed. For more details, see *Publication 553, Highlights of 1994 Tax Changes.*

Appendix C

References and Other Help Available

The IRS is making an ongoing effort to bring its forms, instructions and all other publications into the realm of the readable. There is just so much you can do to make an intricate and complicated tax law easy to understand, but the improvement over the past few years is noteworthy.

Many of the forms and publications are available at public libraries or local IRS offices. All can be obtained by telephone or mail. To order by telephone, call 1-800-TAX-FORM (1-800-829-3676). Allow seven to 10 working days for delivery. To order by mail, refer to the following chart for the correct address.

If you live in:	Forms Distribution Center for your state
Alaska, Arizona, California, Colorado, Hawaii, Idaho, Kansas, Montana, Nevada, New Mexico, Oklahoma, Oregon, Utah, Washington, Wyoming, Guam, Northern Marianas, American Samoa	Western Area Distribution Center Internal Revenue Service Rancho Cordova CA 95743-0001
Alabama, Arkansas, Illinois, Indiana, Iowa, Kentucky, Louisiana, Michigan, Minnesota, Mississippi, Missouri, Nebraska, North Dakota, Ohio, South Dakota, Tennessee, Texas, Wisconsin	Central Area Distribution Center Internal Revenue Service P.O. Box 8903 Bloomington, IL 61702-8903
Connecticut, Delaware, District Of Columbia, Florida, Georgia, Maine, Maryland, Massachusetts, New Hampshire, New Jersey, New York, North Carolina, Pennsylvania, Rhode Island, South Carolina, Vermont, Virginia, West Virginia	Eastern Area Distribution Center Internal Revenue Service P.O. Box 85074 Richmond, VA 23261-5074

As part of the effort to become "user friendly," the IRS also offers telephone assistance. Tele-Tax Service has recorded information on a wide range of topics. The Tele-Tax number is different depending upon which state you are calling from. You can also call the IRS and talk to a *real* person, not just a recording. These numbers (different from Tele-Tax numbers) also vary accordingly. See the directory of Tele-Tax and Tax Help phone numbers at the end of this chapter.

The following is a list of tax-help publications available from the IRS. The general guides published by the IRS are listed first. They are especially informative and easy to read. *Publication 17*, for example, is all about your individual income tax and is thorough, but written in plain language. If you are considering starting a small business, *Publication 334, Tax Guide for Small Business*, is indispensable.

Many of the specialized publications have been referenced throughout the book under "What you'll need." They address only the specific issue mentioned in the title of the publication. They provide in-depth information on each topic.

General Guides

17 Your Federal Income Tax
225 Farmer's Tax Guide
334 Tax Guide for Small Business
509 Tax Calendars for 1993
595 Tax Guide for Commercial Fisherman
910 Guide to Free Tax Services

Specialized Publications

1 Your Rights as a Taxpayer
3 Tax Information for Military Personnel
4 Student's Guide to Federal Income Tax
15 Employer's Tax Guide (Circular E)
54 Tax Guide for U.S. Citizens and Resident Aliens Abroad
378 Fuel Tax Credits and Refunds
448 Federal Estate and Gift Taxes
463 Travel, Entertainment, and Gift Expenses
501 Exemptions, Standard Deduction, and Filing Information
502 Medical and Dental Expenses
503 Child and Dependent Care Credit
504 Tax Information for Divorced or Separated Individuals
505 Tax Withholding and Estimated Tax
508 Educational Expenses
510 Excise Taxes 1993
513 Tax Information for Visitors to the United States
514 Foreign Tax Credit for Individuals
516 Tax Information for U.S. Government Civilian Employees Stationed Abroad
517 Social Security for Members of the Clergy and Religious Workers
519 U.S. Tax Guide for Aliens
520 Scholarships and Fellowships

521 Moving Expenses
523 Selling Your Home
524 Credit for the Elderly or the Disabled
525 Taxable and Nontaxable Income
526 Charitable Contributions
527 Residential Rental Property
529 Miscellaneous Deductions
530 Tax Information for Homeowners
531 Reporting Income from Tips
533 Self-Employment Tax
534 Depreciation
535 Business Expenses
536 Net Operating Losses
537 Installment Sales
538 Accounting Periods and Methods
541 Tax Information on Partnerships
542 Tax Information on Corporations
544 Sales and Other Dispositions of Assets
547 Non Business Disasters, Casualties, and Thefts
550 Investment Income and Expenses
551 Basis of Assets
552 Record Keeping for Individuals
554 Tax Information for Older Americans
555 Federal Tax Information on Community Property
556 Examination of Returns, Appeal Rights, and Claims for Refund
557 Tax-exempt Status for Your Organization
559 Tax Information for Survivors, Executors, and Administrators
560 Retirement Plans for the Self-Employed
561 Determining the Value of Donated Property
564 Mutual Fund Distributions
570 Tax Guide for Individuals With Income From U.S. Possessions
571 Tax-sheltered Annuity Programs for Employees of Public Schools and Certain Tax-exempt Organizations
575 Pension and Annuity Income
583 Taxpayers Starting a Business
584 Non Business Disaster, Casualty, and Theft Loss Workbook
587 Business Use of Your Home
589 Tax Information of S Corporations
590 Individual Retirement Arrangements (IRAs)
593 Tax Highlights for U.S. Citizens and Residents Going Abroad
594 Understanding the Collection Process
596 Earned Income Credit
597 Information on the United States Canada Income Tax Treaty
721 Tax Guide to U.S. Civil Service Retirement Benefits
901 U.S. Tax Treaties
907 Tax Information for Persons with Handicaps or Disabilities
908 Bankruptcy and Other Debt Cancellation
909 Alternative Minimum Tax for Individuals
911 Tax Information for Direct Sellers

915	Social Security Benefits and Equivalent Railroad Retirement Benefits
917	Business Use of a Car
919	Is My Withholding Correct for 1994?
924	Reporting of Real Estate Transactions to IRS
925	Passive Activity and At-Risk Rules
926	Employment Taxes for Household Employers
929	Tax Rules for Children and Dependents
936	Home Mortgage Interest Deduction
937	Business Reporting
939	Pension General Rule (Non Simplified Method)
946	How to Begin Depreciating Your Property
1167	Substitute Printed, Computer Prepared and Computer Generated Tax Forms and Schedules
1212	List of Original Issue Discount Instruments
1244	Employee's Daily Record of Tips/Report of Tips to Employer
1542	Per Diem Rates
1544	Reporting Cash Payments of Over $10,000
1600	Disaster Losses

Appendix D

Glossary of Terms

Adjusted Gross Income (AGI)

This is gross income minus adjustments to income. The allowable adjustments are certain IRA contributions, penalty on early withdrawal of savings, alimony paid—and for the self-employed, one-half of self-employment tax, certain health insurance deductions and certain retirement plan contributions.

Alimony

Spousal support payments made under a decree of divorce or separate maintenance. Alimony is taxable income to the recipient and a reduction (adjustment) of income to the payor. Do not confuse alimony with child support payments, which are not taxable transactions.

Alternative Minimum Tax (AMT)

This is a separate calculation of tax liability designed to ensure that taxpayers who have certain deductions and special types of income excluded from the regular tax computation will pay at least a minimum amount of tax.

Amended Tax Return

A special form (*1040X*) used to correct mistakes made on a tax return already filed. You have up to three years from the due date of the original return to file this amendment. After that, the statute of limitations expires and it is a done deal, unless fraud is involved and then there is no time limit. In other words, if you have filed a fraudulent return, it is open to IRS scrutiny forever.

Amortization

The system of allocating the cost of various intangible assets to expense over a period of years. Examples of costs that are amortizable include organization costs to start a business, lease acquisition costs and noncompete agreements.

At-Risk Rules

Special rules that limit a taxpayer's deductible loss on an activity to the amount of money or other property contributed to the activity. This includes borrowed amounts connected to the activity for which the taxpayer is personally liable. Any losses not allowed in one year due to these rules may be carried over and deducted in a future year, subject to the at-risk rules at that time.

Bad Debt
Money owed you that you cannot collect. It may be tax-deductible as a short-term capital loss if it is not business-related, or as an ordinary loss if it is business-related.

Basis
Basis is your investment in property that Uncle Sam uses to determine your gain or loss when you get rid of the property. It may include more than just your purchase price.

Capital Asset
Property you own that is of a personal or investment nature. Common examples are your home, your car and stocks and bonds.

Capital Gain
This is profit from the sale of a capital asset, such as stock. A long-term gain is from an asset owned for more than a year. A short-term gain is from an asset owned for a year or less.

Capital Gains Distribution
Most commonly, a shareholder's proportionate share in a mutual fund's profit from sales of stocks and bonds. The source of the profit distinguishes it from dividends.

Capital Loss
Just the opposite of a capital gain, this is loss from the sale of a capital asset. Losses are deductible only to the extent that you have capital gains. Beyond that, only $3,000 in capital losses are deductible in one year, but any additional loss can be carried forward and used in future years.

Carryovers/carrybacks
Some credits or losses that you are unable to use in the current year can be carried forward for use in future years or carried back and applied against income in prior years. Carrybacks require filing of an amended tax return.

Corporation
A separate legal entity distinct from its shareholders and formed under state law. A corporation is generally a separate taxable entity unless its shareholders have consented to allow the corporation to be treated as an S Corporation, in which case the corporation is not taxed. Instead, S Corporation shareholders report their pro rata share (based upon ownership percentages) of income or loss on their personal tax returns.

Credits
A reduction in your tax liability. This is different from adjustments, exemptions and deductions which reduce only your income that is subject to tax, not the tax itself.

Deferral
Postponement. When you defer a tax liability, it doesn't go away. It just lies dormant for awhile.

Dependent
Strictly speaking, there are five tests that a person must meet in order to qualify as a dependent and you should refer to the *1040* booklet for exact guidelines if you have a question. *Generally* speaking, a dependent is a relative who receives more than half of his or her support from the taxpayer and does not file a joint return with his or her spouse. (Did your daughter get married this year? Do you get her dependency exemption or do she and her husband get her personal exemption? You can't have it both ways!) Other nonrelated persons may qualify as dependents if they were members of the taxpayer's household for the entire year.

Depreciation
Purchase price of assets used in a business cannot generally be deducted as an expense against income in the year of purchase. Depreciation is a method devised to spread out the expense over the useful life of the asset.

Dividend
A distribution by a corporation to shareholders of their proportionate share of current or retained earnings.

Early Distribution
Generally, any distribution from your qualified retirement plan that you receive before age 59½ that is not on account of death or disability.

Earned Income
Income as a result of an individual's personal services. Examples include wages, salary, tips, other employee compensation, net earnings from self-employment, strike benefits and disability pay reported as wages.

Earned Income Credit
This is a special refundable credit similar to a reverse income tax. It is a subsidy for low-income workers with dependent children. Beginning in 1994, it will be available to those without children as well.

Employment Taxes
Taxes that are deposited with the IRS and state taxing authorities as a result of payments made to employees. Examples include employers' portion of Social Security and Medicare tax and federal and state unemployment taxes.

Estimated Tax
The amount of tax you expect to owe next year. If you have income not subject to withholding, you may be required to make quarterly payments on this estimated tax.

Exemptions
An amount that is deducted from taxable income for the taxpayer, spouse and any dependents.

Fair Market Value
The amount that a buyer would be willing to pay an unrelated seller in an open market situation.

Gross Income
This is all the income you receive from all sources—income that is not specifically exempt from tax.

Individual Retirement Arrangement (IRA)
A personal retirement savings arrangement (bank account, stock brokerage account, etc.) that is self-directed. Generally, contributions can be up to $2,000 per year with earnings untaxed until withdrawal. Contributions may or may not be tax-deductible.

Installment Sale
A sale in which payments are spread out over a period of more than one tax year. Gain can usually be reported (and taxed) as payments are received over the life of the contract, rather than at the date of sale.

Inventory
Goods held for sale as well as materials that are in the process of production of such goods.

Itemized Deductions
Certain expenses that can be used to reduce gross income. Generally, they are certain medical expenses, taxes, interest, charitable contributions, casualty losses, moving expenses, employee business expenses and some miscellaneous expenses.

Joint Return
A tax return filed by a married couple that combines all their reportable items. Both parties are liable for any tax due, even if all income is only from one.

KEOGH Plan
A type of IRS qualified retirement plan available to sole proprietors and partnerships. More formal than an IRA or a SEP, it has the possibility of larger deductible contributions.

Kiddie Tax
This is a special tax applied to investment income over $1,200 earned by a dependent child under age 14. The tax is based on the parents' tax rate and is computed using *Form 8615*. An alternative form of reporting is to include the income on the parents' return and file *Form 8814*.

Lump Sum Distribution
Payment to you (within one tax year) of your entire share in a qualified retirement plan. May qualify for special tax treatment.

Marginal Tax Rate
The rate of tax due on your last dollar of taxable income.

Mileage Rate
The standard mileage rate is an amount you are allowed to deduct as an expense on your tax return. It is 29 cents per mile for business mileage, 9 cents per mile for medical mileage and 12 cents per mile for charitable activities.

Net Operating Loss (NOL)
This is not simply a net loss on your *Schedule C* or *Schedule F*, although such losses do frequently generate an NOL. The actual computation of an NOL is fairly complicated and usually requires professional assistance. An NOL can be carried back three years and forward 15 years to offset taxable income.

OID - Original Issue Discount
The name given to instruments of debt (usually bonds) issued for less than face value. The OID is the difference between the face value and the issue price.

Ordinary Income
Income that is taxed according to the tax tables applicable to an individual's filing status. Ordinary income may be subject to the top tax rate as opposed to the lower capital gain rate.

Partnership
Any combination of two or more persons or legal entities who agree to jointly conduct a trade or business for profit.

Passive Activity
A trade or business in which you do not materially participate. Special rules apply!

Points
Another word for loan origination fees. The term comes from the percentage points of interest used to calculate the loan fees.

Portfolio Income
All gross income attributable to interest, dividends, annuities, royalties, gain or loss on the disposition of property held for investment or which produces portfolio income, unless the income is created in the ordinary course of a taxpayer's trade or business.

Recovery Period
The length of time designated by the tax code over which depreciation takes place. The recovery period varies with type of property.

Rollover
A nontaxable reinvestment of retirement funds whereby you remove funds from one investment and deposit them into another qualified investment within 60 days.

Schedule K-1
The *Schedule K-1* is an attachment to the tax return filed for an S Corporation, a partnership, or estate or trust. It details the individual portions of the income, loss, gains, deductions or credits for each shareholder, partner or beneficiary.

Section 179 Deduction
A special form of depreciation whereby you can fully depreciate or "write off" assets up to $17,500 each year. Certain limitations apply.

Self-Employed
Someone who operates their own business that is not a corporation or partnership. Such a self-employed person is known as a sole proprietor.

Simplified Employee Pension (SEP)
Similar to an IRA but with more generous limits on contributions. It is for self-employed taxpayers, but contributions must be made not only for yourself, but also for any qualified employees.

Standard Deduction
A fixed dollar amount allowed for all taxpayers who don't itemize their deductions.

Taxable Income
The amount left after you have added up all your gross income, subtracted any allowable adjustments to income, standard or itemized deductions, and personal exemptions. This is the amount that you use to calculate your basic tax liability.

Tax Credit
This is an actual reduction of your tax liability and is more valuable than a tax deduction, which reduces only your income subject to tax. The most common credits used are the childcare credit and the earned income credit.

Tax Exempt Income
Income not subject to income tax. Be aware that you can purchase tax exempt securities with earnings not subject to tax. But if you sell them for a profit, you don't escape the capital gain (taxable)!

Tax Preference Items
Items of income or expense that receive favorable tax treatment. Taxpayers benefiting from such items may be subject to alternative minimum tax.

Tax Shelter
Any investment providing a tax break as an integral part of the investment return. Your home is a good example of a legitimate tax shelter. It provides you with annual deductions for mortgage interest and property tax, untaxed appreciation and has the potential for tax-free profit upon sale.

Unearned Income
Generally, income from sources other than wages or self-employment. Income that is not the result of your personal services.

Withholding
Amounts deducted by your employer from your gross pay. One of the deductions is usually for federal income tax. The employer deposits this with the IRS as a prepayment on your tax liability. All withholdings are reported to you on your F*orm W-2*.

!@#$%&*!!!!!
The last sound a taxpayer makes upon sealing a return in its mailing envelope.

Appendix E

Filing Requirements

The rules under ***Do I Have To File?*** *apply to all U.S. citizens and resident aliens. They also apply to* ***nonresident aliens*** *and* ***dual-status aliens*** *who were married to U.S. citizens or residents at the end of 1994 and who have elected to be treated as resident aliens.*

Exception. *Different rules apply to other nonresident aliens and dual-status aliens. They may have to file* ***Form 1040NR,*** *U.S. Nonresident Alien Income Tax Return. Specific rules apply to determine if you are a resident or nonresident alien. Get* ***Pub. 519,*** *U.S. Tax Guide for Aliens, for details, including the rules for students and scholars. Different rules also apply to U.S. citizens who lived in a U.S. possession or had income from a U.S. possession. Get* ***Pub. 570,*** *Tax Guide for Individuals With Income From U.S. Possessions. Residents of Puerto Rico can call Tele-Tax (see page 38) and listen to topic 901 to see if they must file a return.*

Do I Have To File?

Use **Chart A** on this page to see if you must file a return. But you must use **Chart B** on the next page if your parent (or someone else) can claim you as a dependent on his or her return. Also, see **Chart C** on the next page for other situations when you must file.

Note: *Even if you do not have to file a return, you should file one to get a refund of any Federal income tax withheld. You should also file if you can take the earned income credit. If you file for either of these reasons only, you may be able to use Form 1040A or 1040EZ.*

Exception for Children Under Age 14

If your child is required to file a return and **all four** of the following apply, you may elect to report your child's income on your return. But you must use **Form 8814,** Parents' Election To Report Child's Interest and Dividends, to do so. If you make this election, your child does not have to file a return.

1. Your child was under age 14 on January 1, 1995.

2. Your child had income only from interest and dividends (including Alaska Permanent Fund dividends).

3. Your child's gross income was less than $5,000.

4. Your child had no Federal income tax withheld from his or her income (backup withholding) and did not make estimated tax payments for 1994.

If you and the child's other parent are not filing a joint return, special rules apply to determine which parent may make the election. See Form 8814 for details.

Chart A—For Most People

To use this chart, first find your marital status at the end of 1994. Then, read across to find your filing status and age at the end of 1994. You must file a return if your **gross income** was at least the amount shown in the last column. **Gross income** means all income you received in the form of money, goods, property, and services that is not exempt from tax, including any gain on the sale of your home (even if you may exclude or postpone part or all of the gain).

Marital status	Filing status	Age*	Gross income
Single (including divorced and legally separated)	Single	under 65	$6,250
		65 or older	7,200
	Head of household	under 65	$8,050
		65 or older	9,000
Married with a child and living apart from your spouse during the last 6 months of 1994	Head of household (see page 13)	under 65	$8,050
		65 or older	9,000
Married and living with your spouse at end of 1994 (or on the date your spouse died)	Married, joint return	under 65 (both spouses)	$11,250
		65 or older (one spouse)	12,000
		65 or older (both spouses)	12,750
	Married, separate return	any age	$2,450
Married, not living with your spouse at end of 1994 (or on the date your spouse died)	Married, joint or separate return	any age	$2,450
Widowed before 1994 and not remarried in 1994	Single	under 65	$6,250
		65 or older	7,200
	Head of household	under 65	$8,050
		65 or older	9,000
	Qualifying widow(er) with dependent child (see page 13)	under 65	$8,800
		65 or older	9,550

* *If you turned age 65 on January 1, 1995, you are considered to be age 65 at the end of 1994.*

Chart B—For Children and Other Dependents (See the instructions for line 6c on page 13 to find out if someone can claim you as a dependent.)

If your parent (or someone else) can claim you as a dependent on his or her return and any of the four conditions listed below apply to you, you must file a return.

In this chart, **unearned income** includes taxable interest and dividends. **Earned income** includes wages, tips, and taxable scholarship and fellowship grants.

Caution: *If your gross income was $2,450 or more, you usually cannot be claimed as a dependent unless you were under 19 or under 24 and a student. For details, see* ***Test 4—Income*** *on page 14.*

1. Single dependents under 65. You must file a return if—

Your unearned income was:	and	The total of that income plus your earned income was:
$1 or more		more than $600
$0		more than $3,800

2. Single dependents 65 or older or blind. You must file a return if—
- Your earned income was more than $4,750 ($5,700 if 65 or older **and** blind), or
- Your unearned income was more than $1,550 ($2,500 if 65 or older **and** blind), or
- Your gross income was more than the total of your earned income (up to $3,800) or $600, whichever is larger, plus $950 ($1,900 if 65 or older **and** blind).

3. Married dependents under 65. You must file a return if—
- Your earned income was more than $3,175, or
- You had any unearned income and your gross income was more than $600, or
- Your gross income was at least $5 and your spouse files a separate return on Form 1040 and itemizes deductions.

4. Married dependents 65 or older or blind. You must file a return if—
- Your earned income was more than $3,925 ($4,675 if 65 or older **and** blind), or
- Your unearned income was more than $1,350 ($2,100 if 65 or older **and** blind), or
- Your gross income was more than the total of your earned income (up to $3,175) or $600, whichever is larger, plus $750 ($1,500 if 65 or older **and** blind), or
- Your gross income was at least $5 and your spouse files a separate return on Form 1040 and itemizes deductions.

Chart C—Other Situations When You Must File

If any of the four conditions below applied to you for 1994, you must file a return.

1. You owe any special taxes, such as:
   - Social security and Medicare tax on tips you did not report to your employer,
   - Uncollected social security and Medicare or RRTA tax on tips you reported to your employer or on group-term life insurance,
   - Alternative minimum tax,
   - Tax on a qualified retirement plan, including an individual retirement arrangement (IRA), or
   - Recapture taxes. (See the instructions for line 49 on page 26.)
2. You received any advance earned income credit (EIC) payments from your employer. These payments should be shown in box 9 of your W-2 form.
3. You had net earnings from self-employment of at least $400.
4. You had wages of $108.28 or more from a church or qualified church-controlled organization that is exempt from employer social security and Medicare taxes.

Which Form Should I Use?

Because Forms 1040A and 1040EZ are easier to complete than Form 1040, you should use one of them unless using Form 1040 lets you pay less tax. **But** if you cannot use Form 1040A or Form 1040EZ, you **must** use Form 1040.

You May Be Able To Use Form 1040EZ If:

1. You were single or are married filing jointly and do not claim any dependents.

2. You (and your spouse if married filing jointly) were not 65 or older OR blind.

3. You had **only** wages, salaries, tips, taxable scholarship and fellowship grants, and not more than $400 of taxable interest income.

4. Your taxable income is less than $50,000.

5. You did not receive any advance earned income credit (EIC) payments.

6. You do not itemize deductions or claim any adjustments to income.

You can also use Form 1040EZ to claim the earned income credit if you do not have a qualifying child.

Note: *If you are married filing jointly and either you or your spouse worked for more than one employer, you cannot use Form 1040EZ if that person's total wages were over $60,600.*

You May Be Able To Use Form 1040A If:

1. You had income **only** from wages, salaries, tips, taxable scholarship and fellowship grants, pensions or annuities, taxable social security benefits, payments from your individual retirement account (IRA), unemployment compensation, interest, or dividends.

2. Your taxable income is less than $50,000.

3. You do not itemize deductions.

You can also use Form 1040A to claim the earned income credit, the deduction for certain contributions to an IRA, nondeductible contributions to an IRA, the credit for child and dependent care expenses, and the credit for the elderly or the disabled. You may use it even if you made estimated tax payments for 1994 or if you can take the exclusion of interest from series EE U.S. savings bonds issued after 1989.

When Should I File?

You should file as soon as you can after January 1, but not later than April 17, 1995. If you file late, you may have to pay penalties and interest. See page 40.

If you know that you cannot file your return by the due date, you should file **Form 4868,** Application for Automatic Extension of Time To File U.S. Individual Income Tax Return, by April 17, 1995.

Caution: *Form 4868 does not extend the time to pay your income tax. See Form 4868.*

If you are a U.S. citizen or resident, you may qualify for an automatic extension of time to file if, on the due date of your return, you meet one of the following conditions:

- You live outside the United States and Puerto Rico, AND your main place of business or post of duty is outside the United States and Puerto Rico.
- You are in military or naval service on duty outside the United States and Puerto Rico.

This extension gives you an extra 2 months to file and pay the tax, but interest will be charged from the original due date of the return on any unpaid tax. You must attach a statement to your return showing that you meet the requirements.

Appendix F

Forms Section

Form **1040** Department of the Treasury—Internal Revenue Service
U.S. Individual Income Tax Return **1994** (99) IRS Use Only—Do not write or staple in this space.

For the year Jan. 1–Dec. 31, 1994, or other tax year beginning , 1994, ending , 19 | OMB No. 1545-0074

Label

(See instructions on page 12.)

Use the IRS label. Otherwise, please print or type.

LABEL HERE

Your first name and initial	Last name
If a joint return, spouse's first name and initial	Last name
Home address (number and street). If you have a P.O. box, see page 12.	Apt. no.
City, town or post office, state, and ZIP code. If you have a foreign address, see page 12.	

Your social security number

Spouse's social security number

For Privacy Act and Paperwork Reduction Act Notice, see page 4.

Presidential Election Campaign (See page 12.)

	Yes	No
Do you want $3 to go to this fund?		
If a joint return, does your spouse want $3 to go to this fund?		

Note: *Checking "Yes" will not change your tax or reduce your refund.*

Filing Status

(See page 12.)

Check only one box.

1 ☐ Single
2 ☐ Married filing joint return (even if only one had income)
3 ☐ Married filing separate return. Enter spouse's social security no. above and full name here. ▶
4 ☐ Head of household (with qualifying person). (See page 13.) If the qualifying person is a child but not your dependent, enter this child's name here. ▶
5 ☐ Qualifying widow(er) with dependent child (year spouse died ▶ 19). (See page 13.)

Exemptions

(See page 13.)

6a ☐ **Yourself.** If your parent (or someone else) can claim you as a dependent on his or her tax return, **do not** check box 6a. But be sure to check the box on line 33b on page 2

b ☐ **Spouse**

No. of boxes checked on 6a and 6b ____

c **Dependents:**

(1) Name (first, initial, and last name)	(2) Check if under age 1	(3) If age 1 or older, dependent's social security number	(4) Dependent's relationship to you	(5) No. of months lived in your home in 1994

If more than six dependents, see page 14.

No. of your children on 6c who:
- **lived with you** ____
- **didn't live with you due to divorce or separation (see page 14)** ____

Dependents on 6c not entered above ____

d If your child didn't live with you but is claimed as your dependent under a pre-1985 agreement, check here ▶ ☐

e Total number of exemptions claimed

Add numbers entered on lines above ▶ ☐

Income

Attach Copy B of your Forms W-2, W-2G, and 1099-R here.

If you did not get a W-2, see page 15.

Enclose, but do not attach, any payment with your return.

7	Wages, salaries, tips, etc. Attach Form(s) W-2		7	
8a	**Taxable** interest income (see page 15). Attach Schedule B if over $400		8a	
b	**Tax-exempt** interest (see page 16). DON'T include on line 8a	8b		
9	Dividend income. Attach Schedule B if over $400		9	
10	Taxable refunds, credits, or offsets of state and local income taxes (see page 16)		10	
11	Alimony received		11	
12	Business income or (loss). Attach Schedule C or C-EZ		12	
13	Capital gain or (loss). If required, attach Schedule D (see page 16)		13	
14	Other gains or (losses). Attach Form 4797		14	
15a	Total IRA distributions	15a	b Taxable amount (see page 17) 15b	
16a	Total pensions and annuities	16a	b Taxable amount (see page 17) 16b	
17	Rental real estate, royalties, partnerships, S corporations, trusts, etc. Attach Schedule E		17	
18	Farm income or (loss). Attach Schedule F		18	
19	Unemployment compensation (see page 18)		19	
20a	Social security benefits	20a	b Taxable amount (see page 18) 20b	
21	Other income. List type and amount—see page 18		21	
22	Add the amounts in the far right column for lines 7 through 21. This is your **total income** ▶		22	

Adjustments to Income

Caution: See instructions ▶

23a	Your IRA deduction (see page 19)	23a		
b	Spouse's IRA deduction (see page 19)	23b		
24	Moving expenses. Attach Form 3903 or 3903-F	24		
25	One-half of self-employment tax	25		
26	Self-employed health insurance deduction (see page 21)	26		
27	Keogh retirement plan and self-employed SEP deduction	27		
28	Penalty on early withdrawal of savings	28		
29	Alimony paid. Recipient's SSN ▶	29		
30	Add lines 23a through 29. These are your **total adjustments** ▶		30	

Adjusted Gross Income

31	Subtract line 30 from line 22. This is your **adjusted gross income**. If less than $25,296 and a child lived with you (less than $9,000 if a child didn't live with you), see "Earned Income Credit" on page 27 ▶	31	

Cat. No. 11320B Form **1040** (1994)

Tax Computation

(See page 23.)

32 Amount from line 31 (adjusted gross income) . . . 32

33a Check if: ☐ You were 65 or older, ☐ Blind; ☐ Spouse was 65 or older, ☐ Blind.
Add the number of boxes checked above and enter the total here . . . . ▶ 33a

b If your parent (or someone else) can claim you as a dependent, check here . ▶ 33b ☐

c If you are married filing separately and your spouse itemizes deductions or you are a dual-status alien, see page 23 and check here. . . . ▶ 33c ☐

34 Enter the larger of your:
- **Itemized deductions** from Schedule A, line 29, **OR**
- **Standard deduction** shown below for your filing status. **But if you checked any box on line 33a or b,** go to page 23 to find your standard deduction. If you checked **box 33c,** your standard deduction is zero.
  - Single—$3,800
  - Head of household—$5,600
  - Married filing jointly or Qualifying widow(er)—$6,350
  - Married filing separately—$3,175

34

35 Subtract line 34 from line 32 . . . 35

36 If line 32 is $83,850 or less, multiply $2,450 by the total number of exemptions claimed on line 6e. If line 32 is over $83,850, see the worksheet on page 24 for the amount to enter 36

If you want the IRS to figure your tax, see page 24.

37 **Taxable income.** Subtract line 36 from line 35. If line 36 is more than line 35, enter -0- . 37

38 Tax. Check if from a ☐ Tax Table, b ☐ Tax Rate Schedules, c ☐ Capital Gain Tax Worksheet, or d ☐ Form 8615 (see page 24). Amount from Form(s) 8814 ▶ e ______ 38

39 Additional taxes. Check if from a ☐ Form 4970 b ☐ Form 4972 . . . 39

40 Add lines 38 and 39 . . . ▶ 40

Credits

(See page 24.)

41 Credit for child and dependent care expenses. Attach Form 2441 41

42 Credit for the elderly or the disabled. Attach Schedule R . . 42

43 Foreign tax credit. Attach Form 1116 . . . 43

44 Other credits (see page 25). Check if from a ☐ Form 3800 b ☐ Form 8396 c ☐ Form 8801 d ☐ Form (specify) ______ 44

45 Add lines 41 through 44 . . . 45

46 Subtract line 45 from line 40. If line 45 is more than line 40, enter -0- . . . ▶ 46

Other Taxes

(See page 25.)

47 Self-employment tax. Attach Schedule SE . . . 47

48 Alternative minimum tax. Attach Form 6251 . . . 48

49 Recapture taxes. Check if from a ☐ Form 4255 b ☐ Form 8611 c ☐ Form 8828 49

50 Social security and Medicare tax on tip income not reported to employer. Attach Form 4137 50

51 Tax on qualified retirement plans, including IRAs. If required, attach Form 5329 . . . 51

52 Advance earned income credit payments from Form W-2 . . . 52

53 Add lines 46 through 52. This is your **total tax** . . . ▶ 53

Payments

Attach Forms W-2, W-2G, and 1099-R on the front.

54 Federal income tax withheld. If any is from Form(s) 1099, check ▶ ☐ 54

55 1994 estimated tax payments and amount applied from 1993 return . 55

56 **Earned income credit.** If required, attach Schedule EIC (see page 27). Nontaxable earned income: amount ▶ ______ and type ▶ ______ 56

57 Amount paid with Form 4868 (extension request) 57

58 Excess social security and RRTA tax withheld (see page 32) 58

59 Other payments. Check if from a ☐ Form 2439 b ☐ Form 4136 59

60 Add lines 54 through 59. These are your **total payments** . . . ▶ 60

Refund or Amount You Owe

61 If line 60 is more than line 53, subtract line 53 from line 60. This is the amount you **OVERPAID** . . ▶ 61

62 Amount of line 61 you want **REFUNDED TO YOU** . . . ▶ 62

63 Amount of line 61 you want **APPLIED TO YOUR 1995 ESTIMATED TAX** ▶ 63

64 If line 53 is more than line 60, subtract line 60 from line 53. This is the **AMOUNT YOU OWE.** For details on how to pay, including what to write on your payment, see page 32 . . . 64

65 Estimated tax penalty (see page 33). Also include on line 64 65

Sign Here

Keep a copy of this return for your records.

Under penalties of perjury, I declare that I have examined this return and accompanying schedules and statements, and to the best of my knowledge and belief, they are true, correct, and complete. Declaration of preparer (other than taxpayer) is based on all information of which preparer has any knowledge.

Your signature	Date	Your occupation
Spouse's signature. If a joint return, BOTH must sign.	Date	Spouse's occupation

Paid Preparer's Use Only

Preparer's signature	Date	Check if self-employed ☐	Preparer's social security no.
Firm's name (or yours if self-employed) and address		E.I. No.	
		ZIP code	

Printed on recycled paper

SCHEDULES A&B (Form 1040)

Department of the Treasury Internal Revenue Service (99)

Schedule A—Itemized Deductions

(Schedule B is on back)

▶ **Attach to Form 1040.** ▶ **See Instructions for Schedules A and B (Form 1040).**

OMB No. 1545-0074

1994

Attachment Sequence No. **07**

Name(s) shown on Form 1040 | **Your social security number**

Section	Line	Description	Box	Amount	Box	Amount
Medical and Dental Expenses		**Caution:** *Do not include expenses reimbursed or paid by others.*				
	1	Medical and dental expenses (see page A-1)	1			
	2	Enter amount from Form 1040, line 32. [2]				
	3	Multiply line 2 above by 7.5% (.075)	3			
	4	Subtract line 3 from line 1. If line 3 is more than line 1, enter -0-			4	
Taxes You Paid (See page A-1.)	5	State and local income taxes	5			
	6	Real estate taxes (see page A-2)	6			
	7	Personal property taxes	7			
	8	Other taxes. List type and amount ▶	8			
	9	Add lines 5 through 8			9	
Interest You Paid (See page A-2.)	10	Home mortgage interest and points reported to you on Form 1098	10			
	11	Home mortgage interest not reported to you on Form 1098. If paid to the person from whom you bought the home, see page A-3 and show that person's name, identifying no., and address ▶	11			
Note: Personal interest is not deductible.	12	Points not reported to you on Form 1098. See page A-3 for special rules	12			
	13	Investment interest. If required, attach Form 4952. (See page A-3.)	13			
	14	Add lines 10 through 13			14	
Gifts to Charity If you made a gift and got a benefit for it, see page A-3.	15	Gifts by cash or check. If any gift of $250 or more, see page A-3	15			
	16	Other than by cash or check. If any gift of $250 or more, see page A-3. If over $500, you **MUST** attach Form 8283	16			
	17	Carryover from prior year	17			
	18	Add lines 15 through 17			18	
Casualty and Theft Losses	19	Casualty or theft loss(es). Attach Form 4684. (See page A-4.)			19	
Job Expenses and Most Other Miscellaneous Deductions	20	Unreimbursed employee expenses—job travel, union dues, job education, etc. If required, you **MUST** attach Form 2106 or 2106-EZ. (See page A-5.) ▶	20			
	21	Tax preparation fees	21			
(See page A-5 for expenses to deduct here.)	22	Other expenses—investment, safe deposit box, etc. List type and amount ▶	22			
	23	Add lines 20 through 22	23			
	24	Enter amount from Form 1040, line 32. [24]				
	25	Multiply line 24 above by 2% (.02)	25			
	26	Subtract line 25 from line 23. If line 25 is more than line 23, enter -0-			26	
Other Miscellaneous Deductions	27	Moving expenses incurred before 1994. Attach Form 3903 or 3903-F. (See page A-5.)			27	
	28	Other—from list on page A-5. List type and amount ▶			28	
Total Itemized Deductions	29	Is Form 1040, line 32, over $111,800 (over $55,900 if married filing separately)? **NO.** Your deduction is not limited. Add the amounts in the far right column for lines 4 through 28. Also, enter on Form 1040, line 34, the **larger** of this amount or your standard deduction. **YES.** Your deduction may be limited. See page A-5 for the amount to enter. ▶			29	

For Paperwork Reduction Act Notice, see Form 1040 instructions. Cat. No. 11330X **Schedule A (Form 1040) 1994**

Name(s) shown on Form 1040. Do not enter name and social security number if shown on other side. | Your social security number

Schedule B—Interest and Dividend Income

Attachment Sequence No. 08

Part I Interest Income

(See pages 15 and B-1.)

Note: If you received a Form 1099-INT, Form 1099-OID, or substitute statement from a brokerage firm, list the firm's name as the payer and enter the total interest shown on that form.

Note: *If you had over $400 in taxable interest income, you must also complete Part III.*

			Amount
1	List name of payer. If any interest is from a seller-financed mortgage and the buyer used the property as a personal residence, see page B-1 and list this interest first. Also show that buyer's social security number and address ▶	1	
2	Add the amounts on line 1	2	
3	Excludable interest on series EE U.S. savings bonds issued after 1989 from Form 8815, line 14. You MUST attach Form 8815 to Form 1040	3	
4	Subtract line 3 from line 2. Enter the result here and on Form 1040, line 8a ▶	4	

Part II Dividend Income

(See pages 16 and B-1.)

Note: If you received a Form 1099-DIV or substitute statement from a brokerage firm, list the firm's name as the payer and enter the total dividends shown on that form.

Note: *If you had over $400 in gross dividends and/or other distributions on stock, you must also complete Part III.*

					Amount
5	List name of payer. Include gross dividends and/or other distributions on stock here. Any capital gain distributions and nontaxable distributions will be deducted on lines 7 and 8 ▶			5	
6	Add the amounts on line 5			6	
7	Capital gain distributions. Enter here and on Schedule D*	7			
8	Nontaxable distributions. (See the inst. for Form 1040, line 9.)	8			
9	Add lines 7 and 8			9	
10	Subtract line 9 from line 6. Enter the result here and on Form 1040, line 9 ▶			10	

**If you do not need Schedule D to report any other gains or losses, enter your capital gain distributions on Form 1040, line 13. Write "CGD" on the dotted line next to line 13.*

Part III Foreign Accounts and Trusts

(See page B-2.)

	If you had over $400 of interest or dividends OR had a foreign account or were a grantor of, or a transferor to, a foreign trust, you must complete this part.	Yes	No
11a	At any time during 1994, did you have an interest in or a signature or other authority over a financial account in a foreign country, such as a bank account, securities account, or other financial account? See page B-2 for exceptions and filing requirements for Form TD F 90-22.1		
b	If "Yes," enter the name of the foreign country ▶		
12	Were you the grantor of, or transferor to, a foreign trust that existed during 1994, whether or not you have any beneficial interest in it? If "Yes," you may have to file Form 3520, 3520-A, or 926		

SCHEDULE C (Form 1040)

Department of the Treasury Internal Revenue Service (99)

Profit or Loss From Business

(Sole Proprietorship)

▶ **Partnerships, joint ventures, etc., must file Form 1065.**

▶ **Attach to Form 1040 or Form 1041.** ▶ **See Instructions for Schedule C (Form 1040).**

OMB No. 1545-0074

1994

Attachment Sequence No. 09

Name of proprietor | **Social security number (SSN)**

A Principal business or profession, including product or service (see page C-1) | **B Enter principal business code** (see page C-6) ▶

C Business name. If no separate business name, leave blank. | **D Employer ID number (EIN), if any**

E Business address (including suite or room no.) ▶
City, town or post office, state, and ZIP code

F Accounting method: (1) ☐ Cash (2) ☐ Accrual (3) ☐ Other (specify) ▶

G Method(s) used to value closing inventory: (1) ☐ Cost (2) ☐ Lower of cost or market (3) ☐ Other (attach explanation) (4) ☐ Does not apply (if checked, skip line H) | Yes | No

H Was there any change in determining quantities, costs, or valuations between opening and closing inventory? If "Yes," attach explanation

I Did you "materially participate" in the operation of this business during 1994? If "No," see page C-2 for limit on losses.

J If you started or acquired this business during 1994, check here ▶ ☐

Part I Income

1	Gross receipts or sales. **Caution:** *If this income was reported to you on Form W-2 and the "Statutory employee" box on that form was checked, see page C-2 and check here* ▶ ☐	1
2	Returns and allowances	2
3	Subtract line 2 from line 1	3
4	Cost of goods sold (from line 40 on page 2)	4
5	**Gross profit.** Subtract line 4 from line 3	5
6	Other income, including Federal and state gasoline or fuel tax credit or refund (see page C-2)	6
7	**Gross income.** Add lines 5 and 6 ▶	7

Part II Expenses. Enter expenses for business use of your home only on line 30.

8	Advertising	8	19	Pension and profit-sharing plans	19
9	Bad debts from sales or services (see page C-3)	9	20	Rent or lease (see page C-4):	
				a Vehicles, machinery, and equipment	20a
10	Car and truck expenses (see page C-3)	10		b Other business property	20b
11	Commissions and fees	11	21	Repairs and maintenance	21
12	Depletion	12	22	Supplies (not included in Part III)	22
13	Depreciation and section 179 expense deduction (not included in Part III) (see page C-3)	13	23	Taxes and licenses	23
			24	Travel, meals, and entertainment:	
				a Travel	24a
14	Employee benefit programs (other than on line 19)	14		b Meals and entertainment	
15	Insurance (other than health)	15		c Enter 50% of line 24b subject to limitations (see page C-4)	
16	Interest:				
a	Mortgage (paid to banks, etc.)	16a		d Subtract line 24c from line 24b	24d
b	Other	16b	25	Utilities	25
17	Legal and professional services	17	26	Wages (less employment credits)	26
18	Office expense	18	27	Other expenses (from line 46 on page 2)	27

28	**Total expenses before expenses for business use of home.** Add lines 8 through 27 in columns ▶	28
29	Tentative profit (loss). Subtract line 28 from line 7	29
30	Expenses for business use of your home. Attach **Form 8829**	30
31	**Net profit or (loss).** Subtract line 30 from line 29. • If a profit, enter on **Form 1040, line 12,** and ALSO on **Schedule SE, line 2** (statutory employees, see page C-5). Estates and trusts, enter on Form 1041, line 3. • If a loss, you MUST go on to line 32.	31
32	If you have a loss, check the box that describes your investment in this activity (see page C-5). • If you checked 32a, enter the loss on **Form 1040, line 12,** and ALSO on **Schedule SE, line 2** (statutory employees, see page C-5). Estates and trusts, enter on Form 1041, line 3. • If you checked 32b, you MUST attach **Form 6198.**	32a ☐ All investment is at risk. 32b ☐ Some investment is not at risk.

For Paperwork Reduction Act Notice, see Form 1040 instructions. Cat. No. 11334P **Schedule C (Form 1040) 1994**

Part III Cost of Goods Sold (see page C-5)

33	Inventory at beginning of year. If different from last year's closing inventory, attach explanation	33	
34	Purchases less cost of items withdrawn for personal use	34	
35	Cost of labor. Do not include salary paid to yourself	35	
36	Materials and supplies	36	
37	Other costs	37	
38	Add lines 33 through 37	38	
39	Inventory at end of year	39	
40	**Cost of goods sold.** Subtract line 39 from line 38. Enter the result here and on page 1, line 4	40	

Part IV Information on Your Vehicle.

Complete this part **ONLY** if you are claiming car or truck expenses on line 10 and are not required to file Form 4562 for this business. See the instructions for line 13 on page C-3 to find out if you must file.

41 When did you place your vehicle in service for business purposes? (month, day, year) ▶ ..../........./.........

42 Of the total number of miles you drove your vehicle during 1994, enter the number of miles you used your vehicle for:

a Business .... b Commuting .... c Other ....

43 Do you (or your spouse) have another vehicle available for personal use? ☐ Yes ☐ No

44 Was your vehicle available for use during off-duty hours? ☐ Yes ☐ No

45a Do you have evidence to support your deduction? ☐ Yes ☐ No

b If "Yes," is the evidence written? ☐ Yes ☐ No

Part V Other Expenses.

List below business expenses not included on lines 8–26 or line 30.

46 **Total other expenses.** Enter here and on page 1, line 27	46	

Printed on recycled paper

SCHEDULE C-EZ (Form 1040)

Department of the Treasury Internal Revenue Service

Net Profit From Business

(Sole Proprietorship)

▶ Partnerships, joint ventures, etc., must file Form 1065.

▶ Attach to Form 1040 or Form 1041. ▶ See instructions on back.

OMB No. 1545-0074

1994

Attachment Sequence No. 09A

Name of proprietor | Social security number (SSN)

Part I General Information

You May Use This Schedule Only If You:

- Had gross receipts from your business of $25,000 or less.
- Had business expenses of $2,000 or less.
- Use the cash method of accounting.
- Did not have an inventory at any time during the year.
- Did not have a net loss from your business.
- Had only one business as a sole proprietor.

And You:

- Had no employees during the year.
- Are not required to file **Form 4562,** Depreciation and Amortization, for this business. See the instructions for Schedule C, line 13, on page C-3 to find out if you must file.
- Do not deduct expenses for business use of your home.
- Do not have prior year unallowed passive activity losses from this business.

A Principal business or profession, including product or service

B Enter principal business code (see page C-6) ▶

C Business name. If no separate business name, leave blank.

D Employer ID number (EIN), if any

E Business address (including suite or room no.). Address not required if same as on Form 1040, page 1.

City, town or post office, state, and ZIP code

Part II Figure Your Net Profit

1 **Gross receipts.** If more than $25,000, you **must** use Schedule C. **Caution:** *If this income was reported to you on Form W-2 and the "Statutory employee" box on that form was checked, see* ***Statutory Employees*** *in the instructions for Schedule C, line 1, on page C-2 and check here* . . . . . ▶ ☐	1	
2 **Total expenses.** If more than $2,000, you **must** use Schedule C. See instructions	2	
3 **Net profit.** Subtract line 2 from line 1. If less than zero, you **must** use Schedule C. Enter on **Form 1040, line 12,** and ALSO on **Schedule SE, line 2.** (Statutory employees **do not** report this amount on Schedule SE, line 2. Estates and trusts, enter on Form 1041, line 3.)	3	

Part III Information on Your Vehicle. Complete this part ONLY if you are claiming car or truck expenses on line 2.

4 When did you place your vehicle in service for business purposes? (month, day, year) ▶ ..... / ..... / .....

5 Of the total number of miles you drove your vehicle during 1994, enter the number of miles you used your vehicle for:

a Business .... **b** Commuting .... **c** Other ....

6 Do you (or your spouse) have another vehicle available for personal use? . . . . . ☐ Yes ☐ No

7 Was your vehicle available for use during off-duty hours? . . . . . ☐ Yes ☐ No

8a Do you have evidence to support your deduction? . . . . . ☐ Yes ☐ No

b If "Yes," is the evidence written? . . . . . ☐ Yes ☐ No

For Paperwork Reduction Act Notice, see Form 1040 instructions. Cat. No. 14374D **Schedule C-EZ (Form 1040) 1994**

SCHEDULE D (Form 1040)

Department of the Treasury Internal Revenue Service (99)

Capital Gains and Losses

▶ Attach to Form 1040. ▶ See Instructions for Schedule D (Form 1040).

▶ Use lines 20 and 22 for more space to list transactions for lines 1 and 9.

OMB No. 1545-0074

1994

Attachment Sequence No. 12

Name(s) shown on Form 1040 | Your social security number

Part I Short-Term Capital Gains and Losses—Assets Held One Year or Less

	(a) Description of property (Example: 100 sh. XYZ Co.)	(b) Date acquired (Mo., day, yr.)	(c) Date sold (Mo., day, yr.)	(d) Sales price (see page D-3)	(e) Cost or other basis (see page D-3)	(f) LOSS If (e) is more than (d), subtract (d) from (e)	(g) GAIN If (d) is more than (e), subtract (e) from (d)
1							
2	Enter your short-term totals, if any, from line 21		2				
3	**Total short-term sales price amounts.** Add column (d) of lines 1 and 2 . . .		3				
4	Short-term gain from Forms 2119 and 6252, and short-term gain or (loss) from Forms 4684, 6781, and 8824				4		
5	Net short-term gain or (loss) from partnerships, S corporations, estates, and trusts from Schedule(s) K-1				5		
6	Short-term capital loss carryover. Enter the amount, if any, from line 9 of your 1993 Capital Loss Carryover Worksheet				6		
7	Add lines 1, 2, and 4 through 6, in columns (f) and (g)				7	( )	
8	**Net short-term capital gain or (loss).** Combine columns (f) and (g) of line 7 . . . . . ▶					8	

Part II Long-Term Capital Gains and Losses—Assets Held More Than One Year

	(a)	(b)	(c)	(d)	(e)	(f)	(g)
9							
10	Enter your long-term totals, if any, from line 23		10				
11	**Total long-term sales price amounts.** Add column (d) of lines 9 and 10 . . .		11				
12	Gain from Form 4797; long-term gain from Forms 2119, 2439, and 6252; and long-term gain or (loss) from Forms 4684, 6781, and 8824				12		
13	Net long-term gain or (loss) from partnerships, S corporations, estates, and trusts from Schedule(s) K-1				13		
14	Capital gain distributions				14		
15	Long-term capital loss carryover. Enter the amount, if any, from line 14 of your 1993 Capital Loss Carryover Worksheet				15		
16	Add lines 9, 10, and 12 through 15, in columns (f) and (g)				16	( )	
17	**Net long-term capital gain or (loss).** Combine columns (f) and (g) of line 16 . . . . . ▶					17	

Part III Summary of Parts I and II

18	Combine lines 8 and 17. If a loss, go to line 19. If a gain, enter the gain on Form 1040, line 13. **Note:** *If both lines 17 and 18 are gains, see the* ***Capital Gain Tax Worksheet*** *on page 25* . .	18	
19	If line 18 is a (loss), enter here and as a (loss) on Form 1040, line 13, the **smaller** of these losses:		
a	The (loss) on line 18; or		
b	($3,000) or, if married filing separately, ($1,500)	19	( )
	Note: *See the* ***Capital Loss Carryover Worksheet*** *on page D-3 if the loss on line 18 exceeds the loss on line 19 or if Form 1040, line 35, is a loss.*		

For Paperwork Reduction Act Notice, see Form 1040 instructions. Cat. No. 11338H **Schedule D (Form 1040) 1994**

Name(s) shown on Form 1040. Do not enter name and social security number if shown on other side.

Your social security number

Part IV Short-Term Capital Gains and Losses—Assets Held One Year or Less *(Continuation of Part I)*

(a) Description of property (Example: 100 sh. XYZ Co.)	(b) Date acquired (Mo., day, yr.)	(c) Date sold (Mo., day, yr.)	(d) Sales price (see page D-3)	(e) Cost or other basis (see page D-3)	(f) LOSS If (e) is more than (d), subtract (d) from (e)	(g) GAIN If (d) is more than (e), subtract (e) from (d)
20						
21 Short-term totals. Add columns (d), (f), and (g) of line 20. Enter here and on line 2 .		21				

Part V Long-Term Capital Gains and Losses—Assets Held More Than One Year *(Continuation of Part II)*

(a)	(b)	(c)	(d)	(e)	(f)	(g)
22						
23 Long-term totals. Add columns (d), (f), and (g) of line 22. Enter here and on line 10 .		23				

Printed on recycled paper

SCHEDULE E (Form 1040)

Department of the Treasury Internal Revenue Service (99)

Supplemental Income and Loss

(From rental real estate, royalties, partnerships, S corporations, estates, trusts, REMICs, etc.)

▶ **Attach to Form 1040 or Form 1041.** ▶ **See Instructions for Schedule E (Form 1040).**

OMB No. 1545-0074

1994

Attachment Sequence No. **13**

Name(s) shown on return

Your social security number

Part I **Income or Loss From Rental Real Estate and Royalties** **Note:** *Report income and expenses from your business of renting personal property on* ***Schedule C*** *or* ***C-EZ*** *(see page E-1). Report farm rental income or loss from* ***Form 4835*** *on page 2, line 39.*

1	Show the kind and location of each **rental real estate property:**	2 For each rental real estate property listed on line 1, did you or your family use it for personal purposes for more than the greater of 14 days or 10% of the total days rented at fair rental value during the tax year? (See page E-1.)		Yes	No
A			A		
B			B		
C			C		

		Properties A	Properties B	Properties C		Totals (Add columns A, B, and C.)
Income:						
3 Rents received	3				3	
4 Royalties received	4				4	
Expenses:						
5 Advertising	5					
6 Auto and travel (see page E-2)	6					
7 Cleaning and maintenance	7					
8 Commissions	8					
9 Insurance	9					
10 Legal and other professional fees	10					
11 Management fees	11					
12 Mortgage interest paid to banks, etc. (see page E-2)	12				12	
13 Other interest	13					
14 Repairs	14					
15 Supplies	15					
16 Taxes	16					
17 Utilities	17					
18 Other (list) ▶	18					
19 Add lines 5 through 18	19				19	
20 Depreciation expense or depletion (see page E-2)	20				20	
21 Total expenses. Add lines 19 and 20	21					
22 Income or (loss) from rental real estate or royalty properties. Subtract line 21 from line 3 (rents) or line 4 (royalties). If the result is a (loss), see page E-2 to find out if you must file **Form 6198**	22					
23 Deductible rental real estate loss. **Caution:** *Your rental real estate loss on line 22 may be limited. See page E-3 to find out if you must file* ***Form 8582****. Real estate professionals must complete line 42 on page 2*	23	( )	( )	( )		
24 **Income.** Add positive amounts shown on line 22. **Do not** include any losses					24	
25 **Losses.** Add royalty losses from line 22 and rental real estate losses from line 23. Enter the total losses here					25	( )
26 Total rental real estate and royalty income or (loss). Combine lines 24 and 25. Enter the result here. If Parts II, III, IV, and line 39 on page 2 do not apply to you, also enter this amount on Form 1040, line 17. Otherwise, include this amount in the total on line 40 on page 2					26	

For Paperwork Reduction Act Notice, see Form 1040 Instructions. Cat. No. 11344L **Schedule E (Form 1040) 1994**

Name(s) shown on return. Do not enter name and social security number if shown on other side. | **Your social security number**

Note: *If you report amounts from farming or fishing on Schedule E, you must enter your gross income from those activities on line 41 below. Real estate professionals must complete line 42 below.*

Part II Income or Loss From Partnerships and S Corporations

Note: *If you report a loss from an at-risk activity, you MUST check either column (e) or (f) of line 27 to describe your investment in the activity. See page E-4. If you check column (f), you must attach Form 6198.*

27	(a) Name	(b) Enter P for partnership; S for S corporation	(c) Check if foreign partnership	(d) Employer identification number	Investment At Risk? (e) All is at risk	(f) Some is not at risk
A						
B						
C						
D						
E						

	Passive Income and Loss		Nonpassive Income and Loss		
	(g) Passive loss allowed (attach Form 8582 if required)	(h) Passive income from Schedule K-1	(i) Nonpassive loss from Schedule K-1	(j) Section 179 expense deduction from Form 4562	(k) Nonpassive income from Schedule K-1
A					
B					
C					
D					
E					
28a Totals					
b Totals					

29	Add columns (h) and (k) of line 28a	29	
30	Add columns (g), (i), and (j) of line 28b	30	( )
31	Total partnership and S corporation income or (loss). Combine lines 29 and 30. Enter the result here and include in the total on line 40 below	31	

Part III Income or Loss From Estates and Trusts

32	(a) Name	(b) Employer identification number
A		
B		

	Passive Income and Loss		Nonpassive Income and Loss	
	(c) Passive deduction or loss allowed (attach Form 8582 if required)	(d) Passive income from Schedule K-1	(e) Deduction or loss from Schedule K-1	(f) Other income from Schedule K-1
A				
B				
33a Totals				
b Totals				

34	Add columns (d) and (f) of line 33a	34	
35	Add columns (c) and (e) of line 33b	35	( )
36	Total estate and trust income or (loss). Combine lines 34 and 35. Enter the result here and include in the total on line 40 below	36	

Part IV Income or Loss From Real Estate Mortgage Investment Conduits (REMICs)—Residual Holder

37 (a) Name	(b) Employer identification number	(c) Excess inclusion from Schedules Q, line 2c (see page E-4)	(d) Taxable income (net loss) from Schedules Q, line 1b	(e) Income from Schedules Q, line 3b

38	Combine columns (d) and (e) only. Enter the result here and include in the total on line 40 below	38	

Part V Summary

39	Net farm rental income or (loss) from **Form 4835**. Also, complete line 41 below	39	
40	TOTAL income or (loss). Combine lines 26, 31, 36, 38, and 39. Enter the result here and on Form 1040, line 17 ▶	40	
41	**Reconciliation of Farming and Fishing Income.** Enter your **gross** farming and fishing income reported on Form 4835, line 7; Schedule K-1 (Form 1065), line 15b; Schedule K-1 (Form 1120S), line 23; and Schedule K-1 (Form 1041), line 13 (see page E-4)	41	
42	**Reconciliation for Real Estate Professionals.** If you were a real estate professional (see page E-3), enter the net income or (loss) you reported anywhere on Form 1040 from all rental real estate activities in which you materially participated under the passive activity loss rules . . .	42	

Printed on recycled paper

SCHEDULE SE (Form 1040) Department of the Treasury Internal Revenue Service (99)	**Self-Employment Tax** ▶ See instructions for Schedule SE (Form 1040). ▶ Attach to Form 1040.	OMB No. 1545-0074 **1994** Attachment Sequence No. **17**

Name of person with **self-employment** income (as shown on Form 1040)	Social security number of person with **self-employment** income ▶	

Who Must File Schedule SE

You must file Schedule SE if:

- You had net earnings from self-employment from other than church employee income (line 4 of Short Schedule SE or line 4c of Long Schedule SE) of $400 or more, **OR**
- You had church employee income of $108.28 or more. Income from services you performed as a minister or a member of a religious order **is not** church employee income. See page SE-1.

Note: *Even if you have a loss or a small amount of income from self-employment, it may be to your benefit to file Schedule SE and use either "optional method" in Part II of Long Schedule SE. See page SE-2.*

Exception. If your only self-employment income was from earnings as a minister, member of a religious order, or Christian Science practitioner, **and** you filed Form 4361 and received IRS approval not to be taxed on those earnings, **do not** file Schedule SE. Instead, write "Exempt–Form 4361" on Form 1040, line 47.

May I Use Short Schedule SE or MUST I Use Long Schedule SE?

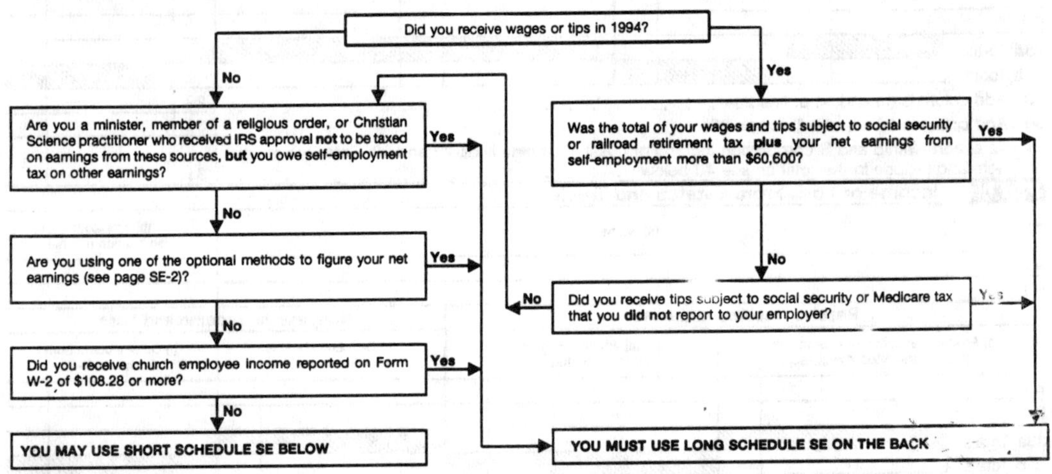

Section A—Short Schedule SE. Caution: *Read above to see if you can use Short Schedule SE.*

1	Net farm profit or (loss) from Schedule F, line 36, and farm partnerships, Schedule K-1 (Form 1065), line 15a	1	
2	Net profit or (loss) from Schedule C, line 31; Schedule C-EZ, line 3; and Schedule K-1 (Form 1065), line 15a (other than farming). Ministers and members of religious orders see page SE-1 for amounts to report on this line. See page SE-2 for other income to report	2	
3	Combine lines 1 and 2	3	
4	**Net earnings from self-employment.** Multiply line 3 by 92.35% (.9235). If less than $400, **do not** file this schedule; you do not owe self-employment tax ▶	4	
5	**Self-employment tax.** If the amount on line 4 is: • $60,600 or less, multiply line 4 by 15.3% (.153). Enter the result here and on **Form 1040, line 47.** • More than $60,600, multiply line 4 by 2.9% (.029). Then, add $7,514.40 to the result. Enter the total here and on **Form 1040, line 47.**	5	
6	**Deduction for one-half of self-employment tax.** Multiply line 5 by 50% (.5). Enter the result here and on **Form 1040, line 25** 6		

For Paperwork Reduction Act Notice, see Form 1040 instructions. Cat. No. 11358Z **Schedule SE (Form 1040) 1994**

Name of person with **self-employment** income (as shown on Form 1040)	Social security number of person with **self-employment** income ▶	

Section B—Long Schedule SE

Part I Self-Employment Tax

Note: *If your only income subject to self-employment tax is church employee income, skip lines 1 through 4b. Enter -0- on line 4c and go to line 5a. Income from services you performed as a minister or a member of a religious order* **is not** *church employee income. See page SE-1.*

A If you are a minister, member of a religious order, or Christian Science practitioner **and** you filed Form 4361, but you had $400 or more of **other** net earnings from self-employment, check here and continue with Part I . . . . . . ▶ ☐

1	Net farm profit or (loss) from Schedule F, line 36, and farm partnerships, Schedule K-1 (Form 1065), line 15a. **Note:** *Skip this line if you use the farm optional method. See page SE-3*	**1**		
2	Net profit or (loss) from Schedule C, line 31; Schedule C-EZ, line 3; and Schedule K-1 (Form 1065), line 15a (other than farming). Ministers and members of religious orders see page SE-1 for amounts to report on this line. See page SE-2 for other income to report. **Note:** *Skip this line if you use the nonfarm optional method. See page SE-3.*	**2**		
3	Combine lines 1 and 2	**3**		
4a	If line 3 is more than zero, multiply line 3 by 92.35% (.9235). Otherwise, enter amount from line 3	**4a**		
b	If you elected one or both of the optional methods, enter the total of lines 15 and 17 here	**4b**		
c	Combine lines 4a and 4b. If less than $400, **do not** file this schedule; you do not owe self-employment tax. **Exception.** If less than $400 and you had church employee income, enter -0- and continue ▶	**4c**		
5a	Enter your church employee income from Form W-2. **Caution:** *See page SE-1 for definition of church employee income* . . . **5a**			
b	Multiply line 5a by 92.35% (.9235). If less than $100, enter -0-	**5b**		
6	**Net earnings from self-employment.** Add lines 4c and 5b	**6**		
7	Maximum amount of combined wages and self-employment earnings subject to social security tax or the 6.2% portion of the 7.65% railroad retirement (tier 1) tax for 1994	**7**	60,600	00
8a	Total social security wages and tips (total of boxes 3 and 7 on Form(s) W-2) and railroad retirement (tier 1) compensation . . . **8a**			
b	Unreported tips subject to social security tax (from Form 4137, line 9) **8b**			
c	Add lines 8a and 8b	**8c**		
9	Subtract line 8c from line 7. If zero or less, enter -0- here and on line 10 and go to line 11 ▶	**9**		
10	Multiply the **smaller** of line 6 or line 9 by 12.4% (.124)	**10**		
11	Multiply line 6 by 2.9% (.029)	**11**		
12	**Self-employment tax.** Add lines 10 and 11. Enter here and on **Form 1040, line 47**	**12**		
13	**Deduction for one-half of self-employment tax.** Multiply line 12 by 50% (.5). Enter the result here and on **Form 1040, line 25** . . . **13**			

Part II Optional Methods To Figure Net Earnings (See page SE-2.)

Farm Optional Method. You may use this method **only** if:

- Your gross farm income[1] was not more than $2,400, **or**
- Your gross farm income[1] was more than $2,400 and your net farm profits[2] were less than $1,733.

14	Maximum income for optional methods	**14**	1,600	00
15	Enter the **smaller** of: two-thirds (⅔) of gross farm income[1] (not less than zero) **or** $1,600. Also, include this amount on line 4b above	**15**		

Nonfarm Optional Method. You may use this method **only** if:

- Your net nonfarm profits[3] were less than $1,733 and also less than 72.189% of your gross nonfarm income,[4] **and**
- You had net earnings from self-employment of at least $400 in 2 of the prior 3 years.

Caution: *You may use this method no more than five times.*

16	Subtract line 15 from line 14	**16**		
17	Enter the **smaller** of: two-thirds (⅔) of gross nonfarm income[4] (not less than zero) **or** the amount on line 16. Also, include this amount on line 4b above	**17**		

[1]From Schedule F, line 11, and Schedule K-1 (Form 1065), line 15b.
[2]From Schedule F, line 36, and Schedule K-1 (Form 1065), line 15a.
[3]From Schedule C, line 31; Schedule C-EZ, line 3; and Schedule K-1 (Form 1065), line 15a.
[4]From Schedule C, line 7; Schedule C-EZ, line 1; and Schedule K-1 (Form 1065), line 15c.

 *Printed on recycled paper*

Form **2119**

Department of the Treasury
Internal Revenue Service

Sale of Your Home

▶ **Attach to Form 1040 for year of sale.**

▶ **See separate instructions.** ▶ **Please print or type.**

OMB No. 1545-0072

1993

Attachment Sequence No. **20**

Your first name and initial. If a joint return, also give spouse's name and initial.	Last name	**Your social security number**

Fill in Your Address Only If You Are Filing This Form by Itself and Not With Your Tax Return	Present address (no., street, and apt. no., rural route, or P.O. box no. if mail is not delivered to street address)	**Spouse's social security number**
	City, town or post office, state, and ZIP code	

Part I General Information

1 Date your former main home was sold (month, day, year) . . . . ▶ **1** / /

2 Have you bought or built a new main home? . . . . ☐ Yes ☐ No

3 Is or was any part of either main home rented out or used for business? If "Yes," see instructions . . ☐ Yes ☐ No

Part II Gain on Sale—Do not include amounts you deduct as moving expenses.

4	Selling price of home. Do not include personal property items you sold with your home . .	**4**	
5	Expense of sale (see instructions)	**5**	
6	Amount realized. Subtract line 5 from line 4	**6**	
7	Adjusted basis of home sold (see instructions)	**7**	
8	**Gain on sale.** Subtract line 7 from line 6	**8**	

Is line 8 more than zero?

Yes ⟶ If line 2 is "Yes," you **must** go to Part III or Part IV, whichever applies. If line 2 is "No," go to line 9.

No ⟶ **Stop** and attach this form to your return.

9 If you haven't replaced your home, do you plan to do so within the **replacement period** (see instructions)? ☐ Yes ☐ No

- If line 9 is "Yes," stop here, attach this form to your return, and see **Additional Filing Requirements** in the instructions.
- If line 9 is "No," you **must** go to Part III or Part IV, whichever applies.

Part III One-Time Exclusion of Gain for People Age 55 or Older—By completing this part, you are electing to take the one-time exclusion (see instructions). If you are not electing to take the exclusion, go to Part IV now.

10 Who was age 55 or older on the date of sale? . . . . ☐ You ☐ Your spouse ☐ Both of you

11 Did the person who was age 55 or older own and use the property as his or her main home for a total of at least 3 years (except for short absences) of the 5-year period before the sale? If "No," go to Part IV now . . ☐ Yes ☐ No

12 At the time of sale, who owned the home? . . . . ☐ You ☐ Your spouse ☐ Both of you

13	Social security number of spouse at the time of sale if you had a different spouse from the one above. If you were not married at the time of sale, enter "None" . . . . ▶	**13**	
14	**Exclusion.** Enter the **smaller** of line 8 or $125,000 ($62,500 if married filing separate return). Then, go to line 15	**14**	

Part IV Adjusted Sales Price, Taxable Gain, and Adjusted Basis of New Home

15	If line 14 is blank, enter the amount from line 8. Otherwise, subtract line 14 from line 8 . .	**15**	
	• If line 15 is zero, stop and attach this form to your return. • If line 15 is more than zero and line 2 is "Yes," go to line 16 now. • If you are reporting this sale on the installment method, stop and see the instructions. • All others, stop and **enter the amount from line 15 on Schedule D, col. (g), line 4 or line 12.**		
16	Fixing-up expenses (see instructions for time limits)	**16**	
17	If line 14 is blank, enter amount from line 16. Otherwise, add lines 14 and 16	**17**	
18	**Adjusted sales price.** Subtract line 17 from line 6	**18**	
19a	Date you moved into new home ▶ / / **b** Cost of new home (see instructions)	**19b**	
20	Subtract line 19b from line 18. If zero or less, enter -0-	**20**	
21	**Taxable gain.** Enter the **smaller** of line 15 or line 20	**21**	
	• If line 21 is zero, go to line 22 and attach this form to your return. • If you are reporting this sale on the installment method, see the line 15 instructions and go to line 22. • All others, **enter the amount from line 21 on Schedule D, col. (g), line 4 or line 12,** and go to line 22.		
22	Postponed gain. Subtract line 21 from line 15	**22**	
23	**Adjusted basis of new home.** Subtract line 22 from line 19b	**23**	

Sign Here Only If You Are Filing This Form by Itself and Not With Your Tax Return

Under penalties of perjury, I declare that I have examined this form, including attachments, and to the best of my knowledge and belief, it is true, correct, and complete.

▶ Your signature _______ Date _______ ▶ Spouse's signature _______ Date _______

If a joint return, both must sign.

For Paperwork Reduction Act Notice, see separate instructions. Cat. No. 11710J Form **2119** (1993)

Printed on recycled paper

Form **2441**

Department of the Treasury
Internal Revenue Service (99)

Child and Dependent Care Expenses

▶ Attach to Form 1040.

▶ See separate instructions.

OMB No. 1545-0068

1994

Attachment Sequence No. **21**

Name(s) shown on Form 1040

Your social security number

You need to understand the following terms to complete this form: **Qualifying Person(s), Dependent Care Benefits, Qualified Expenses,** and **Earned Income.** See **Important Terms** on page 1 of the Form 2441 instructions.

Part I **Persons or Organizations Who Provided the Care**—You **must** complete this part. (If you need more space, use the bottom of page 2.)

1 **(a)** Care provider's name	**(b)** Address (number, street, apt. no., city, state, and ZIP code)	**(c)** Identifying number (SSN or EIN)	**(d)** Amount paid (see instructions)

2 Add the amounts in column (d) of line 1 . . . . **2**

3 Enter the number of **qualifying persons** cared for in 1994 . . . . ▶ ☐

Did you receive **dependent care benefits?**
- **NO** ——▶ Complete only Part II below.
- **YES** ——▶ Complete Part III on the back now.

Part II **Credit for Child and Dependent Care Expenses**

4 Enter the amount of **qualified expenses** you incurred and paid in 1994. DO NOT enter more than $2,400 for one qualifying person or $4,800 for two or more persons. If you completed Part III, enter the amount from line 25 . . . . **4**

5 Enter YOUR **earned income** **5**

6 If married filing a joint return, enter YOUR SPOUSE'S earned income (if student or disabled, see the instructions); **all others,** enter the amount from line 5 . . . . **6**

7 Enter the **smallest** of line 4, 5, or 6 . . . . **7**

8 Enter the amount from Form 1040, line 32 . . . . **8**

9 Enter on line 9 the decimal amount shown below that applies to the amount on line 8

If line 8 is— Over	But not over	Decimal amount is
$0—	10,000	.30
10,000—	12,000	.29
12,000—	14,000	.28
14,000—	16,000	.27
16,000—	18,000	.26
18,000—	20,000	.25

If line 8 is— Over	But not over	Decimal amount is
$20,000—	22,000	.24
22,000—	24,000	.23
24,000—	26,000	.22
26,000—	28,000	.21
28,000—	No limit	.20

9 X.

10 Multiply **line 7** by the decimal amount on line 9. Enter the result. Then, see the instructions for the amount of credit to enter on Form 1040, line 41 . . . . **10**

Caution: *If you paid $50 or more in a calendar quarter to a person who worked in your home, you must file an employment tax return. Get **Form 942** for details.*

For Paperwork Reduction Act Notice, see separate instructions. Cat. No. 11862M Form **2441** (1994)

Part III Dependent Care Benefits—Complete this part **only** if you received these benefits.

11 Enter the total amount of **dependent care benefits** you received for 1994. This amount should be shown in box 10 of your W-2 form(s). DO NOT include amounts that were reported to you as wages in box 1 of Form(s) W-2 11

12 Enter the amount forfeited, if any. See the instructions 12

13 Subtract line 12 from line 11 13

14 Enter the total amount of **qualified expenses** incurred in 1994 for the care of the qualifying person(s) 14

15 Enter the **smaller** of line 13 or 14 15

16 Enter YOUR **earned income** 16

17 If married filing a joint return, enter YOUR SPOUSE'S earned income (if student or disabled, see the line 6 instructions); if married filing a separate return, see the instructions for the amount to enter; **all others,** enter the amount from line 16 . . 17

18 Enter the **smallest** of line 15, 16, or 17. 18

19 **Excluded benefits.** Enter here the **smaller** of the following:

- The amount from line 18, or
- $5,000 ($2,500 if married filing a separate return **and** you were required to enter your spouse's earned income on line 17). 19

20 **Taxable benefits.** Subtract line 19 from line 13. Also, include this amount on Form 1040, line 7. On the dotted line next to line 7, write "DCB" 20

To claim the child and dependent care credit, complete lines 21–25 below, and lines 4–10 on the front of this form.

21 Enter the amount of qualified expenses you incurred and paid in 1994. DO NOT include on this line any excluded benefits shown on line 19 21

22 Enter $2,400 ($4,800 if two or more qualifying persons) . . . 22

23 Enter the amount from line 19 23

24 Subtract line 23 from line 22. If zero or less, **STOP**. You cannot take the credit. **Exception.** If you paid 1993 expenses in 1994, see the line 10 instructions 24

25 Enter the **smaller** of line 21 or 24 here **and** on line 4 on the front of this form . . . 25

Printed on recycled paper

Form **4137**

Department of the Treasury
Internal Revenue Service

Social Security and Medicare Tax on Unreported Tip Income

► See instructions on back.
► Attach to Form 1040.

OMB No. 1545-0059

1994

Attachment Sequence No. 24

Name of person who received tips (as shown on Form 1040). If married, complete a separate Form 4137 for each spouse with unreported tips.	Social security number

Name(s) of employer(s) to whom you were required to, but did not, report your tips:

1 Total cash and charge tips you **received** in 1994. See instructions			1		
2 Total cash and charge tips you **reported** to your employer in 1994			2		
3 Subtract line 2 from line 1. This amount is income you **must** include in the total on Form 1040, line 7			3		
4 Cash and charge tips you received but did not report to your employer because the total was less than $20 in a calendar month. See instructions			4		
5 Unreported tips subject to Medicare tax. Subtract line 4 from line 3. Enter here and on line 2 of Schedule U below			5		
6 Maximum amount of wages (including tips) subject to social security tax	6	60,600 00			
7 Total social security wages and social security tips (total of boxes 3 and 7 on Form(s) W-2) or railroad retirement (tier 1) compensation	7				
8 Subtract line 7 from line 6. If line 7 is more than line 6, enter -0- here and on line 9 and go to line 11			8		
9 Unreported tips subject to social security tax. Compare the amounts on lines 5 and 8 above. Enter the **smaller** of the two amounts here and on line 1 of Schedule U below. If you received tips as a Federal, state, or local government employee, see instructions			9		
10 Multiply line 9 by .062			10		
11 Multiply line 5 by .0145			11		
12 Add lines 10 and 11. Enter the result here and on Form 1040, line 50 ►			12		

For Paperwork Reduction Act Notice, see instructions on back. Form **4137** (1994)

Do Not Detach

SCHEDULE U (Form 1040)
Department of the Treasury
Internal Revenue Service

U.S. Schedule of Unreported Tip Income

For crediting to your social security record

1994

Note: *The amounts you report below are for your social security record. This record is used to figure any benefits, based on your earnings, payable to you and your dependents or your survivors. Fill in each item accurately and completely.*

Print or type name of person who received tip income (as shown on Form 1040)	Social security number
Address (number, street, and apt. no., or P.O. box if mail is not delivered to your home)	Occupation
City, town or post office, state, and ZIP code	

1 Unreported tips subject to social security tax. Enter the amount from line 9 (Form 4137) above ►	1		
2 Unreported tips subject to Medicare tax. Enter the amount from line 5 (Form 4137) above ►	2		

Please do not write in this space

DLN—

Cat. No. 12626C

Form **4797**

Department of the Treasury
Internal Revenue Service (99)

Sales of Business Property

(Also Involuntary Conversions and Recapture Amounts Under Sections 179 and 280F(b)(2))

▶ **Attach to your tax return.** ▶ **See separate instructions.**

OMB No. 1545-0184

1994

Attachment Sequence No. **27**

Name(s) shown on return | **Identifying number**

1 Enter here the gross proceeds from the sale or exchange of real estate reported to you for 1994 on Form(s) 1099-S (or a substitute statement) that you will be including on line 2, 11, or 22 . . . . | 1 |

Part I **Sales or Exchanges of Property Used in a Trade or Business and Involuntary Conversions From Other Than Casualty or Theft—Property Held More Than 1 Year**

(a) Description of property	(b) Date acquired (mo., day, yr.)	(c) Date sold (mo., day, yr.)	(d) Gross sales price	(e) Depreciation allowed or allowable since acquisition	(f) Cost or other basis, plus improvements and expense of sale	(g) LOSS ((f) minus the sum of (d) and (e))	(h) GAIN ((d) plus (e) minus (f))
2							

		(g)	(h)
3 Gain, if any, from Form 4684, line 39	3		
4 Section 1231 gain from installment sales from Form 6252, line 26 or 37	4		
5 Section 1231 gain or (loss) from like-kind exchanges from Form 8824	5		
6 Gain, if any, from line 34, from other than casualty or theft	6		
7 Add lines 2 through 6 in columns (g) and (h)	7	( )	

8 Combine columns (g) and (h) of line 7. Enter gain or (loss) here, and on the appropriate line as follows: . . . . | 8 |

Partnerships—Enter the gain or (loss) on Form 1065, Schedule K, line 6. Skip lines 9, 10, 12, and 13 below.

S corporations—Report the gain or (loss) following the instructions for Form 1120S, Schedule K, lines 5 and 6. Skip lines 9, 10, 12, and 13 below, unless line 8 is a gain and the S corporation is subject to the capital gains tax.

All others—If line 8 is zero or a loss, enter the amount on line 12 below and skip lines 9 and 10. If line 8 is a gain and you did not have any prior year section 1231 losses, or they were recaptured in an earlier year, enter the gain as a long-term capital gain on Schedule D and skip lines 9, 10, and 13 below.

9 Nonrecaptured net section 1231 losses from prior years (see instructions) . . . . | 9 |

10 Subtract line 9 from line 8. If zero or less, enter -0-. Also enter on the appropriate line as follows (see instructions): | 10 |

S corporations—Enter this amount (if more than zero) on Schedule D (Form 1120S), line 13, and skip lines 12 and 13 below.

All others—If line 10 is zero, enter the amount from line 8 on line 13 below. If line 10 is more than zero, enter the amount from line 9 on line 13 below, and enter the amount from line 10 as a long-term capital gain on Schedule D.

Part II **Ordinary Gains and Losses**

11 Ordinary gains and losses not included on lines 12 through 18 (include property held 1 year or less):

		(g)	(h)
12 Loss, if any, from line 8	12		
13 Gain, if any, from line 8, or amount from line 9 if applicable	13		
14 Gain, if any, from line 33	14		
15 Net gain or (loss) from Form 4684, lines 31 and 38a	15		
16 Ordinary gain from installment sales from Form 6252, line 25 or 36	16		
17 Ordinary gain or (loss) from like-kind exchanges from Form 8824	17		
18 Recapture of section 179 expense deduction for partners and S corporation shareholders from property dispositions by partnerships and S corporations (see instructions)	18		
19 Add lines 11 through 18 in columns (g) and (h)	19	( )	

20 Combine columns (g) and (h) of line 19. Enter gain or (loss) here, and on the appropriate line as follows: . . . | 20 |

a For all except individual returns: Enter the gain or (loss) from line 20 on the return being filed.

b For individual returns:

(1) If the loss on line 12 includes a loss from Form 4684, line 35, column (b)(ii), enter that part of the loss here and on line 22 of Schedule A (Form 1040). Identify as from "Form 4797, line 20b(1)." See instructions . . . . | 20b(1) |

(2) Redetermine the gain or (loss) on line 20, excluding the loss, if any, on line 20b(1). Enter here and on Form 1040, line 14 . . | 20b(2) |

For Paperwork Reduction Act Notice, see page 1 of separate instructions. Cat. No. 13086I Form **4797** (1994)

Part III Gain From Disposition of Property Under Sections 1245, 1250, 1252, 1254, and 1255

21 (a) Description of section 1245, 1250, 1252, 1254, or 1255 property:	(b) Date acquired (mo., day, yr.)	(c) Date sold (mo., day, yr.)
A		
B		
C		
D		

Relate lines 21A through 21D to these columns ▶		Property A	Property B	Property C	Property D
22 Gross sales price (**Note:** *See line 1 before completing.*)	22				
23 Cost or other basis plus expense of sale	23				
24 Depreciation (or depletion) allowed or allowable	24				
25 Adjusted basis. Subtract line 24 from line 23	25				
26 Total gain. Subtract line 25 from line 22	26				
27 **If section 1245 property:**					
a Depreciation allowed or allowable from line 24	27a				
b Enter the **smaller** of line 26 or 27a	27b				
28 **If section 1250 property:** If straight line depreciation was used, enter -0- on line 28g, except for a corporation subject to section 291.					
a Additional depreciation after 1975 (see instructions)	28a				
b Applicable percentage multiplied by the **smaller** of line 26 or line 28a (see instructions)	28b				
c Subtract line 28a from line 26. If residential rental property or line 26 is not more than line 28a, skip lines 28d and 28e	28c				
d Additional depreciation after 1969 and before 1976	28d				
e Enter the **smaller** of line 28c or 28d	28e				
f Section 291 amount (corporations only)	28f				
g Add lines 28b, 28e, and 28f	28g				
29 **If section 1252 property:** Skip this section if you did not dispose of farmland or if this form is being completed for a partnership.					
a Soil, water, and land clearing expenses	29a				
b Line 29a multiplied by applicable percentage (see instructions)	29b				
c Enter the **smaller** of line 26 or 29b	29c				
30 **If section 1254 property:**					
a Intangible drilling and development costs, expenditures for development of mines and other natural deposits, and mining exploration costs (see instructions)	30a				
b Enter the **smaller** of line 26 or 30a	30b				
31 **If section 1255 property:**					
a Applicable percentage of payments excluded from income under section 126 (see instructions)	31a				
b Enter the **smaller** of line 26 or 31a	31b				

Summary of Part III Gains. Complete property columns A through D, through line 31b before going to line 32.

32 Total gains for all properties. Add columns A through D, line 26	32	
33 Add columns A through D, lines 27b, 28g, 29c, 30b, and 31b. Enter here and on line 14	33	
34 Subtract line 33 from line 32. Enter the portion from casualty or theft on Form 4684, line 33. Enter the portion from other than casualty or theft on Form 4797, line 6	34	

Part IV Recapture Amounts Under Sections 179 and 280F(b)(2) When Business Use Drops to 50% or Less
See instructions.

		(a) Section 179	(b) Section 280F(b)(2)
35 Section 179 expense deduction or depreciation allowable in prior years	35		
36 Recomputed depreciation. See instructions	36		
37 Recapture amount. Subtract line 36 from line 35. See the instructions for where to report	37		

Printed on recycled paper

Form **5329**

Department of the Treasury
Internal Revenue Service

Additional Taxes Attributable to Qualified Retirement Plans (Including IRAs), Annuities, and Modified Endowment Contracts

(Under Sections 72, 4973, 4974 and 4980A of the Internal Revenue Code)

▶ Attach to Form 1040. See separate instructions.

OMB No. 1545-0203

1993

Attachment Sequence No. **29**

Name of individual subject to additional tax. (If married filing jointly, see instructions.)		Your social security number
Fill in Your Address Only If You Are Filing This Form by Itself and Not With Your Tax Return	Home address (number and street), or P.O. box if mail is not delivered to your home	Apt. No.
	City, town or post office, state, and ZIP code	If this is an Amended Return, check here ▶ ☐

If you are subject to the 10% tax on early distributions **only, see Who Must File** in the instructions before continuing. You may be able to report this amount directly on Form 1040 without filing Form 5329.

Part I Tax on Early Distributions

Complete this part if a taxable distribution was made from your qualified retirement plan (including an IRA), annuity contract, or modified endowment contract before you reached age 59½. ***Note:*** *You must include the amount of the distribution on line 16b or 17b of Form 1040 or on the appropriate line of Form 4972.*

1	Early distributions included in gross income. See instructions	1	
2	Distributions excepted from additional tax. See instructions. (Enter appropriate No. for exception from instructions ▶ ______)	2	
3	Amount subject to additional tax (subtract line 2 from line 1)	3	
4	**Tax due** (multiply line 3 by 10% (.10)). Enter here and on Form 1040, line 51.	4	

Part II Tax on Excess Contributions to Individual Retirement Arrangements

Complete this part if, either in this year or in earlier years, you contributed more to your IRA than is or was allowable and you have an excess contribution subject to tax.

5	Excess contributions for 1993 (see instructions). Do not include this amount on Form 1040, line 24a or 24b			5	
6	Earlier year excess contributions not previously eliminated (see instructions)	6			
7	Contribution credit. (If your actual contribution for 1993 is less than your maximum allowable contribution, see instructions; otherwise, enter -0-.)	7			
8	1993 distributions from your IRA account that are includible in taxable income	8			
9	1992 tax year excess contributions (if any) withdrawn after the due date (including extensions) of your 1992 income tax return, and 1991 and earlier tax year excess contributions withdrawn in 1993 . . .	9			
10	Add lines 7, 8, and 9	10			
11	Adjusted earlier year excess contributions. (Subtract line 10 from line 6. Enter the result, but not less than zero.)			11	
12	Total excess contributions (add lines 5 and 11).			12	
13	**Tax due.** (Enter the **smaller** of 6% of line 12 or 6% of the value of your IRA on the last day of 1993.) Also enter this amount on Form 1040, line 51			13	

For Paperwork Reduction Act Notice, see page 1 of separate instructions. Cat. No. 13329Q Form **5329** (1993)

Part III Tax on Excess Accumulation in Qualified Retirement Plans (Including IRAs)

14	Minimum required distribution (see instructions)	14	
15	Amount actually distributed to you	15	
16	Subtract line 15 from line 14. If line 15 is more than line 14, enter -0-	16	
17	**Tax due** (multiply line 16 by 50% (.50)). Enter here and on Form 1040, line 51	17	

Part IV Tax on Excess Distributions From Qualified Retirement Plans (Including IRAs)

Complete Column A for regular distributions. Complete Column B for lump-sum distributions.			Column A Regular Distributions	Column B Lump-Sum Distributions
18	Total amount of regular retirement or lump-sum distributions	18		
19	Amount excluded from additional tax. (Enter appropriate No. for exception from instructions ▶ ____)	19		
20	Subtract line 19 from line 18	20		
21	Enter the **greater** of the threshold amount or the 1993 recovery of the grandfather amount (from Worksheet 1 or 2). See instructions	21		
22	Excess distributions. (Subtract line 21 from line 20. If less than zero, enter -0-)	22		
23	Tentative tax. (Multiply line 22 by 15% (.15))	23		
24	Early distributions tax offset. See instructions	24		
25	Subtract line 24 from line 23	25		
26	**Tax due.** (Combine columns (a) and (b) of line 25.) Enter here and on Form 1040, line 51	26		

Acceleration Elections (see the instructions for Part IV)

1 If you elected the discretionary method in 1987 or 1988 and wish to make an acceleration election beginning in 1993 under Temp. Regs. section 54.4981A-1T b-12, check here ▶ ☐.

2 If you previously made an acceleration election and wish to revoke that election, check here ▶ ☐

Signature. *Complete **ONLY** if you are filing this form by itself and not with your tax return.*

Please Sign Here	Under penalties of perjury, I declare that I have examined this form, including accompanying schedules and statements, and to the best of my knowledge and belief, it is true, correct, and complete. Declaration of preparer (other than taxpayer) is based on all information of which preparer has any knowledge. ▶ Your signature	▶ Date	
Paid Preparer's Use Only	Preparer's signature ▶	Date	Check if self-employed ▶ ☐ — Preparer's social security no.
	Firm's name (or yours, if self-employed) and address ▶	E.I. No. ▶	ZIP code ▶

Printed on recycled paper

Form **6251**

Department of the Treasury
Internal Revenue Service

Alternative Minimum Tax—Individuals

▶ See separate instructions.

▶ Attach to Form 1040 or Form 1040NR.

OMB No. 1545-0227

1993

Attachment Sequence No. **32**

Name(s) shown on Form 1040 | Your social security number

Part I Adjustments and Preferences

1	If you itemized deductions on Schedule A (Form 1040), go to line 2. If you did not itemize deductions, enter your standard deduction from Form 1040, line 34, and skip to line 6	1	
2	Medical and dental expenses. See instructions	2	
3	Taxes. Enter the amount from Schedule A, line 8	3	
4	Certain interest on a home mortgage not used to buy, build, or improve your home	4	
5	Miscellaneous itemized deductions. Enter the amount from Schedule A, line 24	5	
6	Refund of taxes. Enter any tax refund from Form 1040, line 10 or 22	6	( )
7	Investment interest. Enter difference between regular tax and AMT deduction	7	
8	Post-1986 depreciation. Enter difference between regular tax and AMT depreciation	8	
9	Adjusted gain or loss. Enter difference between AMT and regular tax gain or loss	9	
10	Incentive stock options. Enter excess of AMT income over regular tax income	10	
11	Passive activities. Enter difference between AMT and regular tax income or loss	11	
12	Beneficiaries of estates and trusts. Enter the amount from Schedule K-1 (Form 1041), line 8	12	
13	Tax-exempt interest from private activity bonds issued after 8/7/86	13	
14	Other. Enter the amount, if any, for each item and enter the total on line 14.		

a Charitable contributions		g Long-term contracts	
b Circulation expenditures		h Loss limitations	
c Depletion		i Mining costs	
d Depreciation (pre-1987)		j Pollution control facilities	
e Installment sales		k Research and experimental	
f Intangible drilling costs		l Tax shelter farm activities	
		m Related adjustments	

		14	
15	**Total Adjustments and Preferences.** Combine lines 1 through 14 ▶	15	

Part II Alternative Minimum Taxable Income

16	Enter the amount from **Form 1040, line 35.** If less than zero, enter as a (loss) ▶	16	
17	Net operating loss deduction, if any, from Form 1040, line 22. Enter as a positive amount	17	
18	If Form 1040, line 32, is over $108,450 (over $54,225 if married filing separately), enter your itemized deductions limitation, if any, from line 9 of the worksheet for Schedule A, line 26	18	( )
19	Combine lines 15 through 18 ▶	19	
20	Alternative tax net operating loss deduction. See instructions	20	
21	**Alternative Minimum Taxable Income.** Subtract line 20 from line 19. (If married filing separately and line 21 is more than $165,000, see instructions.) ▶	21	

Part III Exemption Amount and Alternative Minimum Tax

22 Exemption Amount. (If this form is for a child under age 14, see instructions.)

If your filing status is:	And line 21 is not over:	Enter on line 22:
Single or head of household	$112,500	$33,750
Married filing jointly or qualifying widow(er)	150,000	45,000
Married filing separately	75,000	22,500

If line 21 is **over** the amount shown above for your filing status, see instructions. — 22

23	Subtract line 22 from line 21. If zero or less, enter -0- here and on lines 26 and 28 ▶	23	
24	If line 23 is $175,000 or less ($87,500 or less if married filing separately), multiply line 23 by 26% (.26). Otherwise, see instructions	24	
25	Alternative minimum tax foreign tax credit. See instructions	25	
26	Tentative minimum tax. Subtract line 25 from line 24 ▶	26	
27	Enter your tax from Form 1040, line 38 (plus any amount from Form 4970 included on Form 1040, line 39), minus any foreign tax credit from Form 1040, line 43	27	
28	**Alternative Minimum Tax.** (If this form is for a child under age 14, see instructions.) Subtract line 27 from line 26. If zero or less, enter -0-. Enter here and on Form 1040, line 48 ▶	28	

For Paperwork Reduction Act Notice, see separate instructions. Cat. No. 13600G Form **6251** (1993)

Form **8615** | **Tax for Children Under Age 14 Who Have Investment Income of More Than $1,200** | OMB No. 1545-0998 **1993**

Department of the Treasury
Internal Revenue Service

▶ See instructions below and on back.
▶ Attach ONLY to the child's Form 1040, Form 1040A, or Form 1040NR.

Attachment Sequence No. 33

Child's name shown on return | **Child's social security number**

A Parent's name (first, initial, and last). **Caution:** *See instructions on back before completing.* | **B Parent's social security number**

C Parent's filing status (check one):
☐ Single ☐ Married filing jointly ☐ Married filing separately ☐ Head of household ☐ Qualifying widow(er)

Step 1 Figure child's net investment income

1	Enter child's investment income, such as taxable interest and dividend income. See instructions. If this amount is $1,200 or less, **stop here;** do not file this form	1	
2	If the child DID NOT itemize deductions on Schedule A (Form 1040 or Form 1040NR), enter $1,200. If the child ITEMIZED deductions, see instructions	2	
3	Subtract line 2 from line 1. If the result is zero or less, **stop here;** do not complete the rest of this form but ATTACH it to the child's return	3	
4	Enter child's **taxable** income from Form 1040, line 37; Form 1040A, line 22; or Form 1040NR, line 36	4	
5	Enter the **smaller** of line 3 or line 4 here ▶	5	

Step 2 Figure tentative tax based on the tax rate of the parent listed on line A

6	Enter parent's **taxable** income from Form 1040, line 37; Form 1040A, line 22; Form 1040EZ, line 6; or Form 1040NR, line 36. If the parent transferred property to a trust, see instructions	6	
7	Enter the total net investment income, if any, from Forms 8615, line 5, of ALL OTHER children of the parent identified above. **Do not** include the amount from line 5 above	7	
8	Add lines 5, 6, and 7	8	
9	Tax on line 8 based on the **parent's** filing status. See instructions. If from Schedule D Tax Worksheet, enter amount from line 4 of that worksheet here ▶	9	
10	Enter parent's tax from Form 1040, line 38; Form 1040A, line 23; Form 1040EZ, line 8; or Form 1040NR, line 37. If from Schedule D Tax Worksheet, enter amount from line 4 of that worksheet here ▶	10	
11	Subtract line 10 from line 9. If line 7 is blank, enter on line 13 the amount from line 11; skip lines 12a and 12b	11	
12a	Add lines 5 and 7 — 12a		
b	Divide line 5 by line 12a. Enter the result as a decimal (rounded to two places)	12b	× .
13	Multiply line 11 by line 12b ▶	13	

Step 3 Figure child's tax—If lines 4 and 5 above are the same, go to line 16 now.

14	Subtract line 5 from line 4 — 14		
15	Tax on line 14 based on the **child's** filing status. See instructions. If from Schedule D Tax Worksheet, enter amount from line 4 of that worksheet here ▶	15	
16	Add lines 13 and 15	16	
17	Tax on line 4 based on the **child's** filing status. See instructions. If from Schedule D Tax Worksheet, check here ▶ ☐	17	
18	Enter the **larger** of line 16 or line 17 here and on Form 1040, line 38; Form 1040A, line 23; or Form 1040NR, line 37. Be sure to check the box for "Form 8615" even if line 17 is more than line 16 ▶	18	

General Instructions

A Change To Note.—If line 8 of Form 8615 is over $70,000 (over $140,000 if the parent's filing status is married filing jointly or qualifying widow(er)), the election to defer additional 1993 taxes may apply to the child. Get **Form 8841,** Deferral of Additional 1993 Taxes, for details. If the election is made, Form 1040A **cannot** be filed for the child.

Purpose of Form.—For children under age 14, investment income over $1,200 is taxed at the parent's rate if the parent's rate is higher than the child's rate. If the child's investment income is more than $1,200, use this form to figure the child's tax.

Investment Income.—As used on this form, "investment income" includes all taxable income other than earned income as defined on page 2. It includes income such as taxable interest, dividends, capital gains, rents, royalties, etc. It also includes pension and annuity income and income (other than earned income) received as the beneficiary of a trust.

Who Must File.—Generally, Form 8615 must be filed for any child who was under age 14 on January 1, 1994, had more than $1,200 of investment income, and is required to file a tax return. If neither parent was alive on December 31, 1993, do not use Form 8615. Instead, figure the child's tax in the normal manner.

Note: *The parent may be able to elect to report the child's interest and dividends on his or her return. If the parent makes this election, the child will not have to file a return or Form 8615. For more details, see the instructions for Form 1040 or Form 1040A, or get* **Form 8814,** *Parents' Election To Report Child's Interest and Dividends.*

Additional Information.—For more details, get **Pub. 929,** Tax Rules for Children and Dependents.

Incomplete Information for Parent.—If the parent's taxable income or filing status or the net investment income of

For Paperwork Reduction Act Notice, see back of form. Cat. No. 64113U Form **8615** (1993)

Form **8814**

Department of the Treasury
Internal Revenue Service

Parents' Election To Report Child's Interest and Dividends

▶ See instructions below and on back.
▶ Attach to parents' Form 1040 or Form 1040NR.

OMB No. 1545-1128

1993

Attachment Sequence No. **40**

Name(s) shown on your return | Your social security number

A Child's name (first, initial, and last) | B Child's social security number

C If more than one Form 8814 is attached, check here . . . . ▶ ☐

Step 1 Figure amount of child's interest and dividend income to report on your return

1a	Enter your child's **taxable** interest income. If this amount is different from the amounts shown on the child's Forms 1099-INT and 1099-OID, see the instructions	1a	
b	Enter your child's **tax-exempt** interest income. **DO NOT** include this amount on line 1a	1b	
2a	Enter your child's gross dividends, including any Alaska Permanent Fund dividends. If none, enter -0- on line 2c and go to line 3. If your child received any capital gain distributions or dividends as a nominee, see the instructions	2a	
b	Enter your child's nontaxable distributions that are included on line 2a. These should be shown in box 1d of Form 1099-DIV	2b	
c	Subtract line 2b from line 2a	2c	
3	Add lines 1a and 2c. If the total is $1,000 or less, skip lines 4 and 5 and go to line 6. If the total is $5,000 or more, **do not** file this form. Your child **must** file his or her own return to report the income	3	
4	Base amount	4	1,000 00
5	Subtract line 4 from line 3. If you checked the box on line C above or if line 2a includes any capital gain distributions, see the instructions. Also, include this amount in the total on Form 1040, line 22, or Form 1040NR, line 22. In the space next to line 22, enter "Form 8814" and show the amount. Go to line 6 below . . . . ▶	5	

Step 2 Figure your tax on the first $1,000 of child's interest and dividend income

6	Amount not taxed	6	500 00
7	Subtract line 6 from line 3. If the result is zero or less, enter -0-	7	
8	**Tax.** Is the amount on line 7 less than $500? • **NO.** Enter $75 here and see the **Note** below. • **YES.** Multiply line 7 by 15% (.15). Enter the result here and see the **Note** below.	8	

Note: *If you checked the box on line C above, see the instructions. Otherwise, include the amount from line 8 in the tax you enter on Form 1040, line 38, or Form 1040NR, line 37. Also, enter the amount from line 8 in the space provided next to line 38 on Form 1040, or next to line 37 on Form 1040NR.*

General Instructions

Purpose of Form.—Use this form if you elect to report your child's income on your return. If you do, your child will not have to file a return. You can make this election if your child meets **all** of the following conditions:

- Was under age 14 on January 1, 1994.
- Is required to file a 1993 return.
- Had income only from interest and dividends, including Alaska Permanent Fund dividends.
- Had gross income for 1993 that was less than $5,000.
- Had no estimated tax payments for 1993.
- Did not have any overpayment of tax shown on his or her 1992 return applied to the 1993 return.
- Had no Federal income tax withheld from his or her income (backup withholding).

You must also qualify as explained on page 2 of these instructions.

Step 1 of the form is used to figure the amount of your child's income to report on your return. **Step 2** is used to figure an additional tax that must be added to your tax.

How To Make the Election.—To make the election, complete and attach Form 8814 to your tax return and file your return by the due date (including extensions). A separate Form 8814 must be filed for **each** child whose income you choose to report.

Caution: *The Federal income tax on your child's income may be less if you file a tax return for the child instead of making this election. This is because you cannot take certain deductions that your child would be entitled to on his or her own return. For details, see* ***Deductions You May Not Take*** *on page 2.*

SCHEDULE EIC (Form 1040A or 1040) Department of the Treasury Internal Revenue Service (99)	**Earned Income Credit (Qualifying Child Information)** ▶ Attach to Form 1040A or 1040. ▶ See instructions on back.	OMB No. 1545-0074 **1994** Attachment Sequence No. **43**
Name(s) shown on return		Your social security number

Before You Begin . . .

- Answer the questions on page 44 (1040A) or page 27 (1040) to see if you can take this credit.
- If you can take the credit, fill in the worksheet on page 45 (1040A) or page 28 (1040) to figure your credit. **But if you want the IRS to figure it for you, see page 40 (1040A) or page 24 (1040).**

Then, complete and attach Schedule EIC only if you have a qualifying child (see boxes on back).

Information About Your Qualifying Child or Children

If you have more than two qualifying children, you only have to list two to get the maximum credit.

Caution: *If you don't fill in all the lines that apply, it will take us longer to process your return and issue your refund.*	**(a) Child 1**	**(b) Child 2**
1 Child's name (first, initial, and last name)		
2 Child's year of birth	19___	19___
3 If child was born **before 1976** AND—		
a was a student **under age 24** at the end of 1994, check the "Yes" box, **OR**	☐ Yes	☐ Yes
b was permanently and totally disabled (see back), check the "Yes" box	☐ Yes	☐ Yes
4 If child was born **before 1994,** enter the child's social security number		
5 Child's relationship to you (for example, son, grandchild, etc.)		
6 Number of months child lived with you in the U.S. in 1994	months	months

TIP: Do you want the earned income credit added to your take-home pay in 1995? To see if you qualify, get **Form W-5** from your employer or by calling the IRS at 1-800-TAX-FORM (1-800-829-3676).

For Paperwork Reduction Act Notice, see Form 1040A or 1040 instructions. Cat. No. 13339M **Schedule EIC (Form 1040A or 1040) 1994**

Instructions

Purpose of Schedule

If you can take the earned income credit and have a qualifying child, use Schedule EIC to give information about that child. To figure the amount of your credit, use the worksheet on page 45 of the Form 1040A instructions or page 28 of the Form 1040 instructions.

Line 1

Enter each qualifying child's name.

Line 3a

If your child was born **before 1976** but was under age 24 at the end of 1994 and a student, put a checkmark in the "Yes" box.

Your child was a **student** if he or she—

- Was enrolled as a full-time student at a school during any 5 months of 1994, or
- Took a full-time, on-farm training course during any 5 months of 1994. The course had to be given by a school or a state, county, or local government agency.

A **school** includes technical, trade, and mechanical schools. It does not include on-the-job training courses or correspondence schools.

Line 3b

If your child was born **before 1976** and was permanently and totally disabled during any part of 1994, put a checkmark in the "Yes" box.

A person is **permanently and totally disabled** if **both** of the following apply.

1. He or she cannot engage in any substantial gainful activity because of a physical or mental condition.

2. A doctor determines the condition has lasted or can be expected to last continuously for at least a year or can lead to death.

Line 4

If your child was born **before 1994,** you must enter his or her social security number (SSN) on line 4. If you don't enter an SSN or if the SSN you enter is incorrect, it will take us longer to issue any refund shown on your return. If your child doesn't have a number, apply for one by filing **Form SS-5** with your local Social Security Administration (SSA) office. It usually takes about 2 weeks to get a number. If your child won't have an SSN by April 17, 1995, you can get an automatic 4-month extension by filing Form 4868 with the IRS by that date.

Line 6

Enter the number of months your child lived with you in your home in the United States during 1994. Do not enter more than 12. Count temporary absences, such as for school, vacation, or medical care, as time lived in your home. If the child lived with you for more than half of 1994 but less than 7 months, enter "7" on this line.

Exception. If your child, including a foster child, was born or died in 1994 and your home was the child's home for the entire time he or she was alive during 1994, enter "12" on line 6.

Qualifying Child

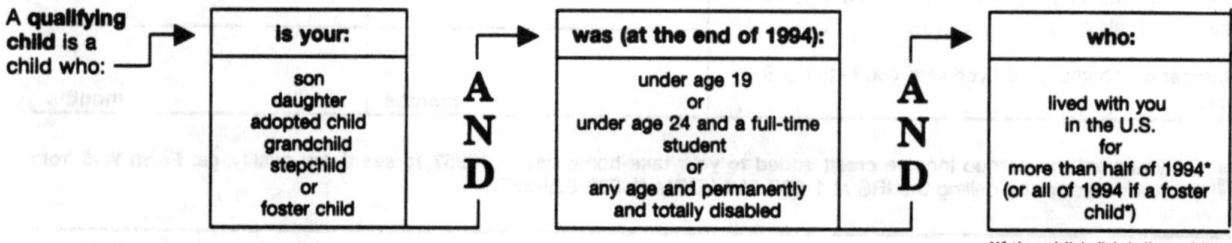

*If the child didn't live with you for the required time (for example, was born in 1994), see the **Line 6** instructions above.

If the child was married or is also a qualifying child of another person (other than your spouse if filing a joint return), special rules apply. For details, see page 47 of the Form 1040A instructions or page 28 of the Form 1040 instructions.

Printed on recycled paper

SCHEDULE F (Form 1040)

Department of the Treasury Internal Revenue Service (99)

Profit or Loss From Farming

▶ Attach to Form 1040, Form 1041, or Form 1065.

▶ See Instructions for Schedule F (Form 1040).

OMB No. 1545-0074

1994

Attachment Sequence No. **14**

Name of proprietor | **Social security number (SSN)**

A Principal product. Describe in one or two words your principal crop or activity for the current tax year.

B Enter principal agricultural activity code (from page 2) ▶

D Employer ID number (EIN), if any

C Accounting method: (1) ☐ Cash (2) ☐ Accrual

E Did you "materially participate" in the operation of this business during 1994? If "No," see page F-2 for limit on passive losses. ☐ Yes ☐ No

Part I **Farm Income—Cash Method. Complete Parts I and II (Accrual method taxpayers complete Parts II and III, and line 11 of Part I.)**
Do not include sales of livestock held for draft, breeding, sport, or dairy purposes; report these sales on Form 4797.

1	Sales of livestock and other items you bought for resale	**1**	
2	Cost or other basis of livestock and other items reported on line 1	**2**	
3	Subtract line 2 from line 1	**3**	
4	Sales of livestock, produce, grains, and other products you raised	**4**	
5a	Total cooperative distributions (Form(s) 1099-PATR) **5a** ___ **5b** Taxable amount	**5b**	
6a	Agricultural program payments (see page F-2) **6a** ___ **6b** Taxable amount	**6b**	
7	Commodity Credit Corporation (CCC) loans (see page F-2):		
a	CCC loans reported under election	**7a**	
b	CCC loans forfeited or repaid with certificates **7b** ___ **7c** Taxable amount	**7c**	
8	Crop insurance proceeds and certain disaster payments (see page F-2):		
a	Amount received in 1994 **8a** ___ **8b** Taxable amount	**8b**	
c	If election to defer to 1995 is attached, check here ▶ ☐ **8d** Amount deferred from 1993	**8d**	
9	Custom hire (machine work) income	**9**	
10	Other income, including Federal and state gasoline or fuel tax credit or refund (see page F-3)	**10**	
11	**Gross income.** Add amounts in the right column for lines 3 through 10. If accrual method taxpayer, enter the amount from page 2, line 51 ▶	**11**	

Part II **Farm Expenses—Cash and Accrual Method. Do not** include personal or living expenses such as taxes, insurance, repairs, etc., on your home.

12	Car and truck expenses (see page F-3—also attach **Form 4562**)	**12**		**25**	Pension and profit-sharing plans	**25**	
13	Chemicals	**13**		**26**	Rent or lease (see page F-4):		
14	Conservation expenses. Attach **Form 8645**	**14**		**a**	Vehicles, machinery, and equipment	**26a**	
15	Custom hire (machine work)	**15**		**b**	Other (land, animals, etc.)	**26b**	
16	Depreciation and section 179 expense deduction not claimed elsewhere (see page F-4)	**16**		**27**	Repairs and maintenance	**27**	
				28	Seeds and plants purchased	**28**	
				29	Storage and warehousing	**29**	
17	Employee benefit programs other than on line 25	**17**		**30**	Supplies purchased	**30**	
				31	Taxes	**31**	
18	Feed purchased	**18**		**32**	Utilities	**32**	
19	Fertilizers and lime	**19**		**33**	Veterinary, breeding, and medicine	**33**	
20	Freight and trucking	**20**		**34**	Other expenses (specify):		
21	Gasoline, fuel, and oil	**21**		**a**		**34a**	
22	Insurance (other than health)	**22**		**b**		**34b**	
23	Interest:			**c**		**34c**	
a	Mortgage (paid to banks, etc.)	**23a**		**d**		**34d**	
b	Other	**23b**		**e**		**34e**	
24	Labor hired (less employment credits)	**24**		**f**		**34f**	

35	**Total expenses.** Add lines 12 through 34f ▶	**35**	
36	**Net farm profit or (loss).** Subtract line 35 from line 11. If a profit, enter on **Form 1040, line 18,** and ALSO on **Schedule SE, line 1.** If a loss, you MUST go on to line 37 (estates, trusts, and partnerships, see page F-5).	**36**	
37	If you have a loss, you MUST check the box that describes your investment in this activity (see page F-5). If you checked 37a, enter the loss on **Form 1040, line 18,** and ALSO on **Schedule SE, line 1.** If you checked 37b, you MUST attach **Form 6198.**	**37a** ☐ All investment is at risk. **37b** ☐ Some investment is not at risk.	

For Paperwork Reduction Act Notice, see Form 1040 Instructions. Cat. No. 11346H **Schedule F (Form 1040) 1994**

Part III Farm Income—Accrual Method (see page F-5)

Do not include sales of livestock held for draft, breeding, sport, or dairy purposes; report these sales on Form 4797 and do not include this livestock on line 46 below.

38	Sales of livestock, produce, grains, and other products during the year			38	
39a	Total cooperative distributions (Form(s) 1099-PATR)	39a	39b Taxable amount	39b	
40a	Agricultural program payments	40a	40b Taxable amount	40b	
41	Commodity Credit Corporation (CCC) loans:				
a	CCC loans reported under election			41a	
b	CCC loans forfeited or repaid with certificates	41b	41c Taxable amount	41c	
42	Crop insurance proceeds			42	
43	Custom hire (machine work) income			43	
44	Other income, including Federal and state gasoline or fuel tax credit or refund			44	
45	Add amounts in the right column for lines 38 through 44			45	
46	Inventory of livestock, produce, grains, and other products at beginning of the year	46			
47	Cost of livestock, produce, grains, and other products purchased during the year	47			
48	Add lines 46 and 47	48			
49	Inventory of livestock, produce, grains, and other products at end of year	49			
50	Cost of livestock, produce, grains, and other products sold. Subtract line 49 from line 48*			50	
51	**Gross income.** Subtract line 50 from line 45. Enter the result here and on page 1, line 11 ▶			51	

*If you use the unit-livestock-price method or the farm-price method of valuing inventory and the amount on line 49 is larger than the amount on line 48, subtract line 48 from line 49. Enter the result on line 50. Add lines 45 and 50. Enter the total on line 51.

Part IV Principal Agricultural Activity Codes

Caution: *File* ***Schedule C*** *(Form 1040), Profit or Loss From Business, or* ***Schedule C-EZ*** *(Form 1040), Net Profit From Business, instead of Schedule F if:*

- *Your principal source of income is from providing agricultural services such as soil preparation, veterinary, farm labor, horticultural, or management for a fee or on a contract basis, or*
- *You are engaged in the business of breeding, raising, and caring for dogs, cats, or other pet animals.*

Select one of the following codes and write the 3-digit number on page 1, line B:

120 **Field crop,** including grains and nongrains such as cotton, peanuts, feed corn, wheat, tobacco, Irish potatoes, etc.

160 **Vegetables and melons,** garden-type vegetables and melons, such as sweet corn, tomatoes, squash, etc.

170 **Fruit and tree nuts,** including grapes, berries, olives, etc.

180 **Ornamental floriculture and nursery products**

185 **Food crops grown under cover,** including hydroponic crops

211 **Beefcattle feedlots**

212 **Beefcattle,** except feedlots

215 **Hogs, sheep, and goats**

240 **Dairy**

250 **Poultry and eggs,** including chickens, ducks, pigeons, quail, etc.

260 **General livestock,** not specializing in any one livestock category

270 **Animal specialty,** including bees, fur-bearing animals, horses, snakes, etc.

280 **Animal aquaculture,** including fish, shellfish, mollusks, frogs, etc., produced within confined space

290 **Forest products,** including forest nurseries and seed gathering, extraction of pine gum, and gathering of forest products

300 **Agricultural production,** not specified

Printed on recycled paper

Schedule R (Form 1040)

Department of the Treasury
Internal Revenue Service (99)

Credit for the Elderly or the Disabled

▶ Attach to Form 1040. ▶ See separate instructions for Schedule R.

OMB No. 1545-0074

1994

Attachment Sequence No. **16**

Name(s) shown on Form 1040 | **Your social security number**

You may be able to take this credit and reduce your tax if by the end of 1994:

- You were age 65 or older, **OR** • You were under age 65, you retired on **permanent and total** disability, and you received taxable disability income.

But you must also meet other tests. See the separate instructions for Schedule R.

Note: *In most cases, the IRS can figure the credit for you. See page 24 of the Form 1040 instructions.*

Part I Check the Box for Your Filing Status and Age

If your filing status is:	And by the end of 1994:	Check only one box:
Single, Head of household, or Qualifying widow(er) with dependent child	1 You were 65 or older 1	☐
	2 You were under 65 and you retired on permanent and total disability . . . 2	☐
Married filing a joint return	3 Both spouses were 65 or older 3	☐
	4 Both spouses were under 65, but only one spouse retired on permanent and total disability 4	☐
	5 Both spouses were under 65, and both retired on permanent and total disability 5	☐
	6 One spouse was 65 or older, and the other spouse was under 65 and retired on permanent and total disability 6	☐
	7 One spouse was 65 or older, and the other spouse was under 65 and **NOT** retired on permanent and total disability 7	☐
Married filing a separate return	8 You were 65 or older and you lived apart from your spouse for all of 1994 . . 8	☐
	9 You were under 65, you retired on permanent and total disability, and you lived apart from your spouse for all of 1994 9	☐

If you checked box 1, 3, 7, or 8, skip Part II and complete Part III on the back. All others, complete Parts II and III.

Part II Statement of Permanent and Total Disability (Complete **only** if you checked box 2, 4, 5, 6, or 9 above.)

IF: 1 You filed a physician's statement for this disability for 1983 or an earlier year, or you filed a statement for tax years after 1983 and your physician signed line B on the statement, **AND**

2 Due to your continued disabled condition, you were unable to engage in any substantial gainful activity in 1994, check this box . . . . ▶ ☐

- If you checked this box, you do not have to file another statement for 1994.
- If you **did not** check this box, have your physician complete the statement below.

Physician's Statement (See instructions at bottom of page 2.)

I certify that ______________________________
Name of disabled person

was permanently and totally disabled on January 1, 1976, or January 1, 1977, **OR** was permanently and totally disabled on the date he or she retired. If retired after December 31, 1976, enter the date retired. ▶ ______________

Physician: Sign your name on **either** line A or B below.

A The disability has lasted or can be expected to last continuously for at least a year . . . . ______________ Physician's signature Date

B There is no reasonable probability that the disabled condition will ever improve . . . . ______________ Physician's signature Date

Physician's name | Physician's address

For Paperwork Reduction Act Notice, see Form 1040 Instructions. Cat. No. 11359K **Schedule R (Form 1040) 1994**

Part III **Figure Your Credit**

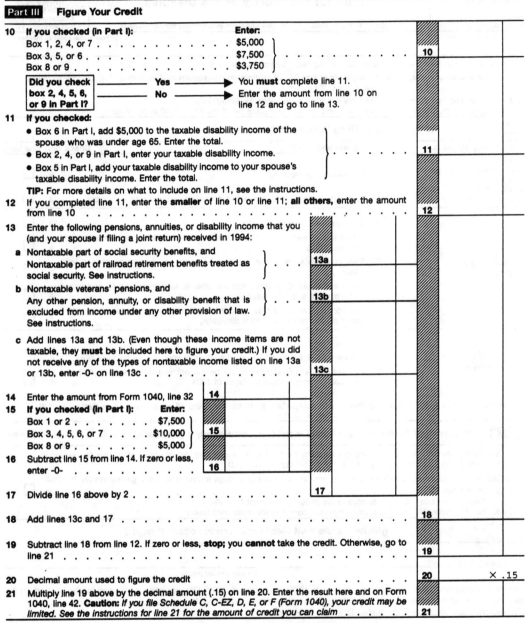

10 **If you checked (in Part I):** **Enter:**
Box 1, 2, 4, or 7 . . . . $5,000
Box 3, 5, or 6 . . . . $7,500
Box 8 or 9 . . . . $3,750 } **10**

Did you check box 2, 4, 5, 6, or 9 in Part I? — **Yes** → You **must** complete line 11.
— **No** → Enter the amount from line 10 on line 12 and go to line 13.

11 **If you checked:**
- Box 6 in Part I, add $5,000 to the taxable disability income of the spouse who was under age 65. Enter the total.
- Box 2, 4, or 9 in Part I, enter your taxable disability income.
- Box 5 in Part I, add your taxable disability income to your spouse's taxable disability income. Enter the total.

} **11**

TIP: For more details on what to include on line 11, see the instructions.

12 If you completed line 11, enter the **smaller** of line 10 or line 11; **all others,** enter the amount from line 10 . . . . **12**

13 Enter the following pensions, annuities, or disability income that you (and your spouse if filing a joint return) received in 1994:

a Nontaxable part of social security benefits, and Nontaxable part of railroad retirement benefits treated as social security. See instructions. } . . . **13a**

b Nontaxable veterans' pensions, and Any other pension, annuity, or disability benefit that is excluded from income under any other provision of law. See instructions. } . . . **13b**

c Add lines 13a and 13b. (Even though these income items are not taxable, they **must** be included here to figure your credit.) If you did not receive any of the types of nontaxable income listed on line 13a or 13b, enter -0- on line 13c **13c**

14 Enter the amount from Form 1040, line 32 **14**

15 **If you checked (in Part I):** **Enter:**
Box 1 or 2 . . . . $7,500
Box 3, 4, 5, 6, or 7 . . . . $10,000
Box 8 or 9 . . . . $5,000 } **15**

16 Subtract line 15 from line 14. If zero or less, enter -0- **16**

17 Divide line 16 above by 2 . . . . **17**

18 Add lines 13c and 17 . . . . **18**

19 Subtract line 18 from line 12. If zero or less, **stop;** you **cannot** take the credit. Otherwise, go to line 21 . . . . **19**

20 Decimal amount used to figure the credit . . . . **20** × .15

21 Multiply line 19 above by the decimal amount (.15) on line 20. Enter the result here and on Form 1040, line 42. **Caution:** *If you file Schedule C, C-EZ, D, E, or F (Form 1040), your credit may be limited. See the instructions for line 21 for the amount of credit you can claim* **21**

Instructions for Physician's Statement

Taxpayer

If you retired after December 31, 1976, enter the date you retired in the space provided in Part II.

Physician

A person is permanently and totally disabled if **both** of the following apply:

1. He or she cannot engage in any substantial gainful activity because of a physical or mental condition, and

2. A physician determines that the disability has lasted or can be expected to last continuously for at least a year or can lead to death.

 *Printed on recycled paper*

Form **2106** | **Employee Business Expenses** | OMB No. 1545-0139

▶ **See separate instructions.**

▶ **Attach to Form 1040.**

Department of the Treasury Internal Revenue Service (99) | **1994** | Attachment Sequence No. **54**

Your name	Social security number	Occupation in which expenses were incurred

Part I **Employee Business Expenses and Reimbursements**

STEP 1 Enter Your Expenses		**Column A** Other Than Meals and Entertainment	**Column B** Meals and Entertainment
1 Vehicle expense from line 22 or line 29	1		
2 Parking fees, tolls, and transportation, including train, bus, etc., that **did not** involve overnight travel	2		
3 Travel expense while away from home overnight, including lodging, airplane, car rental, etc. **Do not** include meals and entertainment	3		
4 Business expenses not included on lines 1 through 3. **Do not** include meals and entertainment	4		
5 Meals and entertainment expenses (see instructions)	5		
6 **Total expenses.** In Column A, add lines 1 through 4 and enter the result. In Column B, enter the amount from line 5	6		

Note: *If you were not reimbursed for any expenses in Step 1, skip line 7 and enter the amount from line 6 on line 8.*

STEP 2 Enter Amounts Your Employer Gave You for Expenses Listed in STEP 1

7 Enter amounts your employer gave you that were **not** reported to you in box 1 of Form W-2. Include any amount reported under code "L" in box 13 of your Form W-2 (see instructions) . . .	7		

STEP 3 Figure Expenses To Deduct on Schedule A (Form 1040)

8 Subtract line 7 from line 6	8		
Note: *If **both columns** of line 8 are zero, **stop here.** If Column A is less than zero, report the amount as income on Form 1040, line 7.*			
9 In Column A, enter the amount from line 8 (if zero or less, enter -0-). In Column B, multiply the amount on line 8 by 50% (.50) .	9		
10 Add the amounts on line 9 of both columns and enter the total here. **Also, enter the total on Schedule A (Form 1040), line 20.** (Qualified performing artists and individuals with disabilities, see the instructions for special rules on where to enter the total.) . . . . ▶		10	

For Paperwork Reduction Act Notice, see instructions. Cat. No. 11700N Form **2106** (1994)

Part II **Vehicle Expenses** (See instructions to find out which sections to complete.)

Section A.—General Information

			(a) Vehicle 1	(b) Vehicle 2
11	Enter the date vehicle was placed in service	11	/ /	/ /
12	Total miles vehicle was driven during 1994	12	miles	miles
13	Business miles included on line 12	13	miles	miles
14	Percent of business use. Divide line 13 by line 12	14	%	%
15	Average daily round trip commuting distance	15	miles	miles
16	Commuting miles included on line 12	16	miles	miles
17	Other personal miles. Add lines 13 and 16 and subtract the total from line 12	17	miles	miles

18 Do you (or your spouse) have another vehicle available for personal purposes? ☐ Yes ☐ No

19 If your employer provided you with a vehicle, is personal use during off duty hours permitted? ☐ Yes ☐ No ☐ Not applicable

20 Do you have evidence to support your deduction? ☐ Yes ☐ No

21 If "Yes," is the evidence written? ☐ Yes ☐ No

Section B.—Standard Mileage Rate (Use this section only if you own the vehicle.)

22	Multiply line 13 by 29¢ (.29). Enter the result here and on line 1. (Rural mail carriers, see instructions.)	22	

Section C.—Actual Expenses

			(a) Vehicle 1		(b) Vehicle 2	
23	Gasoline, oil, repairs, vehicle insurance, etc.	23				
24a	Vehicle rentals	24a				
b	Inclusion amount (see instructions)	24b				
c	Subtract line 24b from line 24a	24c				
25	Value of employer-provided vehicle (applies only if 100% of annual lease value was included on Form W-2—see instructions)	25				
26	Add lines 23, 24c, and 25	26				
27	Multiply line 26 by the percentage on line 14	27				
28	Depreciation. Enter amount from line 38 below	28				
29	Add lines 27 and 28. Enter total here and on line 1.	29				

Section D.—Depreciation of Vehicles (Use this section only if you own the vehicle.)

			(a) Vehicle 1		(b) Vehicle 2	
30	Enter cost or other basis (see instructions)	30				
31	Enter amount of section 179 deduction (see instructions)	31				
32	Multiply line 30 by line 14 (see instructions if you elected the section 179 deduction)	32				
33	Enter depreciation method and percentage (see instructions)	33				
34	Multiply line 32 by the percentage on line 33 (see instructions)	34				
35	Add lines 31 and 34	35				
36	Enter the limitation amount from the table in the line 36 instructions	36				
37	Multiply line 36 by the percentage on line 14	37				
38	Enter the **smaller** of line 35 or line 37. Also, enter this amount on line 28 above	38				

Printed on recycled paper

Form **2106-EZ**

Department of the Treasury
Internal Revenue Service

Unreimbursed Employee Business Expenses

▶ See instructions on back.

▶ Attach to Form 1040.

OMB No. 1545-XXXX

1994

Attachment Sequence No. **54A**

Your name	Social security number	Occupation in which expenses were incurred
	: :	

Part I General Information

You May Use This Form ONLY if All of the Following Apply:

- You are an employee deducting expenses attributable to your job.
- You **do not** get reimbursed by your employer for any expenses (amounts your employer included in box 1 of your Form W-2 are not considered reimbursements).
- If you are claiming vehicle expense,
  - **a** You own your vehicle, and
  - **b** You are using the standard mileage rate for 1994 **AND** also used it for the year you first placed the vehicle in service.

Part II Figure Your Expenses

1	Vehicle expense using the standard mileage rate. Complete Part III and multiply line 8a by 29¢ (.29)	1	
2	Parking fees, tolls, and transportation, including train, bus, etc., that **did not** involve overnight travel	2	
3	Travel expense while away from home overnight, including lodging, airplane, car rental, etc. **Do not** include meals and entertainment	3	
4	Business expenses not included on lines 1 through 3. **Do not** include meals and entertainment	4	
5	Meals and entertainment expenses: $______ x 50% (.50)	5	
6	**Total expenses.** Add lines 1 through 5. Enter here and **on line 20 of Schedule A (Form 1040).** (Qualified performing artists and individuals with disabilities, see the instructions for special rules on where to enter this amount.)	6	

Part III Information on Your Vehicle. Complete this part ONLY if you are claiming vehicle expense on line 1.

7 When did you place your vehicle in service for business purposes? (month, day, year) ▶ ...... / ...... / ......

8 Of the total number of miles you drove your vehicle during 1994, enter the number of miles you used your vehicle for:

a Business .... **b** Commuting .... **c** Other ....

9 Do you (or your spouse) have another vehicle available for personal use? ☐ Yes ☐ No

10 Was your vehicle available for use during off-duty hours? ☐ Yes ☐ No

11a Do you have evidence to support your deduction? ☐ Yes ☐ No

b If "Yes," is the evidence written? ☐ Yes ☐ No

For Paperwork Reduction Act Notice, see back of form. Cat. No. 20604Q Form **2106-EZ** (1994)

Form **3903**

Department of the Treasury
Internal Revenue Service

Moving Expenses

▶ **Attach to Form 1040.**

▶ **See separate instructions.**

OMB No. 1545-0062

1994

Attachment Sequence No. **62**

Name(s) shown on Form 1040

Your social security number

Part I Moving Expenses Incurred in 1994

Caution: *If you are a member of the armed forces, see the instructions before completing this part.*

1 Enter the number of miles from your **old home** to your **new workplace**	1	miles	
2 Enter the number of miles from your **old home** to your **old workplace**	2	miles	
3 Subtract line 2 from line 1. Enter the result but not less than zero	3	miles	

Is line 3 at least 50 miles?

Yes ▶ Go to line 4. Also, see **Time Test** in the instructions.

No ▶ You **cannot** deduct your moving expenses incurred in 1994. Do not complete the rest of this part. See the **Note** below if you also incurred moving expenses before 1994.

4 Transportation and storage of household goods and personal effects	4	
5 Travel and lodging expenses of moving from your old home to your new home. **Do not** include meals	5	
6 Add lines 4 and 5	6	
7 Enter the total amount your employer paid for your move (including the value of services furnished in kind) that is **not** included in the wages box (box 1) of your W-2 form. This amount should be identified with code **P** in box 13 of your W-2 form	7	

Is line 6 more than line 7?

Yes ▶ Go to line 8.

No ▶ You **cannot** deduct your moving expenses incurred in 1994. If line 6 is less than line 7, subtract line 6 from line 7 and include the result in income on Form 1040, line 7.

8 Subtract line 7 from line 6. Enter the result here and on Form 1040, line 24. This is your **moving expense deduction for expenses incurred in 1994**	8	

Note: *If you incurred moving expenses* ***before 1994*** *and you did not deduct those expenses on a prior year's tax return, complete Parts II and III on the back to figure the amount, if any, you may deduct on* ***Schedule A,*** *Itemized Deductions.*

For Paperwork Reduction Act Notice, see separate instructions. Cat. No. 12490K Form **3903** (1994)

Name(s) shown on Form 1040. Do not enter name and social security number if shown on other side. | **Your social security number**

Caution: *If you are a member of the armed forces, see the instructions before completing Parts II and III.*

Part II Moving Expenses Incurred Before 1994

1 Enter the number of miles from your **old home** to your **new workplace** . . . . 1 miles

2 Enter the number of miles from your **old home** to your **old workplace** . . . . 2 miles

3 Subtract line 2 from line 1. Enter the result but not less than zero. . . . . ▶ 3 miles

If line 3 is 35 or more miles, complete the rest of this part and Part III. Also, see **Time Test** in the instructions. If line 3 is less than 35 miles, you **cannot** deduct your moving expenses incurred before 1994.

Note: *Any payments your employer made for your moving expenses incurred before 1994 (including the value of any services furnished in kind) should be included as wages on your W-2 form. Report that amount on* ***Form 1040, line 7.***

Section A—Transportation of Household Goods

4 Transportation and storage of household goods and personal effects. 4

Section B—Expenses of Moving From Old To New Home

5 Travel and lodging **not** including meals 5

6 Total meals 6

7 Multiply line 6 by 80% (.80) 7

8 Add lines 5 and 7 8

Section C—Pre-move Househunting Expenses and Temporary Quarters
(for any 30 days in a row after getting your job)

9 Pre-move travel and lodging **not** including meals 9

10 Temporary quarters expenses **not** including meals 10

11 Total meal expenses for both pre-move househunting and temporary quarters 11

12 Multiply line 11 by 80% (.80) 12

13 Add lines 9, 10, and 12 13

Section D—Qualified Real Estate Expenses

14 Expenses of (check one) **a** ☐ selling or exchanging your old home, or **b** ☐ if renting, settling an unexpired lease. . 14

15 Expenses of (check one) **a** ☐ buying your new home, or **b** ☐ if renting, getting a new lease. 15

Part III Dollar Limits and Moving Expense Deduction For Expenses Incurred Before 1994

Note: *If you and your spouse moved to separate homes, see the instructions.*

16 Enter the **smaller** of:
- The amount on line 13, or
- $1,500 ($750 for certain married individuals filing a separate return—see instructions). . . 16

17 Add lines 14, 15, and 16 17

18 Enter the **smaller** of:
- The amount on line 17, or
- $3,000 ($1,500 for certain married individuals filing a separate return—see instructions). 18

19 Add lines 4, 8, and 18. Enter the total here and on Schedule A, line 27. This is your **moving expense deduction for expenses incurred before 1994**. . . . . ▶ 19

Printed on recycled paper

Form **8829**

Department of the Treasury
Internal Revenue Service (99)

Expenses for Business Use of Your Home

▶ **File only with Schedule C (Form 1040). Use a separate Form 8829 for each home you used for business during the year.**

▶ **See separate instructions.**

OMB No. 1545-1266

1994

Attachment Sequence No. **66**

Name(s) of proprietor(s)

Your social security number

Part I Part of Your Home Used for Business

1	Area used regularly and exclusively for business, regularly for day care, or for inventory storage. See instructions	1	
2	Total area of home	2	
3	Divide line 1 by line 2. Enter the result as a percentage	3	%
	• **For day-care facilities not used exclusively for business, also complete lines 4–6.**		
	• **All others, skip lines 4–6 and enter the amount from line 3 on line 7.**		
4	Multiply days used for day care during year by hours used per day — 4: hr.		
5	Total hours available for use during the year (365 days × 24 hours). See instructions — 5: 8,760 hr.		
6	Divide line 4 by line 5. Enter the result as a decimal amount — 6: .		
7	Business percentage. For day-care facilities not used exclusively for business, multiply line 6 by line 3 (enter the result as a percentage). All others, enter the amount from line 3 ▶	7	%

Part II Figure Your Allowable Deduction

			(a) Direct expenses	(b) Indirect expenses		
8	Enter the amount from Schedule C, line 29, **plus** any net gain or (loss) derived from the business use of your home and shown on Schedule D or Form 4797. If more than one place of business, see instructions				8	
	See instructions for columns (a) and (b) before completing lines 9–20.					
9	Casualty losses. See instructions	9				
10	Deductible mortgage interest. See instructions	10				
11	Real estate taxes. See instructions	11				
12	Add lines 9, 10, and 11	12				
13	Multiply line 12, column (b) by line 7		13			
14	Add line 12, column (a) and line 13				14	
15	Subtract line 14 from line 8. If zero or less, enter -0-				15	
16	Excess mortgage interest. See instructions	16				
17	Insurance	17				
18	Repairs and maintenance	18				
19	Utilities	19				
20	Other expenses. See instructions	20				
21	Add lines 16 through 20	21				
22	Multiply line 21, column (b) by line 7		22			
23	Carryover of operating expenses from 1993 Form 8829, line 41		23			
24	Add line 21 in column (a), line 22, and line 23				24	
25	Allowable operating expenses. Enter the **smaller** of line 15 or line 24				25	
26	Limit on excess casualty losses and depreciation. Subtract line 25 from line 15				26	
27	Excess casualty losses. See instructions		27			
28	Depreciation of your home from Part III below		28			
29	Carryover of excess casualty losses and depreciation from 1993 Form 8829, line 42		29			
30	Add lines 27 through 29				30	
31	Allowable excess casualty losses and depreciation. Enter the **smaller** of line 26 or line 30				31	
32	Add lines 14, 25, and 31				32	
33	Casualty loss portion, if any, from lines 14 and 31. Carry amount to **Form 4684,** Section B				33	
34	Allowable expenses for business use of your home. Subtract line 33 from line 32. Enter here and on Schedule C, line 30. If your home was used for more than one business, see instructions ▶				34	

Part III Depreciation of Your Home

35	Enter the **smaller** of your home's adjusted basis or its fair market value. See instructions	35	
36	Value of land included on line 35	36	
37	Basis of building. Subtract line 36 from line 35	37	
38	Business basis of building. Multiply line 37 by line 7	38	
39	Depreciation percentage. See instructions	39	%
40	Depreciation allowable. Multiply line 38 by line 39. Enter here and on line 28 above. See instructions	40	

Part IV Carryover of Unallowed Expenses to 1995

41	Operating expenses. Subtract line 25 from line 24. If less than zero, enter -0-	41	
42	Excess casualty losses and depreciation. Subtract line 31 from line 30. If less than zero, enter -0-	42	

For Paperwork Reduction Act Notice, see page 1 of separate instructions. *Printed on recycled paper* Cat. No. 13232M Form **8829** (1994)

Form **4562**

Department of the Treasury
Internal Revenue Service (99)

Depreciation and Amortization
(Including Information on Listed Property)

▶ See separate instructions. ▶ Attach this form to your return.

OMB No. 1545-0172

1994

Attachment Sequence No. 67

Name(s) shown on return | Identifying number

Business or activity to which this form relates

Part I **Election To Expense Certain Tangible Property (Section 179) (Note:** *If you have any "Listed Property," complete Part V before you complete Part I.)*

1	Maximum dollar limitation (If an enterprise zone business, see instructions.)	1	$17,500
2	Total cost of section 179 property placed in service during the tax year (see instructions)	2	
3	Threshold cost of section 179 property before reduction in limitation	3	$200,000
4	Reduction in limitation. Subtract line 3 from line 2. If zero or less, enter -0-	4	
5	Dollar limitation for tax year. Subtract line 4 from line 1. If zero or less, enter -0-. (If married filing separately, see instructions.)	5	

	(a) Description of property	(b) Cost	(c) Elected cost
6			
7	Listed property. Enter amount from line 26.	7	

8	Total elected cost of section 179 property. Add amounts in column (c), lines 6 and 7	8	
9	Tentative deduction. Enter the smaller of line 5 or line 8	9	
10	Carryover of disallowed deduction from 1993 (see instructions)	10	
11	Taxable income limitation. Enter the smaller of taxable income (not less than zero) or line 5 (see instructions)	11	
12	Section 179 expense deduction. Add lines 9 and 10, but do not enter more than line 11	12	
13	Carryover of disallowed deduction to 1995. Add lines 9 and 10, less line 12 ▶ 13		

Note: *Do not use Part II or Part III below for listed property (automobiles, certain other vehicles, cellular telephones, certain computers, or property used for entertainment, recreation, or amusement). Instead, use Part V for listed property.*

Part II **MACRS Depreciation For Assets Placed in Service ONLY During Your 1994 Tax Year (Do Not Include Listed Property)**

(a) Classification of property	(b) Month and year placed in service	(c) Basis for depreciation (business/investment use only—see instructions)	(d) Recovery period	(e) Convention	(f) Method	(g) Depreciation deduction
Section A—General Depreciation System (GDS) (see instructions)						
14a 3-year property						
b 5-year property						
c 7-year property						
d 10-year property						
e 15-year property						
f 20-year property						
g Residential rental property			27.5 yrs.	MM	S/L	
			27.5 yrs.	MM	S/L	
h Nonresidential real property			39 yrs.	MM	S/L	
				MM	S/L	
Section B—Alternative Depreciation System (ADS) (see instructions)						
15a Class life					S/L	
b 12-year			12 yrs.		S/L	
c 40-year			40 yrs.	MM	S/L	

Part III **Other Depreciation (Do Not Include Listed Property)**

16	GDS and ADS deductions for assets placed in service in tax years beginning before 1994 (see instructions)	16	
17	Property subject to section 168(f)(1) election (see instructions)	17	
18	ACRS and other depreciation (see instructions)	18	

Part IV **Summary**

19	Listed property. Enter amount from line 25.	19	
20	**Total.** Add deductions on line 12, lines 14 and 15 in column (g), and lines 16 through 19. Enter here and on the appropriate lines of your return. (Partnerships and S corporations—see instructions)	20	
21	For assets shown above and placed in service during the current year, enter the portion of the basis attributable to section 263A costs (see instructions) 21		

For Paperwork Reduction Act Notice, see page 1 of the separate instructions. Cat. No. 12906N Form **4562** (1994)

Part V Listed Property—Automobiles, Certain Other Vehicles, Cellular Telephones, Certain Computers, and Property Used for Entertainment, Recreation, or Amusement

*For any vehicle for which you are using the standard mileage rate or deducting lease expense, complete **only** 22a, 22b, columns (a) through (c) of Section A, all of Section B, and Section C if applicable.*

Section A—Depreciation and Other Information (Caution: *See instructions for limitations for automobiles.*)

22a Do you have evidence to support the business/investment use claimed? ☐ Yes ☐ No **22b** If "Yes," is the evidence written? ☐ Yes ☐ No

(a) Type of property (list vehicles first)	(b) Date placed in service	(c) Business/ investment use percentage	(d) Cost or other basis	(e) Basis for depreciation (business/investment use only)	(f) Recovery period	(g) Method/ Convention	(h) Depreciation deduction	(i) Elected section 179 cost
23 Property used more than 50% in a qualified business use (see instructions):								
		%						
		%						
		%						
24 Property used 50% or less in a qualified business use (see instructions):								
		%				S/L –		
		%				S/L –		
		%				S/L –		

25 Add amounts in column (h). Enter the total here and on line 19, page 1 . . . . . . **25**

26 Add amounts in column (i). Enter the total here and on line 7, page 1 . . . . **26**

Section B—Information on Use of Vehicles—*If you deduct expenses for vehicles:*

- *Always complete this section for vehicles used by a sole proprietor, partner, or other "more than 5% owner," or related person.*
- *If you provided vehicles to your employees, first answer the questions in Section C to see if you meet an exception to completing this section for those vehicles.*

	(a) Vehicle 1		(b) Vehicle 2		(c) Vehicle 3		(d) Vehicle 4		(e) Vehicle 5		(f) Vehicle 6	
27 Total business/investment miles driven during the year (DO NOT include commuting miles)												
28 Total commuting miles driven during the year												
29 Total other personal (noncommuting) miles driven												
30 Total miles driven during the year. Add lines 27 through 29.												
	Yes	No	Yes	No	Yes	No	Yes	No	Yes	No	Yes	No
31 Was the vehicle available for personal use during off-duty hours?												
32 Was the vehicle used primarily by a more than 5% owner or related person?												
33 Is another vehicle available for personal use?												

Section C—Questions for Employers Who Provide Vehicles for Use by Their Employees

Answer these questions to determine if you meet an exception to completing Section B. **Note:** *Section B must always be completed for vehicles used by sole proprietors, partners, or other more than 5% owners or related persons.*

	Yes	No
34 Do you maintain a written policy statement that prohibits all personal use of vehicles, including commuting, by your employees?		
35 Do you maintain a written policy statement that prohibits personal use of vehicles, except commuting, by your employees? (See instructions for vehicles used by corporate officers, directors, or 1% or more owners.)		
36 Do you treat all use of vehicles by employees as personal use?		
37 Do you provide more than five vehicles to your employees and retain the information received from your employees concerning the use of the vehicles?		
38 Do you meet the requirements concerning qualified automobile demonstration use (see instructions)?		
Note: *If your answer to 34, 35, 36, 37, or 38 is "Yes," you need not complete Section B for the covered vehicles.*		

Part VI Amortization

(a) Description of costs	(b) Date amortization begins	(c) Amortizable amount	(d) Code section	(e) Amortization period or percentage	(f) Amortization for this year
39 Amortization of costs that begins during your 1994 tax year:					

40 Amortization of costs that began before 1994 . . . . **40**

41 **Total.** Enter here and on "Other Deductions" or "Other Expenses" line of your return . . . **41**

Printed on recycled paper

Form **6252**

Department of the Treasury
Internal Revenue Service

Installment Sale Income

▶ See separate instructions. ▶ Attach to your tax return.
▶ Use a separate form for each sale or other disposition of property on the installment method.

OMB No. 1545-0228

1993

Attachment Sequence No. **79**

Name(s) shown on return | Identifying number

1 Description of property ▶ ....

2a Date acquired (month, day, and year) ▶ / / **b** Date sold (month, day, and year) ▶ / /

3 Was the property sold to a related party after May 14, 1980? See instructions . . . ☐ Yes ☐ No

4 If the answer to question 3 is "Yes," was the property a marketable security? If "Yes," complete Part III. If "No," complete Part III for the year of sale and for 2 years after the year of sale. . . . ☐ Yes ☐ No

Part I Gross Profit and Contract Price. Complete this part for the year of sale only.

5	Selling price including mortgages and other debts. Do not include interest whether stated or unstated		5
6	Mortgages and other debts the buyer assumed or took the property subject to, but not new mortgages the buyer got from a bank or other source	6	
7	Subtract line 6 from line 5	7	
8	Cost or other basis of property sold	8	
9	Depreciation allowed or allowable	9	
10	Adjusted basis. Subtract line 9 from line 8	10	
11	Commissions and other expenses of sale	11	
12	Income recapture from Form 4797, Part III. See instructions	12	
13	Add lines 10, 11, and 12		13
14	Subtract line 13 from line 5. If zero or less, **stop here.** Do not complete the rest of this form		14
15	If the property described on line 1 above was your main home, enter the total of lines 14 and 22 from Form 2119. Otherwise, enter -0-		15
16	**Gross profit.** Subtract line 15 from line 14		16
17	Subtract line 13 from line 6. If zero or less, enter -0-		17
18	**Contract price.** Add line 7 and line 17		18

Part II Installment Sale Income. Complete this part for the year of sale and any year you receive a payment or have certain debts you must treat as a payment on installment obligations.

19	Gross profit percentage. Divide line 16 by line 18. For years after the year of sale, see instructions		19
20	**For year of sale only**—Enter amount from line 17 above; otherwise, enter -0-		20
21	Payments received during year. See instructions. Do not include interest whether stated or unstated		21
22	Add lines 20 and 21		22
23	Payments received in prior years. See instructions. Do not include interest whether stated or unstated	23	
24	**Installment sale income.** Multiply line 22 by line 19		24
25	Part of line 24 that is ordinary income under recapture rules. See instructions		25
26	Subtract line 25 from line 24. Enter here and on Schedule D or Form 4797. See instructions		26

Part III Related Party Installment Sale Income. Do not complete if you received the final payment this tax year.

27 Name, address, and taxpayer identifying number of related party ....

28 Did the related party, during this tax year, resell or dispose of the property ("second disposition")? . . . ☐ Yes ☐ No

29 **If the answer to question 28 is "Yes," complete lines 30 through 37 below unless one of the following conditions is met. Check only the box that applies.**

a ☐ The second disposition was more than 2 years after the first disposition (other than dispositions of marketable securities). If this box is checked, enter the date of disposition (month, day, year) ▶ / /

b ☐ The first disposition was a sale or exchange of stock to the issuing corporation.

c ☐ The second disposition was an involuntary conversion where the threat of conversion occurred after the first disposition.

d ☐ The second disposition occurred after the death of the original seller or buyer.

e ☐ It can be established to the satisfaction of the Internal Revenue Service that tax avoidance was not a principal purpose for either of the dispositions. If this box is checked, attach an explanation. See instructions.

30	Selling price of property sold by related party	30
31	Enter contract price from line 18 for year of first sale	31
32	Enter the **smaller** of line 30 or line 31	32
33	Total payments received by the end of your 1993 tax year. Add lines 22 and 23	33
34	Subtract line 33 from line 32. If zero or less, enter -0-	34
35	Multiply line 34 by the gross profit percentage on line 19 for year of first sale	35
36	Part of line 35 that is ordinary income under recapture rules. See instructions	36
37	Subtract line 36 from line 35. Enter here and on Schedule D or Form 4797. See instructions	37

For Paperwork Reduction Act Notice, see separate instructions. Cat. No. 13601R Form **6252** (1993)

Printed on recycled paper

Form **1310** (Rev. June 1992)
Department of the Treasury
Internal Revenue Service

Statement of Person Claiming Refund Due a Deceased Taxpayer

▶ **See instructions below.**

OMB No. 1545-0073
Expires 5-31-95
Attachment Sequence No. **87**

Tax year decedent was due a refund:

Calendar year ____________, or other tax year beginning ____________ 19 ____, and ending ____________ 19 ____

Please type or print			
	Name of decedent	Date of death	Decedent's social security number
	Name of person claiming refund		
	Home address (number and street). If you have a P.O. box, see instructions		Apt. no.
	City, town or post office, state, and ZIP code. If you have a foreign address, see instructions		

Part I Check the box that applies to you. Check only one box. Be sure to complete Part III below.

A ☐ Surviving spouse, requesting reissuance of a refund check (see instructions).

B ☐ Court-appointed or certified personal representative. You may have to attach a court certificate showing your appointment (see instructions).

C ☐ Person, **other** than A or B, claiming refund for the decedent's estate (see instructions). Complete Part II and attach a copy of the death certificate or proof of death.

Part II Complete this part only if you checked the box on line C above.

		Yes	No
1	Did the decedent leave a will?		
2a	Has a court appointed a personal representative for the estate of the decedent?		
b	If you answered "No" to 2a, will one be appointed?		
	If you answered "Yes" to 2a or 2b, the personal representative must file for the refund.		
3	As the person claiming the refund for the decedent's estate, will you pay out the refund according to the laws of the state where the decedent was a legal resident?		
	If you answered "No" to 3, a refund cannot be made until you submit a court certificate showing your appointment as personal representative or other evidence that you are entitled under state law to receive the refund.		

Part III Signature and verification. All filers must complete this part.

I request a refund of taxes overpaid by or on behalf of the decedent. Under penalties of perjury, I declare that I have examined this claim, and to the best of my knowledge and belief, it is true, correct, and complete.

Signature of person claiming refund ▶ ____________ **Date** ▶ ____________

Form **1310** (Rev. 6-92)

H763 **For Paperwork Reduction Act Notice, see instructions.**

3A3400 1.000

Form **8582**

Department of the Treasury
Internal Revenue Service

Passive Activity Loss Limitations

▶ See separate instructions.
▶ Attach to Form 1040 or Form 1041.

OMB No. 1545-1008
1993
Attachment Sequence No. 88

Name(s) shown on return | Identifying number

Part I **1993 Passive Activity Loss**
Caution: *See the instructions for Worksheets 1 and 2 on page 7 before completing Part I.*

Rental Real Estate Activities With Active Participation (For the definition of active participation see **Active Participation in a Rental Real Estate Activity** on page 3 of the instructions.)

1a Activities with net income (from Worksheet 1, column (a)) . . .	1a		
b Activities with net loss (from Worksheet 1, column (b))	1b	( )	
c Prior year unallowed losses (from Worksheet 1, column (c)) . .	1c	( )	
d Combine lines 1a, 1b, and 1c			1d

All Other Passive Activities

2a Activities with net income (from Worksheet 2, column (a)) . . .	2a		
b Activities with net loss (from Worksheet 2, column (b))	2b	( )	
c Prior year unallowed losses (from Worksheet 2, column (c)) . .	2c	( )	
d Combine lines 2a, 2b, and 2c			2d
3 Combine lines 1d and 2d. If the result is net income or zero, see the instructions for line 3. If this line and line 1d are losses, go to line 4. Otherwise, enter -0- on line 9 and go to line 10 .			3

Part II **Special Allowance for Rental Real Estate With Active Participation**
Note: *Enter all numbers in Part II as positive amounts. (See instructions on page 7 for examples.)*

4 Enter the **smaller** of the loss on line 1d or the loss on line 3			4
5 Enter $150,000. If married filing separately, see the instructions .	5		
6 Enter modified adjusted gross income, but not less than zero (see instructions)	6		
Note: *If line 6 is equal to or greater than line 5, skip lines 7 and 8, enter -0- on line 9, and then go to line 10. Otherwise, go to line 7.*			
7 Subtract line 6 from line 5	7		
8 Multiply line 7 by 50% (.5). **Do not** enter more than $25,000. If married filing separately, see instructions			8
9 Enter the **smaller** of line 4 or line 8			9

Part III **Total Losses Allowed**

10 Add the income, if any, on lines 1a and 2a and enter the total	10
11 **Total losses allowed from all passive activities for 1993.** Add lines 9 and 10. See the instructions to find out how to report the losses on your tax return	11

For Paperwork Reduction Act Notice, see separate instructions. Cat. No. 63704F Form **8582** (1993)

Caution: *The worksheets are not required to be filed with your tax return and may be detached before filing Form 8582. Keep a copy of the worksheets for your records.*

Worksheet 1—For Form 8582, Lines 1a, 1b, and 1c (See instructions on page 7.)

Name of activity	Current year		Prior year	Overall gain or loss	
	(a) Net income (line 1a)	(b) Net loss (line 1b)	(c) Unallowed loss (line 1c)	(d) Gain	(e) Loss
Total. Enter on Form 8582, lines 1a, 1b, and 1c. . . . . ▶					

Worksheet 2—For Form 8582, Lines 2a, 2b, and 2c (See instructions on page 7.)

Name of activity	Current year		Prior year	Overall gain or loss	
	(a) Net income (line 2a)	(b) Net loss (line 2b)	(c) Unallowed loss (line 2c)	(d) Gain	(e) Loss
Total. Enter on Form 8582, lines 2a, 2b, and 2c. . . . . ▶					

Worksheet 3—Use this worksheet if an amount is shown on Form 8582, line 9 (See instructions on page 8.)

Name of activity	Form or schedule to be reported on	(a) Loss (See instructions.)	(b) Ratio (See instructions.)	(c) Special allowance (See instructions.)	(d) Subtract column (c) from column (a) (See instructions.)
Total . . . . ▶			1.00		

Worksheet 4—Allocation of Unallowed Losses (See instructions on page 8.)

Name of activity	Form or schedule to be reported on	(a) Loss (See instructions.)	(b) Ratio (See instructions.)	(c) Unallowed loss (See instructions.)
Total . . . . ▶			1.00	

Worksheet 5—Allowed Losses (See instructions on page 8.)

Name of activity	Form or schedule to be reported on	(a) Loss (See instructions.)	(b) Unallowed loss (See instructions.)	(c) Allowed loss (See instructions.)
Total . . . . ▶				

Worksheet 6—Activities With Losses Reported on Two or More Different Forms or Schedules (See instructions on page 8.)

Name of Activity:	(a) (See instr.)	(b) (See instr.)	(c) Ratio (See instr.)	(d) Unallowed loss (See instr.)	(e) Allowed loss (See instr.)
Form or Schedule To Be Reported on:					
1a Net loss plus prior year unallowed loss from form or schedule ▶					
b Net income from form or schedule ▶					
c Subtract line 1b from line 1a. If zero or less, enter -0- ▶					
Form or Schedule To Be Reported on:					
1a Net loss plus prior year unallowed loss from form or schedule ▶					
b Net income from form or schedule ▶					
c Subtract line 1b from line 1a. If zero or less, enter -0- ▶					
Form or Schedule To Be Reported on:					
1a Net loss plus prior year unallowed loss from form or schedule ▶					
b Net income from form or schedule ▶					
c Subtract line 1b from line 1a. If zero or less, enter -0- ▶					
Total ▶			1.00		

Form **9465** (Rev. Dec. 1993)	Department of the Treasury - Internal Revenue Service **Installment Agreement Request** ▶**Please attach** this completed agreement request **to the front of your tax return** or **to the notice** we sent you, and mail it to the appropriate IRS office shown on the back.	OMB Approval No. 1545-1350 Expires 11/30/96

General Information

If you can't pay the amount you owe in full at this time, please request an installment agreement by completing this form. Specify the amount of the monthly payment you propose to make in the block marked "Proposed monthly payment amount."

We encourage you to make your payments as large as possible to lower penalty and interest charges. Under law, these charges continue to increase until you pay the balance in full.

Make your check or money order payable to the Internal Revenue Service, and mark the payment with your name, address, taxpayer identification number, form number and tax period. If you have any questions about this procedure, please call our toll-free number **1-800-829-1040.**

Within 30 days, we will let you know if your request for an installment agreement is approved, or if we need more information. However, if a 1040 series tax return is filed after March 31, it may take longer than 30 days to process this request.

Note: If you are currently in bankruptcy, do not use this form. Use the above toll-free telephone number and ask for the telephone number of your local IRS District Office Special Procedures function.

Your first name and initial		Last name			Your social security number
If a joint return, spouse's first name and initial		Last name			Spouse's social security number
Home address (number and street). If you have a P.O. box without home delivery, show box number only				Apt. no.	Employer identification number (for business use only)
City, province or state, and postal zone or ZIP code			Country, if not the United States (do not abbreviate)		Did this address change since you last filed? ☐ NO ☐ YES
Business telephone number (include area code and extension number, if any)		Most convenient time for us to call you	Home telephone number (include area code)		Most convenient time for us to call you
Tax return or notice number	Tax period	Total taxes owed on tax return or notice	Amount paid with your tax return or notice	Proposed monthly payment amount	Date each month I am able to make the payment (Must be the 1st through the 28th day)
Your signature				Date	
Spouse's signature (joint returns only)				Date	

Privacy Act and Paperwork Reduction Act Notice

We ask for the information on this form under authority of Internal Revenue Code sections 6001, 6011, 6012(a), 6109, and 6159 and their regulations. We use this information to process your request for an installment agreement. The principal reason we need your name and social security number is to secure proper identification. We require this information to gain access to the tax information in our files and properly respond to your request. If you do not disclose the information, the IRS may not be able to process your request.

The time needed to complete and file this form will vary depending on individual circumstances. The estimated average time is 10 minutes.

If you have **comments** concerning the accuracy of this time estimate or **suggestions** for making this form more simple, we would be happy to hear from you. You can write both the **Internal Revenue Service,** Attention: Reports Clearance Officer, T:FP, Washington, DC 20224, and the **Office of Management and Budget,** Paperwork Reduction Project (1545-1350), Washington, DC 20503. **DO NOT** send this form to either of these offices. See the back for correct mailing addresses.

Form **9465** (Rev. 12/93)

3W8771 2.000

Form **1040A** (99) Department of the Treasury—Internal Revenue Service

U.S. Individual Income Tax Return 1994

IRS Use Only—Do not write or staple in this space.

OMB No. 1545-0085

Label

(See page 16.)

Use the IRS label. Otherwise, please print or type.

LABEL HERE

Your first name and initial	Last name	Your social security number
If a joint return, spouse's first name and initial	Last name	Spouse's social security number
Home address (number and street). If you have a P.O. box, see page 17.	Apt. no.	
City, town or post office, state, and ZIP code. If you have a foreign address, see page 17.		

For Privacy Act and Paperwork Reduction Act Notice, see page 4.

Presidential Election Campaign Fund (See page 17.)

	Yes	No
Do you want $3 to go to this fund?		
If a joint return, does your spouse want $3 to go to this fund?		

Note: *Checking "Yes" will not change your tax or reduce your refund.*

Check the box for your filing status

(See page 17.) Check only one box.

1 ☐ Single
2 ☐ Married filing joint return (even if only one had income)
3 ☐ Married filing separate return. Enter spouse's social security number above and full name here. ▶ ____
4 ☐ Head of household (with qualifying person). (See page 18.) If the qualifying person is a child but not your dependent, enter this child's name here. ▶ ____
5 ☐ Qualifying widow(er) with dependent child (year spouse died ▶ 19). (See page 19.)

Figure your exemptions

(See page 20.)

If more than seven dependents, see page 23.

6a ☐ **Yourself.** If your parent (or someone else) can claim you as a dependent on his or her tax return, **do not** check box 6a. But be sure to check the box on line 18b on page 2.

b ☐ **Spouse**

No. of boxes checked on 6a and 6b ____

c **Dependents:**

(1) Name (first, initial, and last name)	(2) Check if under age 1	(3) If age 1 or older, dependent's social security number	(4) Dependent's relationship to you	(5) No. of months lived in your home in 1994

No. of your children on 6c who:
- lived with you ____
- didn't live with you due to divorce or separation (see page 23) ____

Dependents on 6c not entered above ____

d If your child didn't live with you but is claimed as your dependent under a pre-1985 agreement, check here . . . . ▶ ☐

e Total number of exemptions claimed.

Add numbers entered on lines above ☐

Figure your total income

Attach Copy B of your Forms W-2 and 1099-R here.

If you didn't get a W-2, see page 25.

Enclose, but do not attach, any payment with your return.

7	Wages, salaries, tips, etc. This should be shown in box 1 of your W-2 form(s). Attach Form(s) W-2.		7
8a	**Taxable** interest income (see page 25). If over $400, attach Schedule 1.		8a
b	**Tax-exempt** interest. DO NOT include on line 8a.	8b	
9	Dividends. If over $400, attach Schedule 1.		9
10a	Total IRA distributions. 10a	10b Taxable amount (see page 26).	10b
11a	Total pensions and annuities. 11a	11b Taxable amount (see page 27).	11b
12	Unemployment compensation (see page 30).		12
13a	Social security benefits. 13a	13b Taxable amount (see page 31).	13b
14	Add lines 7 through 13b (far right column). This is your **total income.** ▶		14

Figure your adjusted gross income

15a	Your IRA deduction (see page 34).	15a	
b	Spouse's IRA deduction (see page 34).	15b	
c	Add lines 15a and 15b. These are your **total adjustments.**		15c
16	Subtract line 15c from line 14. This is your **adjusted gross income.** If less than $25,296 and a child lived with you (less than $9,000 if a child didn't live with you), see "Earned income credit" on page 44. ▶		16

Cat. No. 11327A

1994 Form 1040A page 1

Figure your standard deduction, exemption amount, and taxable income

17 Enter the amount from line 16. 17

18a Check if: ☐ **You** were 65 or older ☐ Blind; ☐ **Spouse** was 65 or older ☐ Blind — **Enter number of boxes checked** ▶ 18a ☐

b If your parent (or someone else) can claim you as a dependent, check here . . . . ▶ 18b ☐

c If you are married filing separately and your spouse files Form 1040 and itemizes deductions, see page 38 and check here. ▶ 18c ☐

19 Enter the **standard deduction** shown below for your filing status. **But if you checked any box on line 18a or b,** go to page 38 to find your standard deduction. **If you checked box 18c,** enter -0-.
- Single—$3,800
- Married filing jointly or Qualifying widow(er)—$6,350
- Head of household—$5,600
- Married filing separately—$3,175

19

20 Subtract line 19 from line 17. If line 19 is more than line 17, enter -0-. 20

21 Multiply $2,450 by the total number of exemptions claimed on line 6e. 21

22 Subtract line 21 from line 20. If line 21 is more than line 20, enter -0-. This is your **taxable income.** ▶ 22

Figure your tax, credits, and payments

If you want the IRS to figure your tax, see the instructions for line 22 on page 39.

23 Find the tax on the amount on line 22. Check if from: ☐ Tax Table (pages 62–67) or ☐ Form 8615 (see page 40). 23

24a Credit for child and dependent care expenses. Attach Schedule 2. 24a

b Credit for the elderly or the disabled. Attach Schedule 3. 24b

c Add lines 24a and 24b. These are your **total credits.** 24c

25 Subtract line 24c from line 23. If line 24c is more than line 23, enter -0-. 25

26 Advance earned income credit payments from Form W-2. 26

27 Add lines 25 and 26. This is your **total tax.** ▶ 27

28a Total Federal income tax withheld. If any tax is from Form(s) 1099, check here. ▶ ☐ 28a

b 1994 estimated tax payments and amount applied from 1993 return. 28b

c **Earned income credit.** If required, attach Schedule EIC (see page 44). 28c

Nontaxable earned income: amount ▶ and type ▶

d Add lines 28a, 28b, and 28c (don't include nontaxable earned income). These are your **total payments.** ▶ 28d

Figure your refund or amount you owe

29 If line 28d is more than line 27, subtract line 27 from line 28d. This is the amount you **overpaid.** 29

30 Amount of line 29 you want **refunded to you.** 30

31 Amount of line 29 you want **applied to your 1995 estimated tax.** 31

32 If line 27 is more than line 28d, subtract line 28d from line 27. This is the **amount you owe.** For details on how to pay, including what to write on your payment, see page 52. 32

33 Estimated tax penalty (see page 52). Also, include on line 32. 33

Sign your return

Keep a copy of this return for your records.

Under penalties of perjury, I declare that I have examined this return and accompanying schedules and statements, and to the best of my knowledge and belief, they are true, correct, and accurately list all amounts and sources of income I received during the tax year. Declaration of preparer (other than the taxpayer) is based on all information of which the preparer has any knowledge.

▶ Your signature	Date	Your occupation
▶ Spouse's signature. If joint return, BOTH must sign.	Date	Spouse's occupation

Paid preparer's use only

Preparer's signature ▶	Date	Check if self-employed ☐	Preparer's social security no.
Firm's name (or yours if self-employed) and address ▶		E.I. No.	
		ZIP code	

Printed on recycled paper

Schedule 2 (Form 1040A)

Department of the Treasury—Internal Revenue Service

Child and Dependent Care Expenses for Form 1040A Filers (99) 1994

OMB No. 1545-0085

Name(s) shown on Form 1040A	Your social security number

You need to understand the following terms to complete this schedule: **Qualifying person(s), Dependent care benefits, Qualified expenses,** and **Earned income.** See **Important terms** on page 70.

Part I

Persons or organizations who provided the care

You MUST complete this part.

1 (a) Care provider's name	(b) Address (number, street, apt. no., city, state, and ZIP code)	(c) Identifying number (SSN or EIN)	(d) Amount paid (see page 72)

(If you need more space, use the bottom of page 2.)

2 Add the amounts in column (d) of line 1. 2

3 Enter the number of **qualifying persons** cared for in 1994 . . . . ▶ ☐

Did you receive **dependent care benefits?**
- NO → Complete only Part II below.
- YES → Complete Part III on the back now.

Part II

Credit for child and dependent care expenses

4 Enter the amount of **qualified expenses** you incurred and paid in 1994. DO NOT enter more than $2,400 for one qualifying person or $4,800 for two or more persons. If you completed Part III, enter the amount from line 25. 4

5 Enter YOUR **earned income.** 5

6 If married filing a joint return, enter YOUR SPOUSE'S earned income (if student or disabled, see page 73); **all others,** enter the amount from line 5. 6

7 Enter the **smallest** of line 4, 5, or 6. 7

8 Enter the amount from Form 1040A, line 17. 8

9 Enter on line 9 the decimal amount shown below that applies to the amount on line 8.

If line 8 is— Over — But not over	Decimal amount is	If line 8 is— Over — But not over	Decimal amount is
$0—10,000	.30	$20,000—22,000	.24
10,000—12,000	.29	22,000—24,000	.23
12,000—14,000	.28	24,000—26,000	.22
14,000—16,000	.27	26,000—28,000	.21
16,000—18,000	.26	28,000—No limit	.20
18,000—20,000	.25		

9 × .

10 Multiply **line 7** by the decimal amount on line 9. Enter the result. Then, see page 73 for the amount of credit to enter on Form 1040A, line 24a. 10 =

Caution: *If you paid $50 or more in a calendar quarter to a person who worked in your home, you must file an employment tax return. Get **Form 942** for details.*

For Paperwork Reduction Act Notice, see Form 1040A instructions. Cat. No. 10749I **1994 Schedule 2 (Form 1040A) page 1**

Name(s) shown on page 1 | Your social security number

Part III

Dependent care benefits

Complete this part **only** if you received these benefits.

11 Enter the total amount of **dependent care benefits** you received for 1994. This amount should be shown in box 10 of your W-2 form(s). DO NOT include amounts that were reported to you as wages in box 1 of Form(s) W-2. 11

12 Enter the amount forfeited, if any. See page 74. 12

13 Subtract line 12 from line 11. 13

14 Enter the total amount of **qualified expenses** incurred in 1994 for the care of the qualifying person(s). 14

15 Enter the **smaller** of line 13 or 14. 15

16 Enter YOUR **earned income.** 16

17 If married filing a joint return, enter YOUR SPOUSE'S earned income (if student or disabled, see the line 6 instructions); if married filing a separate return, see the instructions for the amount to enter; **all others,** enter the amount from line 16. 17

18 Enter the **smallest** of line 15, 16, or 17. 18

19 **Excluded benefits.** Enter here the **smaller** of the following:
- The amount from line 18, or
- $5,000 ($2,500 if married filing a separate return **and** you were required to enter your spouse's earned income on line 17). 19

20 **Taxable benefits.** Subtract line 19 from line 13. Also, include this amount on Form 1040A, line 7. In the space to the left of line 7, write "DCB." 20

To claim the child and dependent care credit, complete lines 21–25 below, and lines 4–10 on the front of this schedule.

21 Enter the amount of qualified expenses you incurred and paid in 1994. DO NOT include on this line any excluded benefits shown on line 19. 21

22 Enter $2,400 ($4,800 if two or more qualifying persons). 22

23 Enter the amount from line 19. 23

24 Subtract line 23 from line 22. If zero or less, **STOP.** You cannot take the credit. **Exception.** If you paid 1993 expenses in 1994, see the line 10 instructions. 24

25 Enter the **smaller** of line 21 or 24 here **and** on line 4 on the front of this schedule. 25

1994 Schedule 2 (Form 1040A) page 2

 ***Printed on recycled paper***

Department of the Treasury—Internal Revenue Service

Form **1040EZ** **Income Tax Return for Single and Joint Filers With No Dependents** (99) **1994**

OMB No. 1545-0675

Use the IRS label (See page 12.) Otherwise, please print.

LABEL HERE

Print your name (first, initial, last)

If a joint return, print spouse's name (first, initial, last)

Home address (number and street). If you have a P.O. box, see page 12. Apt. no.

City, town or post office, state and ZIP code. If you have a foreign address, see page 12.

Your social security number

Spouse's social security number

See instructions on back and in Form 1040EZ booklet.

Presidential Election Campaign (See page 12.)

Note: *Checking "Yes" will not change your tax or reduce your refund.*

Do you want $3 to go to this fund? ▶

If a joint return, does your spouse want $3 to go to this fund? ▶

Income

Attach Copy B of Form(s) W-2 here. Enclose, but do not attach, any payment with your return.

1 Total wages, salaries, and tips. This should be shown in box 1 of your W-2 form(s). Attach your W-2 form(s). 1

2 Taxable interest income of $400 or less. If the total is over $400, you cannot use Form 1040EZ. 2

3 Add lines 1 and 2. This is your **adjusted gross income.** If less than $9,000, see page 15 to find out if you can claim the earned income credit on line 7. 3

Note: *You must check Yes or No.*

4 Can your parents (or someone else) claim you on their return?

Yes. Do worksheet on back; enter amount from line G here.

No. If **single**, enter 6,250.00. If **married**, enter 11,250.00. For an explanation of these amounts, see back of form. 4

5 Subtract line 4 from line 3. If line 4 is larger than line 3, enter 0. This is your **taxable income.** ▶ 5

Payments and tax

6 Enter your Federal income tax withheld from box 2 of your W-2 form(s). 6

7 **Earned income credit** (see page 15). Enter type and amount of nontaxable earned income below. 7

8 Add lines 6 and 7 (don't include nontaxable earned income). These are your **total payments.** 8

9 **Tax.** Use the amount on **line 5** to find your tax in the tax table on pages 28–32 of the booklet. Then, enter the tax from the table on this line. 9

Refund or amount you owe

10 If line 8 is larger than line 9, subtract line 9 from line 8. This is your **refund.** 10

11 If line 9 is larger than line 8, subtract line 8 from line 9. This is the **amount you owe.** See page 20 for details on how to pay and what to write on your payment. 11

Sign your return

Keep a copy of this form for your records.

I have read this return. Under penalties of perjury, I declare that to the best of my knowledge and belief, the return is true, correct, and accurately lists all amounts and sources of income I received during the tax year.

Your signature | Spouse's signature if joint return

Date	Your occupation	Date	Spouse's occupation

For Privacy Act and Paperwork Reduction Act Notice, see page 4. Cat. No. 11329W Form 1040EZ (1994)

Department of the Treasury—Internal Revenue Service

Form **1040EZ** **Income Tax Return for Single and Joint Filers With No Dependents** (99) **1994**

OMB No. 1545-0675

Use the IRS label (See page 12.) Otherwise, please print.

Print your name (first, initial, last)

If a joint return, print spouse's name (first, initial, last)

Home address (number and street). If you have a P.O. box, see page 12. Apt. no.

City, town or post office, state, and ZIP code. If you have a foreign address, see page 12.

Your social security number

Spouse's social security number

See instructions on back and in Form 1040EZ booklet.

Presidential Election Campaign (See page 12.)

Note: Checking "Yes" will not change your tax or reduce your refund.

Do you want $3 to go to this fund?

If a joint return, does your spouse want $3 to go to this fund?

Income

Attach Copy B of Form(s) W-2 here. Enclose, but do not attach, any payment with your return.

1 Total wages, salaries, and tips. This should be shown in box 1 of your W-2 form(s). Attach your W-2 form(s). 1

2 Taxable interest income of $400 or less. If the total is over $400, you cannot use Form 1040EZ. 2

3 Add lines 1 and 2. This is your **adjusted gross income**. If less than $9,000, see page 15 to find out if you can claim the earned income credit on line 7. 3

4 Can your parents (or someone else) claim you on their return?

Note: You must check Yes or No.

Yes. Do worksheet on back; enter amount from line G here. | No. If single, enter 6,250.00. If married, enter 11,250.00. For an explanation of these amounts, see back of form. 4

5 Subtract line 4 from line 3. If line 4 is larger than line 3, enter 0. This is your **taxable income**. 5

Payments and tax

6 Enter your Federal income tax withheld from box 2 of your W-2 form(s). 6

7 **Earned income credit** (see page 15). Enter type and amount of nontaxable earned income below. 7

8 Add lines 6 and 7 (don't include nontaxable earned income). These are your **total payments**. 8

9 **Tax.** Use the amount on line 5 to find your tax in the tax table on pages [illegible] of the booklet. Then, enter the tax from the table on this line. 9

Refund or amount you owe

10 If line 8 is larger than line 9, subtract line 9 from line 8. This is your **refund**. 10

11 If line 9 is larger than line 8, subtract line 8 from line 9. This is the **amount you owe**. See page 21 for details on how to pay and what to write on your payment. 11

Sign your return

Keep a copy of this form for your records.

I have read this return. Under penalties of perjury, I declare that to the best of my knowledge and belief, the return is true, correct, and accurately lists all amounts and sources of income I received during the tax year.

Your signature | Spouse's signature if joint return

Date | Your occupation | Date | Spouse's occupation

For Privacy Act and Paperwork Reduction Act Notice, see page 4. Cat. No. [illegible] Form **1040EZ** (1994)

Index